The *Ultimate* Staffordshire Bull Terrier

Clare Lee & Joyce Shorrock

RINGPRESS

Acknowledgements

The publisher would like to thank the following for their help with photoshoots: Carol and Colin Powell (Bowtmans); Derek and Tracey Packham (Genna's Good As Gold); Bill and Jo Blacker (Crossguns); Wendy and Andy Clewley: Marvin (Den's Duke of Eirl), Tammy (Araidh Sweetest Taboo), Katie (Ariadh Kiss of Life); Mark and Vanessa Pooley: Edith (Puffin Pied Princess), Bruno (Seikostaff Andromeda at Marvach), Elijiah (Seikostaff Hercules); Lesley McFadyen: Carey (Champion Araidh Devil May Care); John and Michell Bartrum: Bomber (Araidh Jacobs Creek); Ian and Sandra Mitchell: Skipper (Skipper Jackson Mitchell), Tilla (Crossguns Thong Song); Mr J and Mrs Y Marshall: Shannon (Reneem Miss Moneypenny) and Buddy (Jems Guardian). Thanks to Iona Antiques, London, for the back cover picture, which also appears on page 28.

Published by Ringpress Books
A Division of INTERPET Publishing
Vincent Lane, Dorking, Surrey RH4 3YX

Designed by Rob Benson

First Published 2003
© 2003 RINGPRESS BOOKS

ISBN 1 86054 281 6

Printed in Hong Kong through Printworks Int. Ltd.

10 9 8 7 6 5 4 3 2 1

CONTRIBUTORS

EDITORS

CLARE LEE

Clare was brought up with Staffordshire Bull Terriers. As a child and a teenager, she handled some of her father's dogs. He founded the famous Constones kennels, and Clare and her husband went into partnership with him in the 1960s.

All the Constones dogs trace back to the first bitch her father bought in 1942. Nine UK Stafford Champions and numerous other winners have carried the Constones prefix, most famous of all being Ch. Constones Yer Man, who broke the then breed record and retired after winning his twentieth CC and Best of Breed at the Centenary Crufts Dog Show. He was also the sire of 11 Champions.

Clare has been awarding Challenge Certificates since 1973, and has judged throughout the UK, including at Crufts in 1985, the fiftieth anniversary of the recognition of the breed. Clare has also judged throughout Europe (Austria, Belgium, Eire, Finland, Germany, Holland, Spain and Sweden), and around the rest of the world (Australia, Canada, South Africa, and the US).

Clare regularly gives seminars on the breed and is the author of *Pet Owner's Guide to the Staffordshire Bull Terrier*, published by Ringpress. *Chapters One, Three, Four, Seven, Eleven.*

JOYCE SHORROCK

Joyce Shorrock purchased her first Staffordshire Bull Terrier in 1950 – a tiger-brindle male bred by Mrs Hesketh Williams of the Verles prefix. In 1952, Joyce registered her own prefix, Eastaff,

and, two years later, she produced her first Champion – Constones Eastaff This'll Do. Undoubtedly, the most famous Champion she has produced is Ch. Eastaff Danom, born in 1955. Danom was a pillar of the breed, winning no fewer than 11 Challenge Certificates and siring a further 11 Champions. In total, a dozen CC winners carry the Eastaff prefix. Joyce bred her last litter in August 2002.

Joyce was secretary of the East Anglian Staffordshire Bull Terrier Club for more than 27 years before she retired from the post. Today, she is a well-respected Championship show judge, who judged at Crufts in the Millennium year. In addition, she has adjudicated in Eire, Finland, Germany, Australia, New Zealand, South Africa, and the US.
Chapters Eight, Nine, Ten.

CONTRIBUTORS

PAUL BOLAND BVSc MRCVS

Paul qualified from Liverpool Veterinary School in 1992 and went straight into a small-animal practice in Liverpool. He became a partner in this veterinary hospital in 1993, and takes specialist referrals in canine reproduction problems.

Paul has owned Staffordshire Bull Terriers for 21 years, and has shown them for eight years – his dogs achieving a CC in Britain and Irish Green Stars. He started to judge Staffordshire Bull Terriers in 1996 and has been breeding them since 1995. In 1999, Eric Galvin and Paul became partners under the new Scousious affix.
Chapter Thirteen: Breed-Related Conditions

WENDY CLEWLEY

Before Staffords, Wendy had always owned GSDs, so set about training them in the same way. Being greedy dogs, with a great desire to please, she found them hugely responsive, and hasn't looked back since!

She currently has three Staffords (Marvin, Tammy, and Katie) and trains and competes in Obedience, Working Trials, Agility, and breed shows. She has been particularly succccessful in Agility – Tammy is one of the fastest Mini dogs in the UK.

Wendy does many demonstrations to promote the breed, and is on the East Anglian Staffordshire Bull Terrier Club (EASBTC) committee.

Tammy and Wendy are part of the Kennel Clubs DOMINO group, which fights breed-specific legislation (BSL) throughout the world. Tammy has become rather a Stafford celebrity from this involvement, visiting the Kennel Club, 10 Downing Street, and the German embassy in her campaigning work, as well as meeting many celebrities on the DOMINO stand.

Wendy is a PAT Dog (Pets As Therapy) assessor, evaluating dogs for their suitability as therapy dogs, and she is currently working towards a KC accreditation for trainers scheme.
Chapter Five: Training Your Stafford

ALISON JONES BVETMED MRCVS

Alison qualified from the Royal Veterinary College, London, in 1987. After spending seven years in mixed practice in Gloucestershire, she joined Hill's Pet Nutrition and became Veterinary Affairs Manager. In January 2001, Alison opened her own small-animal practice in Cheltenham, located in the lower ground floor of her family home. Alison is married with three children (two human, one Dobermann), and has a keen interest in small-animal medicine, especially the nutritional management of disease.
Chapter Six: Diet and Nutrition.

GEOFF POTTS BVSc MRCVS

Geoff qualified from Liverpool University Veterinary School in 1988. After spending one year in mixed practice, Geoff has worked in small-animal practice in Liverpool, the last seven years as a partner in a small-animal hospital. Geoff is the centre vet for the Guide Dogs for the Blind training centre in Liverpool. He has a special interest in emergency medicine and internal medicine.
Chapter Twelve: Health Care

NICK WATERS

Nick is a canine art historian and writer who has been involved with dogs since the mid-1950s. He has bred Challenge Certificate winners in Mastiffs, Standard Poodles and Irish Water Spaniels, and, with Liz Waters, he shares the Zanfi kennel, one of the most successful associated with the Irish Water Spaniel.

Nick contributes regularly on the dog in art for magazines and weekly dog papers in both the US and the UK, and has been a contributing author on the subject to a number of books. For many years, his trade stand featuring canine antiques and collectables was a familiar sight on the British show scene.
Chapter Two: The Stafford in Art

MARNEY WELLS

Marney Wells's first Stafford, Rowley (Barrington Nell Gwynne), was given to her by Major Frank Rowley in 1974. During the 70s and early 80s, Marney was active on the show scene, winning a CC with Cherry (Copyhold Wild Cherry), a daughter of Rowley.

After aquiring Biggles (Arad Llewelyn Bren of Copyhold) and Bertie (Cyclone Sweetheart of Copyhold CDex, UDex) in 1991, Marney became involved in Obedience, Agility and Working Trials. Since that time, Marney has introduced all her Staffords to these three disciplines, with great success. Trilby (Libellula Lass of Copyhold) has achieved her CDex and UDex qualifications, and Bertie, handled by Marney's husband, Tim, has acquired, literally, hundred of rosettes in Agility. Trilby is also a registered therapy (PAT) dog, who is loved by patients and nurses alike!
Chapter Five: Training Your Stafford (Working Trials)

CONTENTS

1 INTRODUCING THE STAFFORD

The Staffordshire Bull Terrier has risen from the humblest of origins to become one of the most popular breeds of terrier. When trying to win Championship Show status in the 1930s, fanciers struggled to get the registration numbers up to 750. Today, in the UK alone, registrations of Staffords reach 10,000 per annum.

Throughout the world, there are breed clubs specialising in, and promoting, all things of benefit to the Staffordshire Bull Terrier. From the original breed club in the Black Country, there are now 18 clubs, covering all of Great Britain and Northern Ireland. In most European countries, from Scandinavia to southern Spain, there will be at least one breed club per country. Further afield, particularly in countries where British people have emigrated to, there is often a number of clubs. Canada, although a large country, does not have so many Staffords and has only one club for the breed. On the other hand, Australia, South Africa, New Zealand, and the United States all have more than one club, although, in the US, there is one 'parent' club that has precedence. Your national kennel club can provide you with details of breed clubs.

To some, this international prominence is a surprise. As a show dog, the Stafford has little to recommend him – no elegance of outline or movement, and no exotic trimming or abundance of coat to attract admiration. Although some do occasionally win the coveted Best in Show awards against all-comers, the strength of the breed lies in its appeal to the general, non-showing public.

The Stafford is a loving and affectionate breed.

The Stafford's many admirers value his no-nonsense, tough physical and mental attributes. He is the ultimate low-maintenance dog. As he is born, so he stays, requiring a minimum of grooming and no expense at the beauty parlour; even in the worst of weathers, it is easy to keep his short coat clean and smelling sweet.

The Stafford might appear lumpy and bumpy in silhouette beside more elegant breeds, but he is a strong, resilient dog, well able to bounce through the densest of undergrowth or waterlogged fields, and to withstand the rough-and-tumble of rowdy children.

Most prized of all is the Stafford character. This is a fun-loving dog, who is intensely human-orientated – the surest way to hurt a Stafford is to ignore him. There is a downside: the Stafford is a fussy dog who likes to lean against his owner, greets visitors with verve, and licks a lot. If you want a dog who 'minds his own business' and lies quietly in his corner all day, then don't get a Stafford!

Although the breed has been civilised over many, many years now from its gory past, vestiges of the fighting instinct may still remain. So, although one would not expect a Stafford to set about every dog he meets (unless he has been badly brought up), there is always a chance that he might retaliate if challenged. Any responsible owner should be aware of this possibility and guard against it.

HISTORY OF THE BREED
(From the writings of the late Mr A.W.A. Cairns)
Naturalists seem to be in agreement that the domestic dog had its origins in the wolf. It is possible that early man, having killed the mother wolf, reared the puppies and started the first association between man and beast. Man found that the wolf-dog made a valuable contribution to his economy by guarding his encampments and assisting in expeditions, and so allowed him to share the kills. This started a mutual dependency, which has continued throughout history, with the dog becoming an increasingly important part of the family tribe.

From such beginnings, the dog has become all-pervasive and can be found in all strata of human society, from native hut settlements to castles. The dog has proved the most adaptable of animals, with the ability to carry out a multiplicity of jobs and to fit in with any sort of society – his only need is to share his life with man.

Over the years, the original wolf shape has been changed in accordance with the particular duties that have been assigned to him. For example, there are longer-headed, lighter-built dogs for the chase, and heavier-built, stronger ones to guard against predators. Thus the different types of dog were developed for specialised jobs, and man learned how to manipulate nature to meet his needs.

BULLDOG BEGINNINGS
The Bulldog type of dog, surely one of the farthest removed breeds from the wolf (in terms of looks), originated in the mists of antiquity, but most historians believe his

The Alaunt: the early ancestor of the Mastiff and all bull breeds. Courtesy: Mike Homan.

progenitors to be the Mollossians or warrior dogs. They were, in fact, more than warriors as they also played a more passive role, guarding the soldiers' encampments.

However, it was their activities in the field of battle with their soldier companions, for whom they would and did give their lives, which earned the Mollossians their niche in history. These were large dogs with large skulls and short forefaces, who, as well as being completely fearless, were prized for the strength of their bite.

MASTIFF MIGHT

A similar type of dog was found by the side of the Britons in their fight against the Roman invaders. The Romans referred to the dogs as Pugnaces – broad-mouthed dogs – and considered them superior to any of their kind in the known world. Many of the dogs finished up in Roman arenas, fighting between themselves or against wild beasts and gladiators.

The same type of dog was known as the Alaunt at the time of the Norman Conquest, and later as Mastiffs. There is a divergence of opinion as to the derivation of the name

'Mastiff'. Some say it is a corruption of the Saxon word 'mastie', meaning fat, while others hold that it came from the Latin *massivus* (massive).

When bull-baiting became a popular sport, the descendents of those dogs became known as Bulldogs, in keeping with the common practice of naming dogs according to their purpose.

These Bulldogs had little resemblance to the modern breed, and it is arguable that the working Bulldog is more identifiable with the Staffordshire Bull Terrier than with any other breed now in existence.

The purpose of this potted history is to illustrate how, for hundreds of years, there have existed large-headed dogs with short forefaces and powerful jaws that carried the prized physical and mental characteristics of the dog now called the Staffordshire Bull Terrier.

TAKING THE BAIT

Throughout the years, the persistent factor has been the breed's mentality rather than the physical make-up and shape, the latter being altered from time to time to meet a specific

The modern Bulldog (left) can now hardly be recognised as the breed it was two centuries ago (right), when it bore a far closer resemblance to the Stafford.
Painting courtesy: B&D Hart.

requirement. Although the physical conformation changed through history to assist in a particular task, the mental virtues of fearlessness, tenacity and indifference to pain have been bred throughout.

Until it became a day out on the village green, bull-baiting was an organised sport. It was a highly profitable business, although, towards the end, the sport was excused on the grounds that the flesh of a baited bull was superior to that of the unbaited one.

Both dogs and bulls were trained for these combats. 'Green' and 'game' bulls were available to the organisers of these events; the 'game' bulls usually being matched with experienced dogs.

The trade at that time was done mainly by butchers, who had their own teams of dogs, although local dogs could be put to the bull for a fee. The butcher's Bulldogs were specially bred, highly trained, hardened to battle, and adept at their jobs. This experience and expertise must have limited the spectacle, unless the dogs were pitted against bulls of similar experience. So, at times, untrained local dogs must have provided a welcome diversion.

SIZE REDUCTION

The original baiting dogs were the size of Mastiffs, and when bull-baiting was at its zenith as a 'sport' of kings and nobles, these rich enthusiasts could afford to feed and maintain the large dogs. When the aristocracy lost interest, the pastime found considerable support from the local populace. However, the cost of feeding and housing such large dogs posed a problem. This brought about a change in the methods of bull-baiting, which led to the production of smaller, more active dogs, and to the tethering of bulls.

By selectively breeding from the Mastiff, the dog was reduced in size to around 50 lbs, and, as previously stated, became known as the Bulldog. It still had the massive skull and short foreface – in fact, the short foreface became even shorter (to increase the power and grip needed to hang on). The undershot mouth and laid-back nose enabled the animal to breathe more easily when hanging on.

Rather than being deliberately bred for, it is possible that this type of jaw and head structure was a natural consequence of mating the best practitioners of the 'sport'

Bull-baiting was originally the 'sport' of the nobility.

Courtesy: Mike Homan.

The descendents of bull-baiting dogs were used for dog-fighting during the early 19th century.

Courtesy: Mike Homan.

(the unsuccessful dogs would not have reached the age of reproduction). If the dogs had undershot jaws, the progeny would largely have this feature, some even more pronounced. Instances of this were found in the earliest Staffordshire Bull Terriers, many of whom were 'grinners', meaning that their bottom incisors were visible in front of the upper incisors, even when their mouths were closed.

Despite this bite being associated with the Bulldog and its descendants, undershot bites have existed in all types of dog for centuries. Today, they can be found in many breeds completely unassociated with Bulldogs, such as the Yorkshire Terrier. There are even undershot cats!

The smaller, faster dogs were cheaper to feed and house, and therefore made the bull-baiting business more profitable. There is evidence that the breeders of these dogs became involved in the 'sport' of dog-fighting. One famous bull-hanker was Ben White, who lived in Shepherd Market. Now, the area is the West End of London, but, back in the 1830s, it was largely green fields. Ben White was reported to have fought his

dogs in most of the 'pits' in London, and these were the same type of dogs, or their descendents, as those which had been put to the bull.

Thus the descendants of the Mollossian/Pugnace/Mastiff Bulldogs entered the most bloody phase of their progress. It was found, however, that the Bulldog's technique of grabbing and holding was not providing the anticipated spectacle. A situation which has faced dog breeders throughout the ages now faced the Bulldog men: how to improve their dogs to increase their efficiency for a given purpose – in this case, to provide a better spectacle?

The laid-back face and the protruding underjaw, which presumably was useful in holding on to the nose of the bull, was not required in dog-fighting, and neither was the all-pervading instinct to bite and hold on. The Bulldog had one target – the bull's nose – and his survival depended on his ability to hold on tightly to it. The pit dog had to learn new tricks, such as grabbing his fast-moving opponent at the nearest point and changing grip to a more vulnerable spot as the opportunity arose.

Further, on the evidence of the modern Bulldog, the Bulldog of those days could have had rather small teeth, and larger teeth would have better suited the new purpose.

The breeders were highly skilled and great care was taken with breeding programmes – after all, considerable sums of money depended on the outcome. By seeing many dogs in action, they were able to note the special features possessed by winning dogs. In this way, they could have seen that larger teeth with a better-articulated bite were advantageous.

Breeders could also have considered that a shorter-legged dog would have had an advantage. Most pictures of the Bulldog of those days show them as somewhat leggy – and leggy dogs are more easily knocked over.

GREAT WHITE DEBATE

I do not support the commonly held belief that breeders introduced terriers to the fighting Bulldog to produce a lighter dog. From the pictures available, the Bulldog was far from being the cumbersome dog which some pundits envisage.

One argument proffered is that the Bulldog was too large to handle in the pit, but this cannot be supported by evidence. According to Stud Book No. 1, 1874, there were Bulldogs weighing less than 20 lbs (9 kgs) while the upper region of these weights would have been 50-60 lbs (22-27 kgs). I am sure that handlers of the early 19th century would have been quite capable of coping with such dogs.

Jaws and dentition were the most important factors when breeding to improve the existing dogs; although the readily available terrier-type dog may have contributed, it is not certain that it did. Any infusion of terrier blood may have been on a relatively small scale, as the available genetic pool of Bulldogs could have been engineered to get the desired results.

Whatever may have taken place, the popular claim that the Staffordshire Bull Terrier was the result of crossing the Bulldog with the English White Terrier is fallacious.

The White Terrier was probably put forward as an ancestor of the Stafford to account for the preponderance of Bulldog Terriers carrying white. This is not a tenable argument, as pictures of the original Bulldogs show that they already carried considerable white.

The argument that the White Terrier was used to reduce the breed's size seems unfounded – Bulldogs were already available in a weight range of around 20-60 lbs (9-27 kgs).

It seems that breed historians have confused the Bull Terrier's history with that of the Staffordshire Bull Terrier. Certainly, the English White Terrier was introduced to develop the Bull Terrier. However, the Staffordshire Bull Terrier was known as the Bulldog Terrier at that time – an entirely different breed to the Bull Terrier.

TERRIER TRAITS

The word 'terrier' was used to describe any dog which failed to qualify for any other description, such as a gundog or a Bulldog. Any terrier could have been used, no matter what its colour. It is probable that there already existed dogs produced by accidental matings between Bulldogs and terriers. Such unplanned crossings could have been examined and the results noted. As a consequence, planned crossings of Bulldogs and terriers could then have taken place, and, in addition, some of the existing crossings could have been put back to the Bulldog.

It is again necessary to remind ourselves that the working Bulldog had little in common with the modern Bulldog. The working Bulldogs were constructed more like Staffordshire Bull Terriers, down to the 'whip' tail 'likened to an old-fashioned pump

It is a popular misconception that the Stafford comes from the Bull Terrier (left). Early photos show far more similarity with the Bulldog (pictured below).

Courtesy: Mike Homan.

handle' (as described in the Breed Standard (see Chapter Seven) and as seen in prints of the early Staffords, Crib and Rosa); the tails were completely different from the modern Bulldog's crank tail.

The Bulldog Terrier was bred for the purposes of dog-fighting. Up to this time, types of dogs were known by names relative to their purposes. With the Bulldog Terrier, this practice was not continued. True, they have occasionally been described as Pit dogs, but the common nomenclature was the Bulldog Terrier, Bull-and-Terrier, and, latterly, the Bull Terrier.

With the success of the Bulldog Terrier as a fighting dog, the popularity of the sport increased, attracting support from the highest and the lowest in society. It soon became necessary to introduce some kind of organisation if these fights were not to

degenerate into riots. To guard against this, detailed contracts were evolved. The greatest stress was laid on weights, and the owner of a dog which failed to check in at the stipulated weight forfeited his stake money.

The rules of dog-fighting favoured the contestant who would not admit defeat – not necessarily the best fighter. This perpetuated the most cherished characteristics of the Staffordshire Bull Terrier – indomitable courage and tenacity.

BIRTH OF THE BULL TERRIER
After the prohibition of bull-baiting and dog-fighting, a new breed emerged from the taproot of the Bulldog Terrier, and that was the modern Bull Terrier.

During the second half of the 19th century, James Hinks, accepted as the father of the show White Bull Terrier, was producing the forerunners of this breed in Birmingham, in the West Midlands region of the UK. The first Stud Book, published by the Kennel Club in 1874, contained a list of Bull Terriers, covering a period of some years prior to 1874. Seventy-seven Bull Terrier dogs were included, a large number of which came from the Birmingham area, as did 22 of the 38 bitches, a considerable number belonging to Mr Hinks or coming from his stock.

However, 'Idstone' (Thomas Pearce) does mention one contemporary – Mr S.E. Shirley – who specialised in a small type of White Bull Terrier, weighing under 15 lbs (7 kgs). Mr Shirley was a member of the Kennel Club, which at that time had only 51 members and a committee of 12.

The aims of Mr Hinks and Mr Shirley were on parallel lines: to produce a white dog with a long muzzle, as far removed as possible from the Bulldog and Bulldog Terrier. These objectives continued and are pursued today, except that modern fanciers have bred dogs of more substance than was observable in earlier specimens.

In the development of this new breed, there was an alteration in class status. The Bulldog Terrier generally stayed with the 'ruffians' or lower orders, and the new breed was nurtured by the 'gentry' – in fact, the Staffordshire Bull Terrier is still considered a working-man's dog by some. Fortunately, it was the commitment of the working-class enthusiasts of the Bulldog Terrier (Staffordshire Bull Terrier) that preserved the breed through to Kennel Club recognition of the Stafford in 1935.

COLOUR CONTROVERSY

In the latter half of the 19th century, the White Bull Terrier attracted people almost exclusively interested in the show ring, a place where, increasingly, the dog was developed as a thing of beauty rather than as a 'workman'.

The Bull Terrier became a fashionable dog among the gentry. Courtesy: Mike Homan.

While the Whites were developed purely as show dogs, the original Bulldog Terrier carried on, often fulfilling his natural bent (digging for badgers, rat-catching, and some illicit dog-fighting). However, in 1935, he also joined the show ranks (as the Staffordshire Bull Terrier), albeit not without objections from some dog fanciers.

The White variety was looked after by well-placed, influential protectors whose partisanship continued up to the 1940s, although Bull Terriers could be registered with the Kennel Club no matter what their colour.

However, up to 1940, owners of pure-bred Whites were under oath not to permit their stock to be mated with anything but pure-bred Whites. How strictly this was observed cannot be quantified, but I can only say that, in 1932, I mated a colour-bred White bitch to one of the leading pure-bred White Champions, a winner of the Regency Trophy. I was dimly aware at the time of the colour-bar, but it is inconceivable that the

The Bulldog Terrier remained a 'working-man's dog' and was used for badger-baiting and rat-catching. Pictured: Lancaster rat pit, 1912.

Courtesy: Mike Homan.

owner of the pure-bred White Champion was equally ill-informed. The efforts to segregate the Whites from the coloureds involved the setting up of a pure-bred White Stud Book. Despite this, the Bulldog Terrier was used on occasions to correct certain deficiencies in the Whites.

In the development of the Whites, inevitably a number of coloured Bull Terriers were born. These were not required by the White fancy and were sold off as pets. In the course of time, these found supporters and, although they could be registered as Bull Terriers in common with the pure-bred Whites, attempts were made to persuade the Kennel Club to open a separate classification for Coloured Bull Terriers. These efforts were fruitless, despite an influential lobby.

The Coloured fancy prospered in spite of not being able to use pure-bred White blood, or at least not with official blessing. Both varieties shared a common Breed Standard and, by the time the Kennel Club took over all Standards, the Bull Terrier colour question was dealt with by saying *"For White, pure white coat. Skin pigmentation and markings on the head should not be penalised. For colour, colour (preferably brindle) to predominate."*

The Coloured Bull Terrier breeders had recourse to Bulldog Terrier blood to improve their stock. As with the White fancy, stock which did not meet their aims could be sold as pets. Throughout the breed's history, the Bull Terrier – both white and coloured – has been brought back to the Bulldog Terrier (Stafford) to improve some features of the Bull Terrier breed. Only whelps showing the desired improvement were run on by the fancy, those discarded being sold as pets.

Clearly, there was a considerable pool of animals available to become Staffordshire Bull Terriers in 1935. A large number were not, as is so often stated, offspring of the Bulldog Terrier. On the contrary, all too many carried Bulldog, Terrier, Dalmatian, Whippet, and Greyhound blood – all the breeds used over a period of time to perfect the Bull Terrier.

Despite all this, there were still dogs of pure Bulldog Terrier blood, preserved through all the vicissitudes of the breed, and these are the true taproot of the Staffordshire Bull Terrier. Such dogs are recognisable because they display the Bulldog characteristics which those developing the modern Bull Terrier had been intent upon destroying. The undesirable characteristics left over from these experiments in crossbreeding include the almond-eye shape, lack of stop (the indentation between the eyes where the muzzle meets the skull), elongated foxy muzzles, lack of well-developed cheek muscle, erect ears and pinched fronts. It has taken years to eliminate, or at least to reduce, these foreign characteristics.

GROWING SUPPORT

The Bulldog Terrier was losing some support to the new breed – the white Bull Terrier – yet continued to be bred because of his prowess in the field, particularly in ratting and badger-baiting. He was also predominantly kept as a family companion. Until official recognition as a pure-bred dog, conformation was of secondary importance to performance, and size was always referred to in weight not height (possibly a throwback to their pit days).

The Bulldog Terrier continued to exist, fulfilling his function in its original, unchanged form. In the main, the people who owned them kept only one or two

(in the small, working-class homes of the time, it would have been difficult to accommodate more). The quarters and the food may not always have been of the best quality, but the dogs did have one tremendous advantage – most lived as members of the family.

So, while the Bull Terrier offshoot was developing as a show and kennel dog, the Bulldog Terrier had to be civilised enough to fit into the domestic scene, while maintaining his original prowess. The Bulldog Terrier's temperament with humans had to be unquestionable. How else could he have survived in the large families common in those days? The same character can be seen in the Staffordshire Bull Terrier today, who can be ferocious when aroused or when necessary, but is incredibly gentle with children.

The Bulldog Terrier was bred at least as much for his mental make-up as for his physical form. The dogs did, however, continue to be physically similar to one another because they were bred to be capable of their original purpose. They were kept in certain areas, particularly in the Midlands,

It was the Bulldog Terrier's good temper with people that assured its survival as a breed.

Courtesy: Mike Homan.

and, because of their relatively low numbers, there would inevitably have been a degree of inbreeding. The absence of pedigrees would have contributed to this, as it would have been very difficult to check any dog's lineage after the first generation. It was a case of mating 'like to like'. Throughout the history of the Bulldog Terrier and his heir, the Staffordshire Bull Terrier, performance was the chief criterion. Maintaining this involved a degree of mating related dogs, and a similarity of appearance automatically followed.

The temperament and mental make-up of the Bulldog Terrier was a highly-prized possession and it is epitomised in the Staffordshire Bull Terrier Breed Standard:

"Traditionally of indomitable courage and tenacity."
"Highly intelligent and affectionate, especially with children."
"Bold, fearless and totally reliable."

A Standard which merely deals with the physical form of a breed reduces the dog to a 'stock' animal; by omission, it fails to place any responsibility on breeders to produce dogs suitable to become household pets and companions. This is the basic reason for the decline of many breeds. No breed can prosper unless members of the public are willing to take it into their homes.

THE STAFFORD EMERGES
We have followed the Bulldog Terrier through his vicissitudes as a pit fighter and as the progenitor of the Bull Terrier, and now we come to his re-emergence under the name of Staffordshire Bull Terrier.

We have discovered how he was preserved by enthusiasts when his fortunes were at their lowest ebb by being taken into their households as playmates and guards for

Between the dog-fighting ban and the breed's formal recognition, the Stafford 'earned his living' as a family companion.
Courtesy: Mike Homan.

their children, and to provide a modicum of sport, by way of ratting or hunting in the fields, for the adults.

It is interesting to note that dog-fighting was made illegal in 1835 and the Staffordshire Bull Terrier was not recognised as a breed until 1935. So, before his resurgence, he had a century of living as a member of the family. One of the most important lessons he learned was to understand humans – something at which he still excels today!

ROAD TO RECOGNITION
The Bulldog Terrier had been preserved in pockets over the country, mostly in mining districts and among steel workers. Many were distributed throughout the Black Country, and it was from this area that the first attempts were made to get the Bulldog Terrier recognised as a pure-bred dog.

The climate was right because the coloured Bull Terrier fraternity, having failed in their attempt to get a separate register at the Kennel Club for Coloured Bull Terriers, were now complaining that some people who wanted to buy a Bull Terrier were, in fact, being sold Bulldog Terriers. It followed, therefore, that the Bull Terrier people (who formed a powerful lobby at the Kennel Club) were prepared to support a move to establish the Staffordshire Bull Terrier.

At that time, all Bull Terriers of any variety could be registered at the Kennel Club as Bull Terriers. A number of Staffords were so registered before recognition of the Staffordshire Bull Terrier. The requirements for the registration of any dog at the Kennel Club prior to the Second World War were extremely loose, and each page of the *Kennel Gazette* carried the following footnotes: *"Where the names of sires and dams in the above records cannot be traced as having been registered, the same [i.e. those same names] appear in italics."*

There was also a special symbol to indicate that the dog was unregistered and "not the dog with this registered name". This last phrase may seem like gobbledegook but in fact is a necessary note at a time when many dogs were simply registered as 'Jim' or 'Nell'. So, the Kennel Club decided that once they had registered a 'Jim' or a 'Nell', while they would accept another dog with this name, they would have to differentiate it from the first. In fact, in Staffords, this problem was largely overcome at the time by calling a dog 'Shaw's Jim' or 'Silver's Jim', etc.

In addition to this, dogs could also be registered *"Sire and dam, date of birth unknown"*. All of which made dog registration a rather light-hearted affair.

No records are available on the steps taken to secure Kennel Club recognition. The first attempt was to recognise the 'Original Bull Terrier', but this was refused. A further attempt was made for the title of 'The Original Staffordshire Bull Terrier', the word 'Staffordshire' being inserted by the Staffordshire county men involved. This title was also rejected, but 'Staffordshire Bull Terrier' was accepted.

There has always been a degree of mystery about these events, to say nothing of the unseemly haste with which they came to fruition. I doubt in modern times if any breed has received Kennel Club recognition without the existence of a Breed Standard. However, in the case of Staffords, the breed was recognised by the Kennel Club in April 1935, but the Breed Standard was not compiled until June 1935.

The *Kennel Gazette* issue for April 1935 carried the following:

"Staffordshire Bull Terriers. At a meeting of the Committee held on April 2nd, it was decided that Staffordshire Bull Terriers be recognised under the heading of Any Other Variety (Staffordshire Bull Terrier). Any Staffordshire Bull Terriers that are registered under the present heading of Bull Terriers can be transferred to the new category if the owners will kindly communicate with the Secretary of the Kennel Club. In future, Staffordshire Bull Terriers will not be eligible to be entered in classes confined to Bull Terriers but only in classes provided for their own variety."

FIRST REGISTRATIONS

The first registrations of this 'new' variety appeared in the *Kennel Gazette* for May 1935. Six Staffords were registered under the heading *"Any Breed or Variety of British, Colonial, or Foreign dog not classified"*, with the sub-heading of Staffordshire Bull Terriers. Of the six, two are of note.

• Buller of Torfield, a male dog, owned by Mrs R. Raine Barker, and bred by Mr Tom Walls. His sire was Buster, and his dam was Bother. He was whelped on September on 22nd 1934.

The actor Tom Walls with Buller, the first Stafford to be registered, in 1935. Courtesy: Mike Homan.

• Woodgate Sanco, a male dog, owned by Mrs M. Smith Jnr, and bred by Mr S.W. Poole. The sire was Pilot, the dam Lady, and he was whelped on September 1st 1934.

It has been said, particularly in the early days, that there were too many women in the breed and they would spoil it! It is noteworthy, therefore, that women were involved in the first six registrations of the breed.

Mr Poole was the breeder of Sanco and was in the forefront of attempts to get the breed recognised. He made an unsuccessful attempt to do so in 1934, under the name of the 'Original Bull Terrier'.

At that time, Mr Tom Walls, the actor and well-known owner of the Derby winner,

April 5th, had the largest kennel of Staffordshire Bull Terriers, and there has been nothing to compare with it for size since. He had been registering Staffords as Bull Terriers before recognition, notably a bitch 'The Looe' (sire Jack; dam Bella – both unregistered). In fact, there were a number of registrations under Bull Terriers. Since both parents were recorded as unregistered, it can be deduced that at least some were Staffordshire Bull Terriers in everything but name. Mr Wall went on to register 'Looe' as the first affix in the breed (and his house at Epsom, Surrey, was also called The Looe).

CHAMPION TIMES
In 1938, the Kennel Club gave the breed its own classification and the following

Crufts 1939. From left to right: Coronation Scot (Mr Roberts); Tough Guy (Henry Melling); Ch. Midnight Gift (Mr H. Beilby); Ch. Lady Eve, the first bitch Champion (Joe Dunn); and Ch. Gentleman Jim, the first dog Champion (Joe Mallen). Mr H. Pegg, the judge, is pictured behind. Photo courtesy: H. Robinson.

announcement appeared in the *Kennel Gazette* for May 1938:

"At a meeting of the Committee held on May 7th, the Staffordshire Bull Terrier was added to the list of breeds. It was decided that Challenge Certificates should be available for the three representative shows this year, namely the Scottish Kennel Club, Birmingham and the Kennel Club, and that for 1939 the breed would be allocated its certificates in accordance with the number of registrations during the usual 12-month period."

Thus the breed came of age, and it was no longer necessary to search among the 'British, Colonial or Foreign Dogs' to find registrations for Staffords. Henceforth, they took their place in alphabetical order with the other fully recognised breeds.

It also meant that the breed could have its own Champions (see page 24). Vindictive Montyson and Lady Eve won the first Challenge Certificates awarded to the breed, at the Birmingham National Championship Show on November 8th 1938. Arthur Demaine was the first judge to have the honour of making these awards. At this time, most of the judges' critiques of Championship Shows were printed in the *Kennel Gazette*, to which we are indebted for the following excerpts from Mr Demaine's critique.

"I was more than pleased to find the breed so splendidly represented at this its first Championship Show… Perhaps it is only natural that I should expect to find some differences of opinion which attaches itself (unduly I think) to certain features, but am not yet convinced that there is anything radically wrong with this charming breed, that, given a chance from the scaremongers, and left alone, will assuredly bed itself down in to a valuable addition to the ranks for terrierdom, and it bids fair to become not the least of that popular group ere long.

"Novice dog was won by Vindictive Montyson, fawn, whose big flat skull, neat ears, strong foreface and lovely body, ribs and tail all appealed, whilst his bone, legs and feet, and soundness and perfect condition all helped him through to take the dog Challenge Certificate and Best of Breed. He is plenty big enough but his type and balance fill my eye, and I doubt if he will ever grow coarse.

"2nd: Gentleman Jim, brindle and white. Also excels in a big, flat skull, nice ears, capital body and ribs. I liked the winner better in foreface, legs and feet but he is a grand type of dog and when on his best behaviour takes a lot of getting away from. He eventually won Reserve Challenge Certificate.

"Novice bitch 1st: Lady Eve, dark brindle and white, nicely turned in body and ribs; good hindquarters, nice fore and aft; good skull and ears, a rather less bold eye and tighter feet would not come amiss, however I failed to find a better to beat her for the Bitch Challenge Certificate."

The first Champions were made up in 1939 – Ch. Gentleman Jim (dog) and Ch. Lady Eve (bitch). Ch. Gentleman Jim was bred by Mr J. Dunn and owned by Mr J. Mallen; Ch. Lady Eve was bred by Mr J. Evans and owned by Mr J. Dunn. Both gained their titles on the same day: May 4th 1939 at the Bath Canine Society Championship Show judged by Mr A.W. Fullwood.

CLUB MATTERS

Although recognition came in April, a breed club was not formed until June 1935, when The Staffordshire Bull Terrier Club was launched.

The breed seems to hold the distinction of not only being recognised by the Kennel Club without a Breed Standard but without any sort of breed organisation to support it! Joseph Dunn organised the first show for Staffords at the Old Cross Guns public house at Cradley Heath, in the West Midlands. At this meeting, he was elected the club's first secretary, a post which he continued to hold up to 1946. He published three booklets and two books on the breed, which made an important contribution to popularising the Stafford.

IMPORTANT DISTINCTIONS

In the *Kennel Gazette* of November 1935, the following appeared:

"Interbreeding of Staffordshire Bull Terriers with Bull Terriers.

"Some short time back, the request for Staffordshire Bull Terriers to be recognised by the Kennel Club as a separate breed was duly granted and Staffordshire Bull Terriers are now recorded on the Kennel Club Registers under the heading Any Other Variety (Staffordshire Bull Terriers). We would, however, point out that this privilege carries with it the important fact that if a dog is to be registered as a Staffordshire Bull Terrier it must be of Staffordshire Bull Terrier parentage. The ordinary brindle Bull Terrier is registered as a Bull Terrier and if a Staffordshire Bull Terrier is mated to an ordinary Bull Terrier of brindle colour, the progeny cannot be recognised as Staffordshire Bull Terriers because they are the result of a cross between two separate recognised existing breeds.

"The Committee of the Kennel Club has decided that the progeny of a Staffordshire Bull Terrier and a Bull Terrier can be registered as a Bull Terrier (Interbred) thus allowing for reversion to pure-bred Staffordshire after the third generation.

"It must therefore be clearly understood that the progeny of a Staffordshire Bull Terrier and a Bull Terrier are not eligible to be registered either as a pure Bull Terrier nor can they be exhibited in classes provided for either of these breeds."

This announcement is noteworthy because it underlines the fact that matings between Staffordshire Bull Terriers and Bull Terriers were common occurrences at that time. The

Bull Terrier fancy readily admit that such crossings took place to improve the Bull Terrier in certain aspects, but I can find no evidence of the reverse taking place.

At the time that this announcement was made, the Kennel Club had no way of enforcing it. It was still accepting registrations where sires and dams were unregistered, and so had little chance of enforcing that edict.

As the Bull Terrier fancy was using the Stafford to improve features in its breed, it follows that a number of these found their way into the pool of dogs now being described as Staffordshire Bull Terriers.

So, at the time of recognition, there were Bulldog Terriers and Bulldog Terrier/Bull Terrier crosses, and these formed the pool of dogs to be described as Staffordshire Bull Terriers.

The taproot of the Stafford was the Bulldog Terrier, or, as the early enthusiasts would have described it, 'The Original Bull Terrier'.

The first Standard of the breed, despite its shortcomings, set out to describe the Bulldog Terrier, and breeders' efforts were concentrated on reproducing the Bulldog Terrier.

Good judges helped by penalising traces of the Bull Terrier to be seen in the main in almond-shaped eyerims, pricked ears, cat feet, long forefaces, downface (where the muzzle slopes downwards from the eyes instead of being on the same plane as the skull), pinched fronts, lack of bone and substance. (See also Chapter Seven on Breed Standards.)

The first Staffordshire Bull Terrier to win at an Open Show, held at Hatfield on June 20th 1935, was Mr W. Boylan's Game Lad (sire of Ch. Game Laddie) before Challenge Certificates were available to the breed (1938). Mr S. Crabtree, the judge, was working without a Breed Standard that was only then being compiled!

Game Lad: the first Stafford to win an Open show, in 1935.

Ch. Madcap Mischief: sired by Game Laddie.

Ch. Game Laddie: son of Game Lad.

Fearless Joe (top), father of top sires Vindictive Monty (left) and Jim the Dandy (right).

THE BREED TODAY

Shortly after the first Champion Staffords were made up, the Second World War virtually ended dog showing, as such events were limited to a 25-mile radius (you couldn't go to shows further than this distance from home). Some shows did take place, however, and litters were bred even in those dangerous times. We had an old bitch at home who was petrified of loud bangs, a fact we put down to her being born during an horrific air-raid over London.

Standardisation of 'type' – a more homogenised shape – had to be achieved. Strangely, considering the odd collection of breeds and types that went into making the breed at recognition, this process started almost immediately.

We are indebted to Mr H.N. Beilby, who, with scientific zeal, tabulated all the registrations at the Kennel Club between May 1935 and December 1937. It should be said from the outset that, of the 580 dogs registered as Staffords during this time, only 355 came from registered sires. Nevertheless, some well-known dogs emerge as being more popular at stud than others.

Vindictive Monty sired 35, Jim the Dandy sired 30, and these two top the poll. However, these dogs were both sired by Fearless Joe, who died in 1936 with just 17 animals registered to his name. He was fifth in the popularity poll, and, when you take into account that two of his sons top the list, you can see what influence his genes must have had on the next generations.

In 1946, Mr Beilby repeated the exercise. By then he had two Champions in his list – Ch. Gentleman Jim (whose record at stud covered an eight-year period) and Ch. Game Laddie (whose record covered nine years). Since geographic considerations have a big influence on a dog's stud potential, it should be noted that both these animals lived in accessible parts of the country. Jim recorded the highest total of all the sires with 255 offspring, whereas Game Laddie sired only 72 offspring.

It would appear that breeders were showing a preference for certain stud dogs and therefore the characteristics of these chosen dogs must have had more influence on future generations than their less-favoured contemporaries.

Ch. Gentleman Jim, who sired 255 offspring in an eight-year period at stud.

Ch. Gentleman Jim was sired by a dog called Brindle Mick. As years went by, the breed became dominated by animals descended from Fearless Joe and Brindle Mick, and so the genetic make-up of the dogs became more and more concentrated on these lines. More uniformity and standardisation had begun.

Trying to standardise a breed that started from such disparate types as a Bulldog and a Terrier is most difficult, however, and many breeders find, even today, that litters planned with the utmost care can still produce the unexpected – a set of semi-erect ears appear in a family renowned for having neat rose ears, for example.

The years after the War saw the great push forward by the breed and the foundations were laid during these years which culminated in the great popularity of the Stafford today. As numbers of animals increased, so more clubs were formed up and down the country and more people abroad began to import dogs. The number of shows increased and the variety and scope of activities in which Staffords participated continues to grow even today.

The breed's progress has been remarkable. Firstly, they have done so well in the show ring. Best in Show awards in the United Kingdom are very hard to achieve, especially for a smooth-coated, plain-looking breed such as the Stafford.

Mr and Mrs Armitage's Ch. Wystaff Warfare achieved this at Leicester City in 1969; Mr Turley's Ch. Springsteen Boy at Paignton in 1989; and Mr and Mrs Bradder's Ch. Flashy Domino Lad, current breed-record holder with 28 CCs, won Best in Show at the National Terrier Show in 1995.

Staffords are now regularly achieving places in the Terrier Group all over the world, but Crufts still has a special cachet. Only one Stafford has managed Best in the Terrier Group there – Bill Knight's Ch. Belnite Dark Huntsman. Two others, Mr and Mrs Cadogan's Ch. Bullseye of Dogan and Miss McGunnigle's Ch. Ladarna Birthday Boy, have won Group Two placings.

Son of Jim, the winner of the Challenge Certificate at the first Staffordshire Bull Terrier Breed Club Championship Show on 24 August 1946. Courtesy: H Robinson.

The Stafford: a versatile, intelligent dog that excels in many disciplines.

The breed has spread throughout the world. On the Continent, the largest numbers are to be found in Finland and now possibly Holland. In South Africa, largely due to the popularity of the Percy Fitzpatrick book *Jock of the Bushveld*, Staffords are one of the most popular of all breeds. Large numbers are also found in Australia. More to the point, the quality of the animals in these countries is becoming very high and it is not unknown for dogs to be imported from abroad to compete or to be used in breeding programmes in the home country.

Yet still, the real attraction of the Stafford lies in his position as a family companion rather than as a big show-ring winner. More are now being seen all around the world taking part in Obedience, Tracking, Agility and Flyball competitions (see Chapter Five). More and more are taking 'good citizen' awards and becoming therapy dogs (also Chapter Five). Best of all, some are dual-Champions, excelling in more than one discipline – all this is a testament to the breed's strength of character, versatility and great intelligence.

2 THE STAFFORD IN ART

It was 1935 before the Kennel Club recognised Staffords as a pure breed, but dogs of the Stafford type had existed long before then. In the preface to *The Staffordshire Bull Terrier Handbook,* first published in 1950, John F. Gordon writes of the breed's *"hard-living, gladiatorial past"*, referring to centuries of hard-bitten, determined dogs, for whom no challenge or combat was too great. It is throughout this period of history that one must look when studying the Stafford in art.

In this chapter, I will attempt to focus firstly on art featuring dogs of the earlier type, culminating in art that irrefutably represents the modern Staffordshire Bull Terrier.

STAFFORD ORIGINS

In *The Staffordshire Bull Terrier Handbook,* John Gordon writes about the confusion surrounding the creation of the breed. Two main theories about the Stafford's origins were presented in the book. The first suggests that the Stafford is a direct descendant of the Bulldog of 200 years ago. The second claims the breed's principal ancestors to be the Bulldog and a small terrier, probably the Old English Terrier (the latter being closely associated with the Bull Terrier and other terrier breeds).

One must remember that the Bulldog and

Bull Terrier of today look very different to their ancestors. Therefore, art showing the development of the Bulldog, Bull Terrier and the extinct White English Terrier, is closely associated with art chronicling the development of the Stafford. Indeed, it is possible to argue that art depicting some of those other breeds does, in fact, more closely resemble the Stafford. While Staffords evolved from the baiting and fighting breeds of the 18th and early 19th centuries, it should not be forgotten that these breeds have their own history of evolution, stretching far back into antiquity.

Some of the earliest illustrations appear in Egyptian tombs and on Assyrian bas-reliefs. They show dogs of Mastiff proportions bringing down horses and other large game. These dogs are the ancestors of a great many modern breeds, from the large Mastiff to the more diminutive Stafford.

The modern Stafford should be well balanced, of great strength for his size, muscular, active, and agile – qualities all shown in art featuring the gladiatorial breeds of old. The accuracy of this early art is, of course, open to question, particularly when one considers the size of the depicted dogs. Illustrators from the past have given us serpents, dragons and wonderful animals from Africa they had never seen, only heard about. However, while art from these times should be treated with caution, it is the only evidence in existence. Therefore, I think it should be included in a study such as this, with the proviso that it is considered representational work, rather than factual.

THE MEDIEVAL PERIOD

By the 12th century, bear- and bull-baiting were recognised as legitimate sports in the UK. By the 16th century, these pastimes were commonplace, and any fair of any note would have its bear- and bull-baiting rings. Engravings from 16th century Europe show powerful, agile dogs, not dissimilar to those seen on Assyrian bas-reliefs. Richard Pynson, in his *Antibossicon* of 1521, shows a bear being baited by six dogs of two, apparently different, breeds. According to Professor Charles Berjeau, writing in 1863, they represented – not very faithfully – a Mastiff and an early Bulldog.

In 1592 in Frankfurt, Jost Ammon published his book on hunting, *Kunstliche Wohlgerissene neu Figuren von Allerlai Jgt Kunst*. The book contains two important illustrations: one of a bear being baited by five dogs, and another showing three dogs bringing down a boar. The dogs in both illustrations look very similar. Two of the dogs in the bear-baiting scene are wearing large, spiked collars. These have been

Early bear-baiting dogs, Jost Ammon, 1592.

associated with baiting and guarding dogs for centuries, and, indeed, they remain in use today in remote parts of Europe and Asia.

Moving on to Italy, where few artists of the time featured dogs in their work, one finds an engraving by Nicoletti da Modena. Engraved in 1536, it shows a dog with cropped ears wearing a muzzle, very similar to the dogs depicted in Jost Ammon's book. However, it should be remembered that, at that time in Italy, the muzzle was not intended to show the sporting qualities of the dog. Rather, it is a reference to a law imposed on dog owners by the Italian authorities, who *"supposed the temperature susceptible of engendering hydrophobia"*.

We will never know if baiting and fighting dogs were similar throughout Europe, or if artists repeated a standard formula in their work, but one can assume a certain amount of similarity. Any dog used in such pastimes would need to be powerful, agile and active, like the modern Stafford.

STAFFORDS IN THE 18th AND 19th CENTURIES

By the 18th century, artists were depicting fighting dogs in a different style from previous eras. Finer points of type, and differences in size, are obvious differences.

An early representation of a dog of Stafford type was painted by Julius Caesar Ibbetson (1759-1817). The painting is a study of a brindle dog standing under a tree with a white Pomeranian lying close by. The brindle dog is close-coupled with well-sprung ribs, standing on straight legs. The dog's head is broad in skull, with a distinct stop and a short foreface. These features can be found in the current Staffordshire Bull Terrier Breed Standard.

Ibbetson was a self-taught portrait painter, who used both oils and watercolours. His subjects were drawn mainly from the north of England. His style was neat and he was a

Engraving by James Tookey, published in 1799, of Julius Caesar Ibbetson's painting of a Pomeranian and a Stafford-type dog.

contemporary of George Moorland and Samuel Howitt, artists with established reputations for their sporting subjects. Ibbetson's painting was engraved by James Tookey and is typical of his delicate work. It was first published in 1799, by W. Darton, Jos Harvey and W. Belok of London. Some subsequent reproductions of this picture show a dog more in keeping with Bulldog proportions of the time. One should appreciate that, in the 18th century, 'Bulldog' was a generic term used to describe all dogs of the type used for baiting and fighting.

A picture of a Bulldog painted by Samuel Howitt (1756-1823) in 1798, shows a white dog with black patches on his head, shoulders, and over the loins and quarters. The dog's head and muzzle are longer than usually seen in this period, even for dogs that were less 'Bulldoggy' in appearance. This pastoral rather than a baiting picture,

showing a farmer (perhaps the dog's owner) riding a donkey into the distance.

MEZZOTINT BY WILLIAM SAY

An anonymous painting from around 1790 was reproduced as a mezzotint by William Say (1768-1834), one-time engraver to the Duke of Gloucester. It shows all the drama and excitement of bull-baiting. While many consider such sports as the recreation of men from the lower classes, this picture disproves the notion. Central to the composition is a bull being baited by two dogs, a light-coloured one and a darker one. Depicting dogs of different colours is common, possibly carried out to identify the dogs more easily. The contest in the picture must have been of some importance, for, gathered around the central characters, is a large crowd of men, women and children. Some stand, some sit on the roofs of coaches, while others crowd into a donkey cart. Grouped together under a tree in the left foreground, at a respectful distance from the others, are mounted gentlemen accompanied by their ladies, the latter sitting in a carriage watching proceedings.

oil on canvas of three early ... Note the straight forelegs, and uncropped ears.

1844 oil on canvas by J. Mott. The dog's collar is inscribed: Nettle, the property of the Earl of Cadogan. Reproduced courtesy Iona Antiques, London.

Say's mezzotint characterises a social trend sweeping through England in the late 18th and early 19th centuries. Competitive sports, such as baiting and horse racing, played a great part in the social evolution of rural England. For the first time, people from all classes were brought together on an equal plateau. Rich and poor alike enjoyed these pastimes, and we will be forever in debt to the English sporting artists who have revealed this to us.

Eight dogs are shown in Say's mezzotint, three of which appear in the foreground. Two of the three are important. At first glance they look similar, but further study reveals significant differences. One of the dogs has straight legs, while the other has legs are slightly bowed. The latter has a more head, a shorter muzzle, and a more marked stop than his straighter-legged companion.

Looking at this picture 200 years later, it is easy to see could have developed into the B other into the Stafford.

ARISTOCRATIC PO

The Stafford will be for baiting, but it is as a fig

reputation became established. Credit for this is reputed to belong to the Duke of Hamilton.

In the last quarter of the 18th century, it is claimed he developed a breed specifically for fighting. An engraving from circa 1790 shows His Grace restraining a dark-coloured dog in the 'make ready' position.

By the early 19th century, it is clear that the aristocracy favoured baiting and fighting breeds, with a surprising number of dogs belonging to women.

Two pictures depict this very clearly. An early 19th-century painting by J.C. Scanlon shows two virtually white dogs.

One of the dogs is Lord Sandwich's Bess, shown running at the head of Bill Gibbon's bull.

The second was painted by George Morley (operating between 1831 and 1889). It features a dark-brindled dog with a white face and muzzle, a white tip to its tail, and four white feet. Named as Rosa, one of the old Bull-and-Terriers, she was owned by the Baroness Burdett-Coutts.

It will be remembered that the Sandwich family gave us the sandwich, while the Coutts gave us banking.

WASP, CHILD AND BILLY

This well-known painting by animal painter Henry Bernard Chalon (1770-1867) depicts three dogs outside an outbuilding, with a youth hanging over a fence attracting the dogs with his hat. Two of the dogs show definite characteristics of the present-day Stafford. Chalon was Dutch by birth but soon established a reputation as an artist in England. At one time he was an animal painter to the Duchess of York, the Prince Regent, and, later, William IV.

Chalon's famous painting of *Wasp, Child and Billy,* dogs owned at the time by H. Boynton Esquire, was engraved by G.W. Ward in 1809. A note in the margin of the print states the dogs to be of the late Duke of Hamilton's breed and the only ones left of that blood. The note declares them to be *"the only real Bulldogs in existence and that upon their decease that species of dog may be considered as extinct"*. Similar dogs are featured in an engraving by Thomas Bewick, published in 1824. The engraving shows two dogs fighting. Both dogs are heavily marked, very similar to the Duke's dogs.

STAFFORD DEVELOPMENT

In the 19th century, the Stafford began to develop into a dog we would recognise today. It is possible that Blue Pauls – bred for their gameness and fighting ability – were involved in this. Blue Pauls developed in an area of Scotland outside Glasgow. They were considered to be the fighting dog of Scotland. The breed displayed many of the physical characteristics one associates with the Stafford, and may have played an ancestral role in the creation of the Stafford in England and the Pit Bull Terrier in America.

Some engravings and paintings have survived to remind us of what this extinct breed was like. The most famous of these hangs in the Louvre, in Paris. It was painted in 1837 by a French landscape genre and animal painter of the French Romantic School, Alexandre-Gabriel Decamps (1803-1860). The painting features a Bulldog beside the muzzled, smoky-grey dog that is the main feature of the painting. The painting's title translates as *English dog and Scottish dog,* leaving us in no doubt that the smoky-grey dog is a Blue Paul.

In examining the Stafford's development in the 19th century, two small oilsl are worthy of consideration. Painted by another French artist, Jules Chardigny, both oils are head studies, loosely painted, of cropped, brindle-and-white dogs. Both dogs are wearing spiked metal collars with a brass plaque, on which the dogs' names are revealed – Tom and Turc. While Tom appears self-conscious, Turc seems very sure of himself, and it is interesting to speculate that the two dogs were brothers.

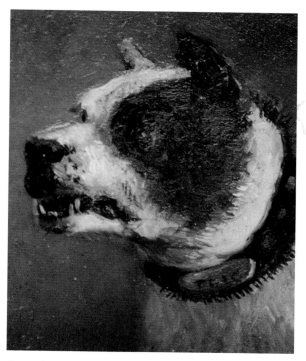

Head study of Turc wearing a baiting collar of the period, by 19th-century French artist Jules Chardigny.

In 1825, the UK's first lion fight took place at the Factory Yard in Warwick. The lion, Nero, was baited by two dogs, one being called Turk. It is interesting to surmise that the Turc in Chardigny's painting and the Warwick Turk are one and the same dog, but that might be rather fanciful. However, it is interesting that a bronze from the Turk period shows a dog with a head very similar to Chardigny's Turc. An admission ticket for the fight shows that a pit ticket cost two guineas, a fairly sizeable sum in those days. Indeed, any gentleman could have employed three housemaids for a year for such an amount.

Another painting by a French artist worthy of consideration is *Revenge*. Painted by Alfred de Dreux (1810-1860), it shows a Greyhound being attacked by a Stafford-type dog. The latter dog is almost white all over, displaying many of the structural characteristics of the Stafford. De Dreux travelled to England to complete several commissions, so it is possible this painting was completed in England. The landscape is more English than French, but one should not attach too much importance to landscapes, which were often painted to give atmosphere to a painting, rather than to provide a true record of contemporary landscapes.

Connecting Chardigny's painting to the lion fights at Warwick may be tenuous. However, a picture by W. Pedham has a much stronger connection with the famous lion fight at Warwick. It was painted in 1828, three years after the fight at Warwick. The painting depicts a black-and-white bitch called Rose, standing beside her kennel. The picture bears the inscription *"Rose, the mother of Nelson and Nettle who fought the Great Lion at Warwick"*.

The painting is an excellent portrait of a dog from the days when dogs (as opposed to hounds) were becoming established as the

Rose: the mother of Nelson and Nettle who fought the Great Lion at Warwick. W. Pedham, 1828.

subject matter in art in their own right, rather than as an accompaniment to a narrative picture.

In addition to the famous painting of Rose, three slightly earlier portraits are all worth consideration. All feature dogs that are well balanced and muscular, with straight forelegs, hindlegs with well-bent stifles, and heads with distinct stops, short forefaces, and pronounced cheek muscles. Again, all these characteristics are desirable in the modern Stafford.

The first of these three was painted by Philip Reinagle (1749-1833). It depicts a brindle-and-white dog on guard, chained outside a byre containing cattle. Reinagle's painting was engraved by John Scott (1774-1828) and published in William Taplin's *The Sportsman's Cabinet* of 1803/4, the third ever dog book to be published in the English language.

The second picture is another engraving, published in *The Sporting Magazine* in 1812. The dog is shown outside his kennel, behind which is an extensive landscape. The picture is captioned as *"Dustman, a celebrated dog, a*

Dustman, a celebrated cross between a Bulldog and a terrier. From The Sporting Magazine, 1812.

cross between Bulldog and Terrier", with a note that *"the breed of dogs of this description has been much encouraged of late".*

The third picture is a much-reproduced oil painting, dated 1812. It features a dark-brindled, cropped-eared dog standing in an extensive landscape. It was painted by George Townley Stubbs (1756-1815), son of George Stubbs, to whom the painting is frequently credited. This painting has been described by many as an outstanding representative portrait of the Bull-and-Terrier at the beginning of the 19th century, coming close to today's Stafford.

RISE OF THE FIGHTING DOG

Today, a painting of baiting or fighting sports would do little to enhance a contemporary artist's reputation, but this was not the case in the early 19th century. At the age of 16, one of England's finest animal painters, Sir Edwin Landseer (1802-1873), produced a painting he exhibited at the Society of Painters in Oil and Water Colours Exhibition. This picture, painted in 1818, shows two fighting dogs getting wind (i.e. catching their

breath before carrying on). A review of the exhibition, published in *The Examiner,* describes the picture vividly, *"But the gasping, and cavernous, and redly-stained mouths, the flaming eyes, the prostrate Dog, and his antagonist standing exultingly over him, the inveterate rage that superior strength inflames but cannot subdue, with the broad and bright relief of the objects, give a wonder-producing vitality to the canvas".*

An interesting comment in the review refers to a 'canine judge', indicating that, in 1818, there was some form of competition for dogs before dog shows (as we know them) began in the second half of the 19th century and also before the earlier shows held in inns and taverns that were frequently referred to by writers in the second quarter of the 19th century.

Before anti-cruelty laws were introduced, the early decades of the 19th century were among the most brutal as far as pitting one animal against another was concerned. Dogs fought animals of all sizes, from ducks to donkeys. One of the best-known paintings from this era depicts dogs with a badger, although not in combat in this case. The painting has been attributed to Charles Towne (who died circa 1850) and Malers

A badger (far left) standing its ground against two dogs.

Nelion, an early 19th-century artist. Towne, who was a landscape and animal painter, is the artist most credited and seems the more likely of the two. The picture was later engraved by Richard Earlom (1743-1822). It features two all-white dogs confronting a badger, with two figures rushing to the scene. The landscape is a social document of the English landscape of the period, with small enclosures, old trees, wooden fences and undulating countryside.

An engraving dated to 1820 was published in 1821, in Pierce Egan's *Real Life in London*. Egan produced various publications recording social sporting life in the first decades of the 19th century. The engraving shows bear-baiting at Charley's Theatre at Westminster. One dog is at the throat of the chained bear, while three more dogs are being restrained in the pit. There are a number of other dogs around the outside of the pit boards, all being restrained by their handlers. The scene is highly indicative of the number of dogs required for an evening's entertainment such as this.

HENRY ALKEN AND SON

Sporting art in the first quarter of the 19th century owes a great debt to Henry Alken and his son (also called Henry Alken), who recorded the various sports practised at the time. Alken engravings tend to be small, often in sets, featuring prize-fighting, bear-baiting, cock-fighting, dog-fighting, bull-baiting, cat-baiting, and ratting, as well as the more popular sports of boxing, cricket and steeplechasing.

Alken engravings of dogs usually show the dogs in combat, pitted against each other or against bears, badgers and bulls. Sometimes, their work is highly narrative, rather than a simple 'snapshot' of the contest. An example from 1820 shows an impromptu dog fight in a street, with a pie-seller walking past who stops to watch. In keeping with other

Bear-baiting, after Alken, 1820.

Alken engraving of a dog fight, published 1820.

paintings of the time, where more than one dog is shown there are always light-coloured dogs and very dark ones.

It has been suggested that so-called 'Old English Bulldogs' were involved in the creation of the modern Staffordshire Bull Terrier, and an engraving from circa 1820 would appear to corroborate this hypothesis. The engraving, by J. Clarke (after Alken) shows of a group of seven terriers, of the type that would have been crossed with 'Old English Bulldogs'. Of the seven dogs shown, five could well be ancestors of the Staffordshire Bull Terrier.

Two similar dogs, a dark one and a white one, are shown in combat in an engraving from circa 1820. It shows a dog fight at Westminster Pit, one of the fashionable venues in London. A man to the right of the picture looks through a crack in the door, perhaps trying to recognise the applicant for admission, suggesting the sport had become illegal by this time. Alternatively, of course, it could be that the event organisers were choosy as to who was granted admission.

GROWTH OF RAT PITS

With the outlawing of baiting and fighting sports, alternative ways of testing dogs in competition came to the fore. It is at this time that rat pits became popular, along with early dog shows, held in inns and taverns. Undoubtedly, the most successful and best-known dog in the rat pits was Charles Dew's Billy, billed as *"The Phenomenon of the Canine Race, and Superior Vermin Killer of his day, having killed nearly 4,000 Rats in about Seven Hours"*.

Supplying rats became big business in the latter half of the 19th century, and the livelihoods of many Essex families were dependent on the rats they caught and supplied. For example, Jemmy Shaw at the Queens Head Tavern would buy as many as 500 live rats each week, and, on occasions, he would have as many as 2,000 live rats in his house. The dead carcasses were disposed of every Wednesday morning, when rubbish collectors took them away.

The rat pits appealed to widely differing social classes. Among the Royal Collection is a table centre, designed by Prince Albert for Queen Victoria, bearing silver-gilt figures of the royal dogs, one being a terrier that has just killed a rat.

An anonymous oil on canvas, circa 1860, features a brindle dog in a rat pit. Although the dog is not large, he is, perhaps, more like a Stafford than any other dog portrayed in the rat pits. The ring is surrounded by a large, all-male crowd, and each man is painted as a sharply defined, individual portrait. The men are so clearly individualized, they must have been easily identifiable once. This picture was on display in the British Sporting Painting 1650-1850 travelling exhibition of 1975.

LITERATURE

Jock of the Bushveld is a well-known book. It was first published in 1907. Many

19th-century French bronze of a dog standing over the rats he has killed.

subsequent editions have been published, and, in the 1980s, the book was made into a film. The late Clifford L.B. Hubbard described it as *"a rattling good yarn"*. The book was written by Sir Percy Fitzpatrick, and it contains some very graphic illustrations by Edmund G. Caldwell (1852-1930) of a remarkable dog.

Probably the first proper 'breed book' published about Staffords is *The Staffordshire Bull Terrier,* written by Jack Barnard and published circa 1935, the year in which the breed was recognised by the Kennel Club. Referring to it as a book could be considered a little ambitious, but it is, nonetheless, very interesting. It is a small, paperback kennel handout, and reveals a great deal about the time in which it was written.

In contrast, another book from the same time was described as *"a horror withal"* by Hubbard, in 1968. Hubbard's description pertains to Arthur Heald's *Make Ready,* published in Northampton in 1936 for private circulation. Its typewritten text was of such content that the RSPCA offered £5.00 per copy – a large amount of money at the time – for any copies handed in to them to be destroyed.

SCULPTURES

A late 19th-/early 20th-century bronze desk-set has, mounted upon it, a standing dog similar to that seen in *Jock of the Bushveld.* Decorated with classical and human masks for feet, behind the dog is a pair of antlers acting as pen-rests, to both sides are inkwells, and in the centre is a tray.

Antoine-Louis Barye (1796-1875) was the earliest, most famous sculptor of the French animalier school, a movement that brought realism to sculpture, releasing it from centuries of romanticism and classicism. Dogs were at the centre of the animalier school, and fighting, baiting, and hunting dogs lent themselves to this new freedom of approach.

Bronze of two dogs fighting, by 19th-century French artist Joseph-Victor Chemin.

A modern bronze (1982) of two dogs playing, by Anne Godfrey of North Light.

Gilded bronze of a dog watching over a rabbit, by 19th-century sculptor Clovis-Edmond Masson.

One of the best-known and most copied sculptures to emerge from the animalier school was modelled by Charles Valton (1851-1918). There have been many copies of this model, ranging from exact replicas to variations on the theme. The sculpture is cast in bronze, featuring a chained, rampant guarding dog with cropped ears. Valton studied under Barye and exhibited regularly at the Paris Salon between 1868 and 1914. One finds many desk-sets with this dog mounted on them, for the pose of the dog contributes height to the piece.

For collectors of Staffordshire Bull Terrier art, a French bronze modelled by Joseph-Victor Chemin (1825-1901), another pupil of Barye's, is a particularly fine example. It features two dogs fighting, or for today's delicate tastes, the dogs could just as easily be playing.

A similar pose was repeated by Anne Godfrey in a cast-bronze model sculpted for North Light in 1982. For collectors of Staffordshire Bull Terrier art, this company has become synonymous with the breed. Over the years, they have produced a number of fine pieces. Another early North Light model is a standing Stafford, also sculpted by Anne Godfrey. The sculpture was cast in a limited edition, in which bitches are more rare than dogs. Today, North Light are, perhaps, best known for their cold-cast models rather than for their bronzes.

One piece of work produced by the French animalier school stands out from the rest, in that it depicts a dog more like a Stafford than any other models of the period. The sculpture was modelled by Christophe Fratin (1800-1864), who was described as *"the greatest animal sculptor of his day"* at the Great Exhibition in London in 1851. The dog of the sculpture stands four-square over a bowl, and he does not have the cropped ears common to so many other models of the time. More interestingly, the dog shows all

French desk-set, mounted with a dog similar to the illustrations in Jock of the Bushveld.

the breed characteristics of the modern-day Stafford.

Another interesting and unusual bronze is a group sculpture of two dogs fighting over a basket of game by a sign in the road. Loosely translated, the title of this piece is *A Bad Encounter on a Road*. Many of the French animaliers took up the theme of the rat pits and rat-catching, for there are a number of models of dogs shown beside rats, or with a foot on a rat. One such desk-set conveniently has a rat knob on the lid of the inkwell.

A particularly fine, gilded bronze by Clovis-Edmond Masson (1836-1913) – another of Barye's pupils – shows a cropped dog peering over a rock at a rabbit hidden beneath. The Victorians were keen to anthropomorphize animals, and another humorous piece is a small, painted spelter 'nodder' of a dog playing an accordion.

A very rare bronze recounts the story of Brummy and Physic, a man-against-dog fight, described, even at the time, as a horrible spectacle. Brummy was a dwarf who went 11 rounds against the dog *"frenzied with passion and foaming with awful persistence"*. In the final round, Brummy dealt a tremendous blow to the dog's chin, knocking it against a wall where it lay for one minute.

Bronze modelled in 1979 by British sculptor Sally Arnup. Reproduced courtesy Sally Arnup.

Moving on to the present day, two contemporary British sculptors are worthy of note. Sally Arnup and Rosemary Cooke have both sculpted the Stafford, and both artists included the breed in their respective London exhibitions. With their loose approach to their work, both artists have managed to capture the character and spirit of the breed.

POTTERY

An exceedingly rare, white-lustre, 18th-century, Staffordshire pottery group is one of the earliest pottery pieces showing a baiting group. An enraged bull, head down, turns to encounter a determined dog about to grab the bull's nose.

Keenly sought after by collectors, but less rare, is the Obediah Sherratt bull-baiting group. The bull has a similar stance to the other Staffordshire piece, and also has a dog at its face. However, this ceramic features a second dog, which appears to have been tossed on to the bull's withers. Standing by the bull is a farmer. Finding a perfect example of this piece is close to impossible, as so many parts were moulded in very fragile material. There are also slight variations in reproductions of the original, the most notable being that in some pieces the farmer wears a hat, while in others the farmer's hat can be found beneath the bull.

Later than both those models is a French terracotta showing Billy, the famous rat-pit dog. Billy is surrounded by rats and holds many in his mouth. Billy appeared in more than a score of contemporary engravings, but this piece is a particularly rare representation. It was modelled by the Comte Arthur-Marie-Gabriel du Passage (1838-1909), another student of Barye's. He was best known for his bronze sculptures, one of which shows two terriers trying to get at a rat caught in a wooden trap. Billy was sired by a dog *"of the best strain of Bulldog in England"* out of

*Left: Beswick Staffordshire Bull Terrier. Centre: late-Victorian pottery jar
and cover. Right: Beswick Stafford modelled on Ch. Bandits Brintiga.*

*19th-century French terracotta of Billy, the
famous rat-killer.*

Obediah Sherratt bull-baiting group.

Yardington Sal, a half-Bulldog/half-terrier
bitch. Pierce Egan described Billy as *"a game
article and would mill well with other dogs, draw
the badger and serve out the bear, but on account
of his goodness at rat catching, Billy left the
above pursuits"*.

Two early English porcelain models
showing dogs of fighting or baiting
proportions were made at the Rockingham

factory, during the 1826-1830 period. The
models give a great impression of the
strength and stature of these dogs. Both dogs
are lying on rectangular bases, and both have
cropped ears. The dog in one model is
brindle, except for some white on the head,
chest and feet, while the second dog is white,
with orange patches on the head, chest and
rump.

ROYAL DOULTON AND BESWICK
Probably the earliest model marketed as a Staffordshire Bull Terrier was produced by Royal Doulton, a company famed for producing porcelain of the highest order and employing the best modellers and craftsmen.

Virtually all the models in their Champion Dogs range were modelled by Frederick Thomas Daws, including a model of the brindle Bull Terrier, Ch. Bokus Brock.

This piece was produced in three sizes, as were all the models in the Champion Dogs range, and all were introduced in 1937. Keen as Doulton were to produce models of the highest standard, as a commercial company they were also eager to cut corners where they could, and so a white version of Brock was marketed as a Staffordshire Bull Terrier.

This was not the only time Doulton did such a thing, for the famous Best in Show-winning English Setter in the range also appeared as a Gordon Setter and Irish Setter.

It has to be said that, even by changing the colour, one cannot make a 1930s Bull Terrier into a Staffordshire Bull Terrier!

Doulton's sister company, Beswick, produced their first Staffordshire Bull Terrier in 1964. Unlike the Doulton piece, this dog is unquestionably a Stafford. The piece was modelled on Mr T. Field's Ch. Bandits Brintiga (bred by Mr Southall), the first Stafford to win a group in the UK, at Manchester in 1964. The modeller was Arthur Gredington, who, in 1939, was appointed the first resident modeller for Beswick. Brintiga was withdrawn from Beswick's range in 1969.

Beswick introduced another Stafford in 1988, from a model by Alan Maslankowski, a freelance modeller who worked for many companies, including Royal Doulton. This model was produced in two colours (tan, and brindle and white) and two finishes (glossy and matt).

An Understanding Mother by Jane Howse.

OTHER CONTEMPORARY ARTISTS

Another contemporary factory producing models of Staffords – such as dogs in show stance – is Heredities, a company based in the north of England.

Among collectors of Stafford ceramics, sculptures by Jane Howse (Howz) are particularly well known. At one time, Jane owned and bred Staffords, and she was able to incorporate her familiarity with the breed into her work. Her earlier pieces were in a form of plaster, but later models were produced in ceramic and cold cast.

One of her models, showing a long-suffering mother with her four puppies, is reminiscent of a 19th-century bronze. Another of her models depicts a crouching dog playing with a ball, while a third was modelled on one of Jane's own bitches, sitting on the patio. Jane modelled most of the piece from a vantage point behind the bitch. She once said the piece should be displayed from the back, which is how she saw the bitch when modelling her.

An early 19th-century, brass baiting collar, engraved: H.B. Hughes Esqr. Gogarth.

DOG COLLARS

A number of early illustrations featuring baiting and fighting dogs show the dogs wearing collars. Often, these collars have turned-out, serrated edges, or are studded with small spikes. While they do not appear on the market very often, they are well worth looking out for by collectors of Staffordshire Bull Terrier art and other art related to the breed's colourful heritage.

3 THE STAFFORD PUPPY

The Staffordshire Bull Terrier has a charming and unusual character. Combining the bull and the terrier breeds, he inherits the best of both worlds. From the Bulldog, he inherits courage, determination and a stoical approach to life, but he is prevented from being a bore by the spark of terrier blood, which lightens up his character and makes him such a fun dog to own.

However, the Stafford is not the ideal dog for everyone. It is important to make sure that this is the right breed for you, and that your lifestyle is one that can easily accommodate such a lively dog.

Rescue organisations are full of popular breeds that have suddenly taken the fancy of the general public (often because of an amusing television advert). When a breed finds sudden popularity, some unethical breeders, out to make a swift 'buck', capitalise on the demand for 'fashionable' breeds, and, in an attempt to sell as many puppies as possible, they are only too ready to stress the attractive points about a breed, without telling the owners what they are really letting themselves in for.

It would probably be more helpful if, instead of listing all the positive characteristics of the Stafford, potential owners were given an honest account of the breed, including what the breed is not!

A Stafford is not a guard dog

If you want a dog who barks every time the front gate rattles and who is reserved in his judgement about visitors to the house, choose a breed that has been developed for this purpose. A Stafford is an exuberant, boisterous and welcoming host to all who visit. If he barks, it is likely that something really unusual has alerted him, and you will ignore it at your peril.

The Stafford is too friendly a dog to make a natural guard.

However, the Stafford is naturally protective of his family – usually the weakest member of that family. He does not need to be taught this, as, throughout his history, he has been bred and trained to love human beings – it is against his nature to be aggressive or even suspicious of humans.

A Stafford is not shy and retiring

He does not easily amuse himself: he will not want to retire to his basket when a visitor calls and wait politely to be spoken to. He will fuss the visitor relentlessly, and will want to be with human companions as much as possible.

Staffords are of medium size, and, being short-coated and constitutionally sound, are low-maintenance in terms of time and money. However, they are very strong for their size and may lack tolerance for other canines or felines who are not part of the family.

A Stafford will not 'turn the other cheek'

This is not the sort of dog that you can let off the lead in a busy public place and expect him to get along with everything he meets. The motto of the Stafford is the same as the Scottish kings: *nemo me impune lacessit* which translates as: 'no one attacks me with impunity'. Traditionally, the Stafford is expected to be able to defend himself, but not to attack other animals on sight.

INHERITING A HISTORY

In recent years, considerable publicity has been given to the supposed dangers of 'dogs bred for fighting'. As has been illustrated in Chapter One, the Staffordshire Bull Terrier stems from just such root stock.

Of course, dog-fighting has been outlawed for many, many years, since which time the Stafford has been recognised as a show/companion dog. A dog trained for fighting is deliberately conditioned to a physical and mental state of high tension immediately prior to the fight. At this time, such a dog may well be beyond himself and therefore dangerous.

However, those characteristics of the fighting ancestry that might remain in the modern-day Stafford have always been considered by long-term breed enthusiasts as positive virtues. Staffords are brave (most dogs bite from fear); they are strong (many dogs bite because they experience pain); and their tough ancestry has left them with an almost unique ability to forget and overcome bad experiences (many dogs are aggressive because of some painful experience they remember from the past).

The only drawback is the breed's tendency to retaliate if attacked. However, this trait can be overcome by proper socialisation, and vigilantly supervising their free exercise in

Thorough socialisation and careful handling around other dogs is required, as the Stafford will not back down if he is attacked.

public places. Even when I have owned a Stafford whom I could not let off a lead in case he found himself in a fight, the dog never showed aggression to human beings.

It is often overlooked that, unlike some other breeds who were developed for fighting, the Stafford has never had any traditional guarding characteristics bred into him. So, unlike other so-called 'fighting' breeds, Staffords are not good guards, they are not reserved with strangers (quite the reverse), and they are not 'one-man' dogs – in fact, they are renowned for moving on to new homes without a backward glance. This is why dozens of them are so easily stolen every year.

FINDING A PUPPY

If you are quite sure that you still want a Stafford, and you are fully prepared to accept him 'warts and all', where do you go to buy a puppy?

It is always advisable to buy a pedigree dog, of whatever breed, directly from a recognised breeder, but it is especially important in the case of the Staffordshire Bull Terrier. The classified columns of local papers carry numerous advertisements for all sorts of Staffords – unregistered, crossbred, and an increasing number of so-called 'types' of Stafford.

Some of these dogs may make excellent pets, but many fall short of what the purchasers expect. Belatedly, such purchasers will discover breed club secretaries, who spend many hours listening to the moans of disappointed owners who find their attractive pup has grown into an adult that bears little resemblance to a Stafford. These dogs are often too large for the owners to manage physically, and others do not have the breed's sound temperament.

Even more upsetting are those cases where the pup has grown into a handsome Stafford who, because he is unregistered, cannot be

shown, and whose progeny (should someone be silly enough to breed from him) cannot be registered.

Buyers, take note: there is only one breed called the Staffordshire Bull Terrier and it is recognised worldwide under the same Standard.

REPUTABLE BREEDERS

Every country has its own governing body or kennel club that will supply you with the names and addresses of secretaries of breed clubs, and may also be able to put you in touch with breeders. Most countries have several clubs, so it should not be difficult to find one that is fairly local to you.

Of course, it would be foolish to contend that all registered pups bought from recognised breeders will turn out to be wonderful show prospects. However, you

Stafford puppies are irresistibly cute, but do not be tempted to buy a pup from anywhere other than from a reputable breeder.

have a much better chance of getting a good, typical Stafford, as a reputable breeder will be dedicated to breeding to the recognised Standard (see Chapter Seven).

If you are dealing with a reputable breeder, you should expect an after-sales service, where the breeder will provide advice and support, and offer to take the dog back should your circumstances change. A 'pedigree' is a list of names on a piece of paper. Without the backing of a Kennel Club registration there is absolutely no guarantee of breed or parentage. Without any documentation to attest to your dog's background, you have no grounds for complaint. At the very least, a breeder who attends shows and who is a member of a breed society has a reputation to uphold among his peers.

The club secretaries can put you in touch with breeders in your area and provide you with details of any shows. It is a good idea to attend these events and meet as many Staffords as possible. You'll discover that Stafford breeders are very friendly and helpful.

PATIENCE IS A VIRTUE
Don't be in too much of a hurry to buy your puppy. You may have to wait for a litter to be born or to be old enough to go to a new home. Don't be tempted to rush into a purchase, and certainly do not buy from commercial outlets. Profit will be the main motive in such organisations, and you will have no chance to see the mother or any other relatives of your puppy (essential for you to assess the pup's likely temperament and conformation – see page 52).

Buying a pup that is registered with your national kennel club is by far the best option. Purchasing an unregistered puppy could result in your taking on a mixed-blood pup – or even a mongrel – and you will have no means of redress. The puppy may have serious health problems, and his temperament may be questionable due to bad breeding and

A well-bred litter will sell itself, so be wary of a strong sales pitch.

lack of adequate socialisation. Do not take any chances – buy only from a recognised breeder.

Breeders are naturally proud of their stock and will undoubtedly want to do a bit of bragging about their success in the ring. If you have done some background work on the breed, you should be able to tell fact from fiction – or, at least, exaggeration!

MEETING THE BREEDER
Ideally, you will build a relationship with your prospective breeder long before you actually pick up the puppy. This will give you a chance to 'meet the family' and get real hands-on experience with the breed.

Large commercial kennels of Staffords do not really exist. Ninety-nine per cent of Staffords, even in the most successful show kennels, live in the family home. Indeed, this is some guide to the breed's temperament: it is comparatively easy to keep a bad-tempered dog if he is shut away in a kennel, whereas a dog living in the home is a much more daunting prospect if he is not good-natured.

You may not be able to see the sire of the puppies, as most serious breeders will travel many miles to pick the ideal mate for their bitch. Someone who uses their own stud dog on all their bitches should be viewed with caution.

It may be that you meet someone who has just mated their pet dog to their pet bitch, and you will have the advantage of being able to see the whole family group. If getting a pet with an excellent temperament is your only concern, then this might be a good buy for you, but remember that such sellers are not strictly 'breeders', and you are less likely to get knowledgeable back-up once you take the pup home.

You should take especial note of the character of the mother. It is from her that the puppies will learn their first lessons – if she is shy of strangers, then the pups will follow her lead and be reluctant to come up to you. If there is any sign of ill temper towards you or if you are told 'she doesn't like children' when you visit with your family, leave the litter well alone.

You must be prepared for a good breeder to quiz you before agreeing to any sale. They will want to know about you, your family, and the home that their puppy will be going to. Don't be offended by this interrogation. Indeed, if the only question is concerned with the price, then I would walk away. Breeders who care will be interested in the welfare of the pups they sell and anxious to see how they have turned out as adults – so photos, phone calls and visits will be

The mother's temperament will give you a good indication of the pups' future characters.

welcomed. Such breeders will be there to give you advice as you need it, and will offer assistance even in the extreme eventuality that your circumstances may change and you need to find a new home for the dog they bred.

MALE OR FEMALE?

Your next big decision is whether to buy a dog or a bitch. There are pros and cons for both, which you should discuss with your family.

Male Staffords are full of character. They are rough and tough, and ideally suited to the hurly-burly of family life. They love games with balls, rings and other toys, and are always ready for walks, rides in the car, and any other family activity. Males are generally stronger characters and will need firm handling right from the start.

All Staffords are boisterous and energetic, but males (right) can be particularly exuberant. A female (left) may better suit a first-time owner.

Bitches are quieter and possibly easier for the first-time owner to train. However, they are somewhat self-centred and very sure of what is best for them – they will only play with the ball until they have had enough and will then retire to their beds.

Females are often greedier than males, and are easier to withdraw from a pugnacious incident if only because they are less strong than their male counterparts.

Bitches will have seasons twice a year. This is a nuisance, but spaying (neutering/altering) is an option (see page 82). If you have a young family who may leave doors open, it will certainly be best to choose a male or have a female spayed.

If you already have a dog, then choose a Stafford of the opposite sex, as they are more likely to get along. Never buy two male puppies. Indeed, never try to keep two male Staffords together at whatever age.

Staffords do not need the company of other dogs – they yearn for the company of their human soul-mate. Every rescue worker in the Stafford field will have heart-rending stories about people who have taken on two male puppies only to have to choose which one to keep and which one to rehome when they approach maturity. Both will vie for 'top dog' status, and will not back down.

COLOUR CHOICE

Staffords come in a wide variety of colours, and you may have a preference for one in particular. The most common is a brindle of various hues, but red or fawn, black, blue, or pied (these colours with white) are also available.

There are no colours that are truly 'rare', so be wary of unscrupulous breeders trying to obtain an inflated price for a pup that may be differently marked from the rest of the litter.

There are no real differences between the colours; it is simply a cosmetic preference. If you do wish to buy a particular colour, you should notify the breeder at the outset, as most specialise in one or two colours.

The pups should be clean and alert, with a healthy, shiny coat.

SIGNS OF GOOD HEALTH

Whether you are selecting a puppy as a house pet or for the show ring, the first priority must be the same – a healthy, well-reared pup.

You should not attempt to look at a litter before their eyes are open. There is a much greater danger from infection with very tiny puppies, and the mothers will be much more protective towards their young family and may actually cause them harm in their efforts to stop you looking at them. However, if you are dealing with an experienced breeder, I would not expect them to allow you to view a litter of such young pups.

It is advisable to visit a few litters before you make your final selection. Each time, bear in mind the tips given later in the book on breeding (see Chapters Nine and Ten).

- Assess how clean the environment is.
- Are the puppies lively and bright-eyed, with clean, shiny coats?
- Do the pups have pot-bellies (often a sign of worm infestation)?

- Ask about the litter's feeding routine. (Your puppy should be having at least four meals per day and two of these should be protein – it is not sufficient for a puppy over four weeks of age to be fed only milky meals. The breeders should be able to give you a set timetable for this feeding – irregular feeding times are not a good thing for a young pup. They should also be able to tell you what steps have been taken to ensure that all the puppies have been able to get their fair amount of food.)
- Look to see if there are signs of old faeces – pups that play in their own excrement will not prosper.
- If you do see a puppy 'perform', take note that the stools are well formed. Loose motions may indicate a tummy upset.
- Look out for bumps on the tummy or in the groin – signs of a possible hernia. Little hernias in the tummy area will most probably disappear as the pup grows, but make sure that you can easily depress the bump.

Watch the puppies at play, and you will see their individual characters emerge.

51

If you are in any doubt, especially over a hernia in the groin area, either choose another pup or make it a condition of sale that you will have it checked out by a vet. Groin (iguinal) hernias are not particularly prevalent in Staffords, although tummy (umbilical) hernias are quite common.

CLUES TO TEMPERAMENT

Stafford puppies should come straight up and greet you enthusiastically, usually by pulling on your trouser bottoms and chewing your shoelaces. Because of this, don't dress up for a visit – clothes that are tough and old must be the order of the day.

If the litter is in the house – where most Stafford litters are reared – the pups will have the advantage of being used to everyday household noises (e.g. television, washing machine, vacuum cleaner). This holds them in good stead for when they come to your

The breeder will help you to assess the puppies.

home. Home-reared puppies are also more likely to be well handled and socialised. Again, this is a great advantage for their future development.

Puppies that are kept outside need not be disadvantaged, provided that a great deal of time has been spent handling and playing with them. You will have to judge for yourself whether you think the litter has had plenty of human contact or if, although well fed, the pups have been left largely to their own devices.

Puppies who have been deprived of good socialisation will be reticent about coming to you, they will crawl on their stomachs, or hide in a corner of the box. Should you take a pup from such a litter, you will need to put in extra time introducing him to household noises and generally getting him used to human company.

Never buy the timid, sickly-looking puppy for sentimental reasons – you could be taking on a lot of heartache and also be encouraging an uncaring breeder to produce more timid, sickly puppies in the future.

Home-reared pups will have a head start in terms of socialisation and good temperament.

NUMBERS GAME

Don't be tempted to buy more than one puppy, however cute they may look together and whatever favourable terms the seller might offer for 'bulk-buying'. Two pups are more than double the trouble of one. There is nothing to compare with the one-to-one contact and bonding you will get from training up one puppy. It is better to bring up one Stafford to be a well-trained adult before attempting to keep any more.

PEDIGREE PAPERS

A pedigree is a dog's family tree. Looking at pedigrees can be a bit of a mystery to the uninitiated.

In brief, the father is called the sire, and his ancestry is written behind his name – i.e. his grandparents and great-grandparents feature in the top half of the pedigree. The mother is called the dam and her ancestry appears on the lower half of the pedigree form. Champion animals are usually written in red or in capital letters, and the title is abbreviated to Ch.

Phoney pedigrees are not unknown. If you have some knowledge of the breed, you should be able to check if a particular dog really is a Champion and even if his parentage is as written on your form. It would be a good idea for you to make the acquaintance of someone who is a breeder, or contact the secretary of a breed club and ask them. Attending a few dog shows is also advisable, especially those run by a breed club. Here, you can talk to people who are familiar with the breed and who can confirm for you that, for example, a certain dog is really a Champion. Some books on the breed will give you a list of all the Champions in the breed.

Absolute fakes should be picked up by your national kennel club when the registration is applied for. As a further security, some national kennel clubs list their litter

You may find it difficult to choose a puppy, but do not be tempted to take two – one Stafford is handful enough!

registrations in a breed record supplement, usually published several times a year. These publications are avidly studied by breed fanciers, so you stand a chance of having any obvious mistake or misrepresentation picked up. The bottom line is that, when buying a puppy, one must use as much common sense and judgement as when buying anything that you plan to live with for maybe 14 to 15 years.

Finally, DNA-testing is becoming more widely available and has been used to establish the correct or incorrect parentage of a number of dogs.

The breeder should give you a signed pedigree with the kennel club registration form that should contain all the pup's details – including the first generations from the pedigree. The breeder should sign this form so that you can notify your kennel club that you have transferred ownership of the pup into your name.

The only person entitled to register the puppies is the breeder. Even if both parents are registered, you cannot register the pup without the breeder's signature and consent. If one or both of the parents are unregistered, you cannot register the pup. There is often a deadline for registering a puppy, after which it is very difficult and costly to obtain a registration – contact your national kennel club for details.

Breeders may impose endorsements on a registration, e.g. 'name unchangeable', 'not eligible for the issue of an export pedigree', or even 'progeny not eligible for registration'. These are usually imposed by breeders who wish to protect their bloodlines against inappropriate matings, or exports to countries where animal protection is poor.

The breeder must inform you of any such endorsement before you purchase the puppy. These endorsements can usually only be removed by application to your kennel club from the breeder, but, in very exceptional circumstances, removal can be applied for by the new owner.

If the pup has had any inoculations, you should receive a card informing you of the date and type of injections given, and it should be signed by the vet who administered them. The breeder should also provide you with a diet sheet and a note of when the pup was last wormed.

THE SHOW PUPPY
If you wish to select a puppy for the show ring, then your task is much harder. Thousands of puppies are registered every

Spotting a show winner takes skill and a lot of luck!

year, but only a relatively small proportion will ever make it into the show ring. For example, in the UK in 2001, 11,026 Stafford puppies were registered at the Kennel Club. In the same year, only 16 Staffords (seven dogs and nine bitches) became Champions – and that was a good year in that more Champions were made than usual. The percentage will be somewhat higher in other countries, but not considerably so. In other words, the odds are very much against you picking a Champion and only slightly higher that you will get a show dog of any quality. But the fact that it can be done keeps everyone trying!

It is vital that the prospective purchaser does a great deal of homework. Read as many books about the breed as you can lay your hands on, and visit several shows, where you should find plenty of fanciers to speak to.

Talk to as many people as possible. It is a truism that, often, the people with the least experience and first-hand knowledge are the quickest to jump in with words of wisdom and advice. Speak to the quiet ones, as well as those who have most to say, and make up your own mind who is speaking from experience and who is just trying to impress!

This careful attitude is even more important when you surf the internet. Always look for official websites, and remember that those who are the busiest, caring for their dogs, rearing their puppies, and attending the shows, often have little or no time for participating on the 'net'.

If you attend some shows and read club publications and magazines, you will begin to learn which Staffords and breeders were successful in the show ring, and, more importantly, who were their sires and dams. You should begin to get a picture in your mind of how you would like your adult Stafford to look. You may be seeing these characteristics appearing in certain lines or families. Then you can look out for anyone expecting or planning a litter from these lines.

A Stafford should neither be light and narrow like a terrier, nor thick-set and wide like a Bulldog.

Remember: it takes two to make a pup! It is really important that you see the mother of the pups (and, if possible, the sire), even if it means making a long trip across the country.

PET POTENTIAL

Strangely, some of the most successful show dogs have been bought as pets and their potential only realised afterwards. One of the first was Ch. Troglodyte, who was bought as a family companion for a young boy. He was more than a year old when a well-known fancier spotted him being exercised in the park, advised that he be shown, and the rest is history.

Fortunately for the owners of Troglodyte, the fancier they bumped into was genuine and experienced. Usually the 'experts' who stop you and opine that you have a really big potential Champion know next to nothing about the breed. It can be quite an expensive lesson to learn that you have been given wrong advice.

CHECK POINTS

What should you be looking for when selecting a puppy for the show ring?

As with choosing a pet dog, the mother should be calm and steady. Physically, she should be a typical example of her breed, and should be well bred (from good family lines).

Similarly, you should check on the character and breeding of the sire. Dogs or bitches bred from poor-quality parents are unlikely to produce better than themselves. Even if they do, the resulting pups will be even less likely to produce outstanding puppies.

Obviously, the litter you select from should be a healthy, well-reared one. A poorly-reared pup can make up his body weight and substance, but it will be an uphill task for you, and the harm done to his development might never be reversed.

Staffords do not always breed 'true'. This is partly because the breed has such a mixture of blood in his make-up. Being predominantly a mix of terrier (a light, narrow dog) and a Bulldog (thick set and wide), it is hard to get all the litters in the middle of these two extremes. If all the pups bred 'true', they would be bang in the middle, but, in fact, too often litters split into very heavy or very lightweight animals. In addition, most Stafford breeders do not overbreed their stock, so less experimentation or standardisation has occurred.

With other breeds, this poses less of a problem. In breeds that have been bred for show for many, many more years than the Stafford, and where large kennels of these breeds were maintained (especially in the formative years of the breed), a great deal of experimentation could take place. Matings were made, and if the puppies were no good for the show ring, they were simply put to sleep. Thus, only ones with the desired characteristics were allowed to live and procreate. By contrast, Stafford puppies generally belonged to families who would not, for sentimental reasons, want to put any to sleep. This left a lot of poor-quality animals to be bred from as well as the good ones.

Such policies, while being more humane, leave a great number of below-par animals in the gene pool. In any winning Stafford's pedigree, such animals will be lurking and their bad points can come out in whelps just as surely as other good points can exhibit themselves. This is why it is hard to pick Stafford show pups and also why some slip through the breeder's fingers and finish up in pet homes.

For the same reason, you should not be carried away by the overenthusiastic hopes a breeder may have for his pups. Experienced, sensible breeders will be reluctant to extol the show potential of their dogs, and some will not sell a pup as a 'show' dog at all, merely saying that this pup shows more promise than another, will make a healthy, happy pet, and the rest is in the lap of the gods!

SPOTTING POTENTIAL

Generally, in a well-bred litter, Stafford puppies will appear very alike. After six weeks, differences begin to appear. It is wise not to select a puppy until about seven to eight weeks of age. Do not get carried away by attractive markings – this may be a useful way of picking a pet, but it is structure, not colour, that is important if you are selecting for the show ring.

So how do you judge a good shape? Up to about six weeks of age, any reasonable litter (barring any obvious faults, such as bad colouring) will appear very promising and even (that is, the pups will all look alike – they will be the same size and have roughly the same shape). Difference in head shape, length of back, etc. will only become obvious after six weeks of age. There is even an old saying: "They are all Champions at six weeks". After this age, however, variance between littermates becomes more obvious.

"All Staffords are Champions at six weeks."

A pup should have a square body shape.

At around eight weeks, these differences are pronounced, and you will be in a better position to make a selection.

As you look at the puppies, they will probably vary most in size and substance. On the whole, Stafford puppies refine as they get older. In other words, picking a fine-boned, narrow pup in the hopes that it will develop rib and bone with age is likely to lead to disappointment. You are safer choosing a fairly substantial pup – although not the biggest, stockiest dog, as he could well finish up a monster.

Height is the most difficult characteristic to assess in puppies – unless the pups as a whole are midgets or giants, in which case you should forget the litter! It is true that the smallest puppies in a litter may grow to be the tallest adults. Perhaps the size of the parents may give you a guide here.

HEAD
The first individual characteristic that will strike you about a puppy is his head – and this is one characteristic that does not improve with time. If a pup is snipy (has a thin, pointed muzzle) at six weeks, he will be snipy at 16 months. The cheek muscles might develop and make the head look passable, and the body characteristics might be good enough to make your dog a winner, but he will not be a good-headed winner.

The head does not have to be big – it is the shape and especially the depth that matters. The good-headed pup will have round eyes, set wide apart; the ears will be set rather low; the foreface will look blocky and short at this age; and there should be width across the mouth. Viewed from the side, the pup will have the good stop required by the Breed Standard (see Chapter Seven), and his foreface must be on a parallel plane to his skull. His muzzle should not tip upwards so that his nose is higher than his stop, but nor should it slope downwards. This latter, more common, fault is usually associated with a pointed muzzle and small eyes. The face will appear quite short at this age – shorter than it will finally finish up.

MOUTH
At this stage, puppies have their first (milk) teeth. Mouth faults in the Stafford are fairly common – especially in those lines which are breeding for good, strong forefaces. Overshot pups (where the top jaw protrudes in front of the bottom one) are not uncommon in the breed. Very often, the lower jaw will close up to the top, but almost invariably such a pup will have a weak, snipy foreface (although he will probably have perfect dentition!).

Do not select an undershot puppy (one where the bottom teeth are in front of the top), as this is considered a bad fault in the show ring. While puppies will appear overshot at a very young age, it is rare for an eight-week-old puppy to be undershot. Unfortunately, this fault usually develops much later – sometimes as late as six to nine months old. Furthermore, it is a fault that will get progressively worse.

BODY

When standing, the best puppy will look square – roughly as long as he is high. His front legs should look sturdy, and, when you pick him up, his rib cage should feel solid in your hands. He should be active and able to run and move freely.

If you see the litter when they are very young, you'll notice that they will take some time before they are right up on their feet (the heavier the pup, the longer it will take). But if you are selecting at six to eight weeks, all the puppies should be running around.

PHYSICAL DEVELOPMENT

After eight weeks of age, puppies start to go through many different phases. The head may lose its stop and the legs will grow suddenly very long. One week, the puppy's

By 12 weeks, you will have a clearer idea of whether the pup has potential.

head will look too heavy for the body, and the next he seems to have a pea-sized head on a monster's body.

At teething time, his ear carriage may become erratic – one ear may unfold and lie flat, or both ears may suddenly start to fly high above his head. Then, of course, there is the ever-present worry when the milk teeth change to the permanent set that the dentition will be correct. All this will sort itself out for better or for worse by the time the pup is about a year old.

Because of all these changes, it is important that you start with as good a pup as you can. As he grows, you will have many worries, and some of your worst fears may materialise. Perhaps the pup will develop a mouth fault; he might stop growing, or conversely, keep growing like a beanstalk. Suddenly, your dream Champion becomes an also-ran. But a pup that is a poor specimen at six to eight weeks has even less chance of growing into a star, so increase your odds by picking the best pup from the start.

PREPARING FOR THE PUPPY

Once you have booked your puppy, there is time for you to make all the necessary preparations for his arrival into your family. Decide on the house rules and stick to them – changing rules can be very confusing for any animal.

SLEEPING ARRANGEMENTS

Firstly, decide where the new puppy will sleep. A draught-proof spot is needed, if possible, next to a source of heat (for example, a radiator or Aga oven). Staffords have a very close, short coat, and, unlike many other double-coated breeds, have very little protection against the cold.

Most Staffords have a penchant for sleeping on humans' beds. Think twice before you allow this, as it is a very difficult habit to break. Think ahead: pups grow into large

A synthetic fleece blanket is an ideal form of bedding.

adults, who take up an amazing amount of space when fully extended, fast asleep.

Simple plastic beds are easily cleaned and can withstand busy little teeth better than most – although they can develop frilly edges which are lethal for tights and other fine clothing. When the pup is older and has grown out of the chewing stage, bean bags and wicker baskets can be used.

For bedding, a blanket of synthetic fleece (such as veterinary bedding) is warm and can be easily laundered.

The bed should be placed on tiles or other flooring which can be easily washed – at first, puppies cannot usually hold themselves all night. You may wish to spread newspaper down around the bed for ease of clearing up, just until the pup is old enough to be fully house-trained.

BOWLS

You should buy non-breakable food and water dishes, made of plastic or stainless steel. Water should be available at all times. Do not make the mistake of buying pretty pottery water bowls, especially with youngsters, as they can be picked up and smashed with disastrous results.

COLLAR AND LEAD

You could also buy a small collar and lead – although the puppy should not be taken outside until after he has finished his inoculations. Until such time, you can practise lead-training in your garden (see page 86).

Do not leave the pup unattended with the collar on, as he might do a lot of scratching and/or get it caught on protruding objects. If you have another dog, he could get a tooth caught in the youngster's collar, and it is possible for the pup to be strangled.

CRATE

If you plan to use a crate or cage for the puppy, now is the time to buy it. Do make sure it is large enough for when he grows into an adult dog, and that there will be plenty of room for him to lie and stretch himself. (See Chapter Four for details of crate-training.)

TOYS

There are so many toys on the market, you certainly won't be short of choice. Just remember not to buy anything which is too big for the puppy's tiny jaws, and not so small that he can swallow it. Watch out for

Choose durable, safe toys that can withstand a pup's vigorous chewing.

rubber and cloth toys that a Stafford might chew to bits, and be careful of rawhide toys that can be munched to a pulp and then swallowed whole.

Regardless of what toy you buy, make sure it is safe even when chewed – and chewed it surely will be. Our favourite and most successful toy is still the plain old ball. For tiny pups, we use a screwed-up piece of paper, progress to a lightweight ball, and then move on to a really tough, rubber one. Staffords love to chase balls, and, with encouragement, can easily be taught to retrieve.

SAFETY MEASURES

Before you collect your pup, you should take a good look round your house and garden to note any possible danger areas. In general, Staffords are strong but accident-prone.

Indoors, the main problems will be chewing shoes or slippers, electricity wires, and knocking over precious ornaments. They will sometimes attempt to jump down the stairs, through or over banisters, even out of an upstairs window, if the temptation is too great. Stair-gates to prevent access to unsupervised areas are therefore a must.

The biggest danger comes from what they decide to chew. Top of the list must be their penchant for chewing electric wires and cables. Strangely enough, even something as harmless-looking as a pair of tights (pantyhose) can also cause devastation as they can become entangled in a dog's intestine and virtually strangulate his digestive system.

In the garden, ponds can be death-traps for young Staffords, as they are so inquisitive. Make sure the pup cannot gain access to the pond, or cover it over until he is old enough to know better.

A secure perimeter fence is vital. Pups can squeeze through or under the tiniest of spaces, so make sure that garden gates and fences go right down to the ground. Should refuse collectors or window cleaners need to use your back garden for access, make sure that you have secure gates with locks that you can release and secure after the visitors have left.

Slug pellets are a danger to any dog, so always keep them (and any other poisonous substances) away from your Stafford. If you use weedkillers, check that they are animal-safe. Also check with your garden centre that

Trailing electrical cables are irresistible – but deadly – to an inquisitive pup.

A puppy will investigate every inch of your garden, so ensure it is safe before you bring your Stafford home.

You should be able to collect your pup when he is seven to eight weeks old.

you have dog-friendly plants – the beautiful laburnum tree has poisonous seed pods, and puppies find objects like these very interesting and chewable.

A number of Staffords disappear, are stolen, or are killed or injured on the roads because a gate was inadvertently left open by visitors – do not let the same happen to your new addition.

FINDING A VET

Before you collect your pup, decide which vet you will use. The best way is through personal recommendation. This presupposes that you trust the judgement of the person giving you advice. A neighbour recommending a vet because he is cheap and looks like George Clooney is not to be preferred to the one who recommends a vet for his diagnostic skills and the quality of care he offers – even if he looks like Homer Simpson.

COLLECTING YOUR PUP

Puppies should not leave their mothers until they are seven to eight weeks of age, although they should be fully weaned by about five to six weeks of age. They need this extra time with their canine family to learn the many social and doggie skills which a good mother will teach her puppies.

Choose a quiet time to collect the puppy. If you have young children, for example, arrange to collect the pup during school-

time, so that you and he can get settled in before the excited horde descends. The puppy will need time to explore his new surroundings, and he does this best at his own speed and in peace and quiet. For this reason, it is never a good idea to introduce a new puppy to your home at Christmas time – in fact, most sensible and caring breeders will not let pups go to their new homes over the festive period.

When you collect your Stafford, take someone with you, so the pup can be held safely in the car without being thrown around by the vehicle. In any case, he will most probably be sick – so take a towel and plenty of newspaper to mop up!

Speak to your veterinary surgeon and make arrangements for the pup's inoculations. You might also enquire about whether the clinic runs a puppy party. These are opportunities for puppies who are not yet fully inoculated to socialise together. The classes should be carefully regulated so as to minimise the chances of infection. Proper training classes will require that the puppy has had all of his inoculations.

Check that the people in charge understand the Staffordshire Bull Terrier. The way a Stafford puppy plays is very rough and forceful. If all the puppies in his group are small breeds, he may well appear to be a bully. So make sure that he is teamed with others of similar make and shape.

Hold and reassure the pup on the journey home.

4 THE RIGHT START

When you are bringing a new dog or puppy into your household, it is important to plan ahead. Firstly, you should have given a great deal of thought before deciding that a Stafford is the breed best suited to your family. Next, you should have taken time to select a caring, experienced breeder from whom to buy your pup. Now, you should plan how you will rear the pup so that he becomes a well-adjusted, well-behaved, and happy new member of your family.

HOUSE RULES
Sit down with your family and decide on the 'house rules' – where the pup will sleep, when he will be fed, and, later, when and who will exercise him. If you do not plan, your Stafford pup will make his own choices – and one of those will almost certainly be that he is going to sleep in somebody's bed.

Do you want the dog to sit on your furniture? Remember: if he can get on with clean feet, he can do so with dirty paws. Perhaps you will decide to allocate one chair for the puppy, or perhaps you will prefer him to rest on the fireside rug. You could even train him to wipe his feet every time he comes in from the garden, or, more realistically, train him to stand and wait for you to wipe his feet.

Whatever you decide, stick to it – nothing is more confusing for an animal than to have rules suddenly changed. It is also much easier to teach a pup good habits than to unteach bad ones.

Also, plan to avoid problems by encouraging everyone in the household to be responsible for keeping favourite toys, slippers, shoes etc. out of the puppy's reach. All puppies chew and it is better to be safe than sorry.

HOME AT LAST
Take time to let your puppy familiarise himself with his surroundings. This is potentially a traumatic experience – even for a breed as confident and stable as a Stafford.

All your pup has ever known up to now has been the warmth and security of his mother and his littermates. He will have lived within a set routine and surroundings in which he had full confidence. Now, everything has changed – all that was familiar to him has been taken away.

This is why it is important that he is introduced to his new home gradually and peacefully. Never bring a puppy home at Christmas, a busy holiday time, or on celebration days (such as a birthday party). It is also preferable to bring him home while the children are at school, so that he has a quiet time to settle in before the excitement of a house full of kids.

Take your Stafford pup into the kitchen (or wherever you plan to put his bed) and show it to him. If the breeder has given you a blanket or something from his original nest, then spread it out for him. Let him have a good sniff around – dogs, unlike humans, learn more through their sense of smell than any of their other senses.

As discussed in Chapter Three, make sure that the bed is durable, washable and chewproof (see page 58). If the bed seems too big for your puppy, a plastic washing-up bowl, lined with a blanket, will suffice until he grows. The bed should be in a draught-free area – Staffords, being so close-coated, are not well adapted for the cold.

Next, you should introduce the pup to your garden. Stay with him and encourage him to explore. He will probably need to relieve himself, so this is as good a time as any to start his house-training lessons.

HOUSE-TRAINING

This is your first big hurdle – and a most important one, as nothing is worse than a dirty dog. Actually, Staffords are usually very clean – even tiny pups will crawl off their blankets to avoid fouling their sleeping place. Sensible breeders will have supplied the litter with a 'sleeping' and a 'play' area, so he will already have some idea of keeping his quarters clean.

There are a few simple, general rules to successful house-training:

- Always take the pup outside after a meal, after play, exercise or excitement, and when he wakes from a sleep.
- Choose a toilet spot for your pup and stick to it. Not only will it make it easy for you to keep the area clean, picking up after your dog and hosing down any wet patches, but you will find that your pup will quickly learn to associate the area with relieving himself.

Just before 'performing', the puppy will sniff the ground.

- Always praise the pup when he has performed. Puppies are keen to please their owners, and praising him after he relieves himself in the right place will encourage him to repeat his actions in the future.
- Choose a word that you will use when your pup performs (e.g. 'busies' or 'wee wee'). Once your dog associates the word with the action, you will be able to get him to 'perform' virtually on demand. This is especially useful when travelling. As ever, as soon as your pup performs, praise effusively.
- Never use punishment. If your pup has an accident, clean it up, and make an effort to take him out frequently to avoid it happening again. If you shout or smack your pup, he won't know why you are being so unreasonable (he won't be able to associate your anger with something that he may have done an hour or so ago but that you have only just discovered). Your puppy may think you are objecting to what he does, not to where he does it. Then he will try to relieve himself secretly, so as not to upset you – and this means even more accidents! If you see him in the act of relieving himself, just startle him to stop him mid-flow and then whisk him outside for him to finish his business.

Spread newspaper around his bed at night to help the cleaning-up process in the morning – until he is a bit older, it is unlikely that the pup will be able to 'hold' himself all night.

Similarly, when you leave the pup for any length of time, you can also leave paper down. This process is useful, but can become a nuisance if your puppy comes to rely on being able to perform on paper whenever he is left for any time – he may not try to wait until you return.

Some pups – especially bitches – are less confident than others about performing. You may find that, at about four to six months, although you are taking her for reasonable walks, your female pup will be waiting until she returns to her own garden before she will actually do her 'duties'. This should be overcome when she gains more confidence with maturity.

Recently, I was approached by a gentleman who was having difficulties house-training a little collie crossbreed bitch. After some discussion, it transpired that he was a keen

If you are a proud gardener, fence off any areas that you don't want the puppy to toilet on.

gardener, and, almost as soon as the pup arrived, he had chastised her for transplanting one of his prize plants. As a consequence, she was afraid of the garden and would run back into the house to do her business.

If you are having problems with house-training, it is a good idea to sit down quietly and try to see things from the dog's point of view – you may well discover that you have been giving your Stafford the wrong signals.

FIRST NIGHT

It will be to everyone's advantage if you spend a little time planning for this first night – or, indeed, the first few nights.

Make sure the puppy has been awake for most of the evening – if he has been snoozing on your lap while you watch TV, how can you expect him to be tired when you all go off to bed? So spend a little time playing with him during the evening. Make sure play is not vigorous just before going to bed, though, as the pup will not settle.

Give him some supper about half an hour before leaving him for the night, so that he has time to relieve himself before sleep. But don't make supper so far before bedtime that he will wake up feeling hungry a couple of hours into the night.

Take him outside to do his business, and then settle him in his bed. Pups fresh from the nest will often cry at night – they will feel cold and lonely away from their brothers and sisters. You can help console him by wrapping a stone hot-water bottle in a small blanket and put it in with pup. Some people like to put a clock nearby, as it is believed the tick will make the puppy think he is hearing the heartbeats of his siblings.

Once he's in his bed/crate, say "Good night", and go to bed. Providing he is warm and comfortable and in a bed that has become familiar to him for at least a few hours, then you should try to ignore any cries. It will help if you understand the different cries that puppies make. A plaintive, spasmodic wail is generally no more than a sign of loneliness. If the pup is in trouble or pain, his cries will be completely uncontrolled – high-pitched and continuous.

Try to ignore the first type of cry. You might want to confirm to yourself that everything is okay by visiting the puppy just once (try not to be noticed). Provided everything is okay, you will just have to grin and bear it.

The worst possible thing you could do at this stage is to bring him back to bed with you. Yes, this will certainly stop him crying, but you will then have a pup that expects to spend every night in your bed. Some people take the puppy's bed up to their bedroom, where they can talk to him to settle him. But, I repeat, do not let him into your bed, unless you are prepared to continue this sleeping arrangement for the next 15 years!

Some puppies don't cry at all; most cry for two or three nights and just a few will keep it up for longer. Keeping the pup active in the evening, feeding him at a sensible time, and making sure he is warm and cosy is the best way to ensure a peaceful night's sleep for everyone.

COSY CRATES

Collapsible metal crates or cages are universally used by those showing their Staffords. Even where benches are provided at shows, most people like to have their Stafford in a cage inside the bench. This is because the dog is more relaxed in his own, familiar cage; he is safely restrained; and the cage can be covered easily if the owner thinks the dog needs to sleep. Otherwise, at busy shows, there can be a continuous flow of spectators peering in and generally preventing the dog from relaxing.

However, crates are particularly useful when raising a puppy, as it will ensure you can leave him at night, safe in the

A crate is invaluable for puppies, but will also prove useful when the dog is an adult.

knowledge that he is not chewing electrical wires, or chasing the cat, or getting into any other mischief. Crate-training also helps the pup to be clean through the night, as he will try to avoid fouling his sleeping area, and so is more likely to hold on until morning.

Crates are useful when you are visiting a friend's house or a dog-friendly hotel, or if you have a strange dog visiting your home. They prove very useful to protect your property during the chewing stage if you need to leave your puppy for a short period of time (if shopping, for example).

The cage must be large enough for the adult dog to lie at full length – say 24 x 18 x 21 ins (60 x 45 x 52.5 cms) for bitches, and 31 x 21 x 24 ins (77.5 x 52.5 x 60 cms) for dogs. But be sure that the size of the metal squares is small enough, so that the pup will not get his lower jaw caught in them. This can be a very frightening experience both for the puppy and the owner.

In cold weather, it is advisable to buy or make a cover for the crate, which will help to prevent draughts.

In recent years, cages have had something of a bad reputation. This is not because there is anything intrinsically wrong with them, but because they have been abused. Some people treat a cage as a puppy-sitter, leaving their pup inside for hours on end – sometimes while they are at work all day. This is unforgivable. As we have said again and again, Staffords love to be with people. Being left isolated for very long periods of time in a cage is not right for any dog, but particularly terrible for a breed that craves human contact so much. A crate should only ever be used for short periods, or during the night.

Train the pup to a cage from the earliest time – the litter will have been confined in some way, so he will not find this detainment too onerous.

CRATE-TRAINING

- The best way of crate-training is simply to regard the crate as a bed. Put a piece of fleecy veterinary bedding or a blanket in the bottom and then put the puppy in, just as you would an ordinary bed.
- Leave the door open at first – very young puppies can get their jaws caught in the wires if they chew at a closed door.
- Once your Stafford pup has accepted the crate as his bed, then you can shut the door. First, try for a short time, say 15 minutes while you are still in the house.

Then gradually extend the time.
- If a puppy or adult retires to his crate, all the family should accept that he needs to rest and he should be left alone.
- If you give the puppy toys in his crate, make sure they are safe. Even tiny Staffords can tear up foam toys or lightweight rubber or plastic balls.
- It is an important lesson that the dog learns to spend some time of every day on his own. If a puppy has never been left unattended, then, as an adult, he might demonstrate signs of anxiety – sometimes extreme – when left on his own, so get him used to being alone right from the word go.

PEACE AND QUIET

Whether pup has a bed, a crate, or both, these should always be regarded as his property – if he goes to one of these to sleep, he should be allowed to do so in peace. This rule is particularly important if you have children.

Like a baby, a pup needs plenty of sleep to grow properly and to keep him happy and good-tempered – do not allow any interruptions to the dog's beauty sleep.

An adult Stafford may get fed up with the noise and games of the family, and the natural place for him to seek relief will be his bed. Again, your children should be taught to respect the dog's needs.

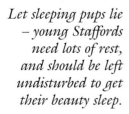

Let sleeping pups lie – young Staffords need lots of rest, and should be left undisturbed to get their beauty sleep.

FAMILY INTRODUCTIONS

CHILDREN

Staffords love children, and their affinity with them plus their ability to withstand the rough and tumble of family life is what has made them such popular pets. However, mutual respect must be taught.

The Stafford pup should be taught not to chew children's fingers, ears, clothes etc., and children must be supervised during play – the puppy is not a toy. The puppy will regard the child as a littermate. Unfortunately, his milk teeth are as sharp as needles and can prove painful.

I recently watched two children playing with a litter of pups. One child was not familiar with dogs and was rather tentative in handling them. A puppy gave her quite a hard nip, she pulled away from it, and the puppy went towards her again, tail up, ready for some more rough and tumble. The little girl ended up crying and running to her mum.

The second child, a daughter of a breeder, quickly imposed her personality on the puppies. One bold pup managed to nip the girl's finger, and she immediately said "No!" and tapped him firmly – but not harshly – on the nose and refused to play with him until he mended his ways. The pup approached her next time with much more respect, while the other child was still being 'mugged' mercilessly by the litter.

Puppies should be taught to respect people, especially children. This is not done by inflicting pain – the tap on the nose didn't hurt the pup, but it stopped him in his tracks and made him think that this person was not to be messed with. Just as with house-training, rewarding the positive behaviour and ignoring the dog who is behaving 'badly' is the key to success.

Stafford pups are very wriggly and very strong. Many are dropped by children who

Since the breed's early history, the Stafford has had an affinity with children – a fondness that continues to the present day.

don't realise quite how strong they are – sometimes puppy limbs are broken as a result. Teach small children to sit on the floor before they pick up a pup. With older children, teach them to hold a pup correctly – that is, with a hand under the pup's bottom to support his weight, and the other supporting the dog's chest, while holding one front leg firmly near the elbow to prevent the pup from wriggling out of their grasp.

Young children should never be left unsupervised with any dog. No child under 16 years of age should be left to exercise an adult Stafford in a public place.

If you have a dog first and then have a baby, you should let the dog 'examine' the baby – that is, let him sniff and even lick the child's feet (you can always wash the baby afterwards). Make sure you give the dog plenty of affection. Obviously, the new baby will be the centre of attention, but don't ignore your dog or he will resent the new addition to the family.

FELINE FRIENDS
If you already have pets in the household, it is best to introduce them as soon as possible to the new arrival. Many, many Staffords live happily with the family cat, although they may chase strange cats out of their garden. In fact, with tiny Stafford puppies, you must be prepared to protect the pup, as they are not fearful and may get badly scratched by the cat. For this reason, never leave the two unsupervised.

- A face-to-face introduction with both pets on the floor is destined to end in failure and conflict. Before introducing the two pets, make sure the cat has an escape route – somewhere high to jump up to (such as the back of a chair, or a windowsill).
- The average Stafford will bark at the cat and rush towards it. Every time he barks, tell him to be quiet.
- The cat is likely to stay put, out of reach,

and, eventually, the novelty will wear off and the puppy will lose interest.
- When the cat jumps down, the pup will probably bark again and try to chase her. Tell him "No" again, and be consistent every time he attempts to harass the cat. He will soon learn that such behaviour is unacceptable.

Patience is required, and the two may never become the best of buddies, but, with care, you should at least get them to respect each other. If you're lucky, they may take to each other immediately and become good chums.

OTHER DOGS
It is very uncommon, even for Staffords who like to fight, to attack a puppy, especially one of the opposite sex.

Introduce them to each other as soon as possible. Don't leave them alone unsupervised, and, if the other dog is elderly, give him a rest from the pup, who will undoubtedly have enormous reserves of energy.

It is important that you have the pup at the correct age – when he is fully weaned. Otherwise, he will hassle even a male dog to find a teat.

Although they are not renowned for their friendliness with other dogs, Staffords will accept newcomers as part of their family if introductions are carefully supervised.

- The initial introduction should take place on neutral territory. If the pup is inoculated, a nearby park will be ideal. Otherwise, use your garden – it is a far less stressful environment than a small, enclosed room, and your older dog will feel less territorial outside.
- Put the pup on the ground and stand back. Stay close enough so that you can intervene if there are any problems.
- The older dog will most likely assume a dominant pose and will be reserved with the newcomer.
- Make sure there are no favourite toys around that they could argue over. Food should also be avoided.
- Expect the older dog to growl at the pup – he is teaching the youngster to know his place.
- Try to discourage the pup from jumping up at the older dog, and speak to both in a calm, relaxing voice.
- If you think the growls are becoming too intense, then you may have to interfere. Take the pup away, and introduce them again later.
- With short, frequent meetings, they will soon get used to each other.
- If you have doubts about the older dog's ability to accept a puppy, or the first introduction has gone very badly, then put the pup in his crate for a bit. Put it in the middle of a room, and let the older dog investigate.
- Always remind your older dog that you still love him – he will feel neglected and antagonistic to the newcomer if you give the pup all your attention.

HIERARCHY
In any household, a 'pecking order' will evolve. The most important element in this pecking order, even where you keep only one pet, is that the top position is held by you. You can strengthen this by ensuring that the dogs do what you tell them, and also by using dominant body language. When you go through a door, for example, make the dogs 'wait' and always walk ahead of them – reinforcing your status above them.

Where you keep more than one Stafford, it is not always the male or the eldest who will be the dominant animal. When we find a dog is 'bossing' another, it is human nature to intervene. While you obviously can't let any harm come to the 'lesser' dog, you should not try to build it up to challenge the dominant family member.

Always be fair to all your dogs, but you will keep the peace if you acknowledge the pecking order the dogs have made for themselves. For example, give them all treats, but give them in the order of the dominant dog first and so on down the pecking order.

AVOIDING CONFLICT
The overriding causes of strife between Staffords and other pets are food and jealousy. Watch two or more animals when you put their food down. Sometimes a very dominant one will steal the food from his lesser mate, and this submissive animal will actually give up his food. A less submissive animal will try to protect his food and then you may have a full-scale fight.

Feed them in separate rooms, with interconnecting doors shut. The dogs soon learn the routine and run to their appropriate places. Always feed in the same sequence – the dominant dog first and then work down the pecking order.

Giving treats is the easiest way to create conflict. Always make sure that you have the dogs under control and always give fairly – a piece each. You should teach the dogs to take things carefully and gently from your fingers. Giving treats in this way prevents a mad scramble for the goodies, and such scrambles can easily lead to a major fall-out if one dog misses his treat and the highly desired morsel

falls between two or more contestants!

Jealousy can be a difficult problem among a family of Staffords. As we have said so many times before, Staffords love people. They seek attention from their owners all the time. They rarely lie on their own in a room. Invariably, they will be found on their owner's lap, curled up beside them in a chair, or leaning against their legs begging for the caressing hand to stroke them all the time.

With more than one dog, there is naturally competition for the lap, or the owner's attention. You have to be most careful to spread your favours fairly and evenly. If you feel there is a build-up of resentment, the best thing is to ignore them all – send them away from you to sit by themselves and only agree to resume petting if and when they are sensibly sharing your attentions.

SOCIALISATION

It is important to expose your puppy to as

many different experiences as possible – cars, lorries, crowds of people, children coming out of school etc. If he doesn't experience them as a puppy, he could be wary of them as an adult. Imagine if you saw a motorbike for the first time in middle age, or a hot-air balloon. You would be terrified – not knowing what it was or if it posed a danger. The same applies to your Stafford. If you show him as much of the world as you can, you will prepare him for later life.

Devise a plan of action to ensure you take your puppy out and about to many different places as soon as it is safe for him to be out in public. Of course his socialisation will already begin before his inoculations – this is why it is so important to choose a puppy that has been home-reared (he will already be used to domestic noises – see pages 52 and 204).

Before your dog is protected by his inoculations, you can take him out in the car, so he gets used to travelling and also experiences the sights and sounds of the outside world.

Later, when he is vaccinated, take him out and about as much as possible. Take him to visit friends who have children, dogs and other pets. Visit a busy park where he can see cyclists, children, rollerbladers, skateboarders etc. Take a trip to a market and to a shopping centre where he is likely to see people of all different sizes, ages and races. Plan some journeys on public transport (buses, trains, subway/tube etc.). Make a list of everything he is likely to experience throughout his life (wheelchairs, umbrellas, people wearing crash helmets etc.) and cross them off as the puppy encounters them.

If you live in a quiet area, you should, when the puppy is used to the lead and confident taking these quiet walks, take him to a busier area. This way he will get used to motorbikes, and the sound of large lorries changing gear or using airbrakes, etc.

How you deal with any signs of fear is important. You should not immediately smother the pup with kisses and caresses – this is a sure way to teach him that he should act scared if he wants attention. Talk to the pup when outside; when he is content, tell him he is a good boy. If he becomes apprehensive in a certain situation, become even jollier so he realises there is nothing to worry about.

WELCOME VISITORS

Meeting visitors is a cause for complaint from many new Stafford owners. This is just the Stafford's character – this is not a bashful, reserved breed. He is not bred for guarding, and therefore everyone is his friend. You must be prepared to accept that, for the first five minutes of meeting someone, or greeting you when you return from an outing, your dog will be very, very fussy.

The Stafford's natural bounce and exuberance should be channelled so that visitors are not 'mugged' on arrival.

Early socialisation will help to ensure that your Stafford grows up to view other dogs as friends, not foes.

You must discourage him from jumping up at strangers, but do so in a positive way – you don't want to discourage his natural love for human-kind. The best method is to distract him – say hello, and if he is too fussy, tell him to get a toy. Usually, he will then run in circles around you or the visitor, toy clasped in his mouth but not jumping up.

You should also train your visitors to ignore the dog if he jumps up. Once the dog has settled down, with four feet on the ground, he can then be greeted.

DOG-FRIENDLY
Although peace can be achieved between family dogs, it can be more difficult getting your Stafford to respect other dogs. As a new Stafford owner, you must be aware of the horror stories about the breed 'beating up' other dogs. It must be said that most of these stories are apocryphal and their number and savagery grow with every pint consumed in the bar!

Modern owners spend a lot of time and thought planning how best to bring up their Stafford to be friendly to other dogs. One of the most endearing characteristics of a Stafford, and one which makes him such a safe pet, is his ability to forget bad

experiences. Some dogs never forget a frightening experience and may act with aggression any time they are reminded of this bad event. Tests have shown that the Stafford has an amazing ability to erase bad memories from his mind. Being so 'bomb-proof', he is most unlikely to react unfavourably when faced with a frightening experience.

One experience that can have a lasting effect upon a Stafford, however, is if he has the misfortune to be beaten up by another dog when he is a young pup or immature juvenile. At this stage, he will probably try to run away, but, once he is fully mature and feeling confident in himself, he may well react if confronted by an aggressive dog – especially one who reminds him of his original tormentor.

Therefore, when you are out in the park or other public place where dogs may be present, always be prepared to protect your young Stafford from any aggressive dogs you may encounter – being beaten up at this stage is just the sort of experience that can produce an aggressive adult. If he has a bad experience, you will have to put in a great deal of work to bring your dog back to a normal, happy-go-lucky type. In any case, one should always remember that a Stafford – although he should be slow to start a fight – is usually determined to finish one.

If you do find that, as an adult, your Stafford is pretty gutsy, then you must be responsible and exercise him on a lead – the extending type of lead is excellent for this type of dog.

SOCIALISATION CLASSES

Puppy socialisation classes are essential for all Staffords. Through them, your pup will learn how to behave himself with other dogs – which will save you considerable embarrassment and concern throughout his adult life.

You can find details of puppy socialisation classes through your veterinary surgeon. They are usually organised by the veterinary practice to introduce young puppies to each other, allowing them to play and socialise, and learn doggie body language. Because the puppy will associate interaction with other dogs with an enjoyable experience (play), he should grow up to be friendly to any canines he meets.

Socialisation classes should be followed by puppy training classes, which are more structured sessions where basic obedience exercises are taught. Care should be taken when choosing one of these classes. Try to go along for one visit without your pup and get a feel for the class. In general, it is important that free play is monitored and is not allowed to get out of control. It is also important that puppies are segregated according to age – a six-month-old Stafford puppy would be far too strong for a 12-week-old Cavalier King Charles.

You should not have to put a choke chain on your Stafford. These are cruel and unnecessary. The class organisers should allow you to use a normal leather collar and lead at this early stage. If you feel that tempers are getting frayed and that your pup is not being encouraged to respond, but rather is being coerced into obedience, then you would be best advised to try another class. Reward-based training is the only type of teaching that is kind and effective. Research the methods used before taking your puppy along to a class.

EARLY TRAINING

Young pups are fast learners – do not think that a puppy is ever too young to learn. As early as eight weeks of age, you can start to teach him to sit, to get used to a collar and lead, and other basic obedience exercises. Make the sessions fun, and train in your garden and home until he is old enough to be taken out and about (see Chapter Five for more details on training).

"NO"

This word should be taught as soon as you get your puppy home. At first, the Stafford

The puppy should be taught, early on, that mouthing people is unacceptable.

pup will think that shoelaces, trouser bottoms, and fingers are very nice toys. This may be acceptable when he is very tiny, but is downright painful as he grows bigger.

From the very start, stop the puppy from using you as a chewing rag. Tell him "No!" very firmly. You must teach him that you are the head of the family. Staffords are not easily taught by chastisement – a questionable form of training anyway. Ignoring your Stafford (not talking to him) is what he will hate most.

EXERCISE

Puppies should not go out in public places until their inoculations are complete – this is so that they do not come into contact with the diseases to which they may have little or no resistance. Full protection is usually two weeks after the final injection.

A young Stafford does not need a great amount of exercise. Indeed, too much exercise at an early age can be harmful – causing dropped pasterns, for example. A

An extending lead is essential for dogs that cannot be trusted to return when called.

short walk of just a few minutes is all that is necessary until your Stafford is more than six months old. At this early age, socialisation is more important (see pages 72 and 204).

Stairs should be out of bounds (a puppy might manage to scrabble up but will need help to come down if he isn't to tumble and hurt himself). Be particularly careful with stairs that have an open tread – he could fall through. Taking a puppy on to a chair or sofa might be allowed, but watch that he doesn't launch himself off – as sturdy as Stafford puppies are, they have been known to break a leg when jumping this way.

When your puppy is old enough to go out into the big, wide world, always keep him on a lead. The breed has very little road sense and many dogs are killed every year on the roads.

Always take a plastic bag or poop-scooper to clean up after your dog. Dog fouling fuels the anti-dog lobby more than anything else, so be sensible and clean up after him.

The adult Stafford requires a fair amount of exercise to release some of his boundless energy.

ADULT EXERCISE

People often ask how many miles of exercise an adult Stafford should have. Actually, while a certain amount of road walking is good – especially for the Stafford's nails – the main advantage of this type of exercise is that he will be meeting people.

For the best physical results, we believe in tough exercise – playing with another Stafford under supervision is excellent. Alternatively, a ball thrown for 10 to 20 minutes is the very best form of exercise for a fully-grown dog.

CAR TRAVEL

You can, of course, take your Stafford out in your car; it is a great way of introducing him to the world, while keeping him safe from disease.

At first, car travel may make your puppy dribble or even be sick. If he does have a problem with travel sickness, take him on daily, short rides. In 99 per cent of cases, the pup will grow out of this problem by the age of six months or so – providing that he has enough experience in the car. Make sure that his trips out are more than just for visits to the vet – he must associate the car with enjoyable experiences.

It is safer for a dog to travel in a cage in the car or behind a dog guard. There are also dog safety harnesses on the market for those who want their dogs on the back seat. Controlling your dog is essential. It prevents the distraction of having a dog loose in the car, and, in the event of an accident, he will not be hurled about (sometimes with fatal consequences for the owner and the dog).

From the beginning, you should train your pet to stay in the car until you have secured his lead and given him the command to come – this will prevent a nasty accident if he jumps unexpectedly out of the car when you open a door.

Staffords generally love cars and travelling around. Indeed, the car is the one piece of property that many Staffords are willing to guard, barking if a stranger approaches. They are much more likely to defend the car than the house!

Not all Staffords are like this, however – a friend of mine recently had her car stolen with her Stafford bitch on the back seat. The car was found, but it took several days and a lot of effort to locate the dog.

Never let a dog travel in the back of an open truck – this is the cause of so many accidents, often resulting in the dog's death and severe injury for other drivers. Letting a dog travel with his head out of the window may look cute, but, at the very least, could result in sore, runny eyes. At worst, the dog could actually lose his head.

FEEDING YOUR PUP

The breeder should have given you a diet sheet to follow. This will ensure that the puppy is fed the same food as when he was with the breeder – a change of diet can cause tummy upsets (see page 78).

Here is a diet sheet that breeder Joyce Shorrock gives to her new puppy owners. This is a good diet sheet because it gives a clear idea of the amounts and times that the pup has been fed, and gives plenty of ideas as to how you may proceed. It also recommends that your puppy has experience of many different types of food, and will therefore be more able to cope with any changes that you might wish to introduce (see page 204).

Some breeders prefer to use an all-in-one diet, sometimes with the addition of milk. These complete foods are quick, easy, and convenient. They contain all the vitamins, minerals and proteins needed by the dog. The only disadvantage is that people often feed other things to the dog too, which spoils the balance of the diet.

Some breeders claim that dogs fed 'complete' diets become hyperactive and that the protein levels can be too high. Some

DIET SHEET

BREAKFAST

Cereal and milk: Avoid sugar-coated cereals, but use full-cream milk for at least the first six months. As the puppy grows, you may prefer to switch to semi-skimmed.

Start with a handful of cereal and $1/_3$ pint of milk, as a rough guide. Increase as necessary. I usually give more milk mid-morning and last thing at night. Your puppy should be drinking between $1/_2$ and 1 pint of milk a day fairly soon.

Try some yoghurt mixed in with the cereal and milk – puppies often like that.

LUNCH

One of the following:

• A particular puppy food. [*Obviously, the breeder would specify the brand and type of food, and may even include details of the flavours that the pup has tried.*] Don't be tempted to feed adult food – the protein balance isn't correct for a puppy.
• Beef or lamb (raw or cooked; minced or cut into smallish cubes).
• Chicken or turkey (make sure it is properly cooked, and is cut up or minced to ensure there are no bones. Mix in the juices in which it was cooked).
• Tinned pilchards, mackerel, sardines or tuna in oil.
• Cooked mackerel, herring, or coley (preferably cook it in a pressure cooker, then mince or mash it through the fingers, being very careful not to leave any bones).
• Scrambled eggs with grated cheese (this will disappear in record time).
• Grilled cheese on toast (brown or wholemeal bread, no butter).

Mix about 4-6 oz of any of the above with a handful of puppy food, some cooked rice or pasta, fromage frais, or even some brown bread (fresh or toasted). You could occasionally include some cooked or raw vegetables, such as carrot or cauliflower, but never add raw potato, as it is undigestible.

DINNER

See Lunch (above).

SUPPER

See Breakfast (above)

• Or scrambled eggs with milk
• Or yoghurt, with or without milk
• Or rice pudding.

Eggs are good for dogs if cooked – try to include one a week.
Fish is good for dogs, especially for their coat – try to include once a week.

Quantities

If the puppy finishes all his food, offer some more. If not, adjust your quantities.
A rough guide to the amount of meat you should give: it should fill a space approximately the same size as the puppy's head. A growing puppy will eat more each week, and will eat a total of about 1 to 1 $1/_2$ lb per day while growing fast.

Feeding time: the highlight of a Stafford's day.

people have 'gone back to nature', feeding a bones and raw-food diet (BARF diet). If you are considering this type of diet, you must research the topic thoroughly to ensure you are providing your Stafford with all the essential nutrients he needs.

Recently, some breeders have been concerned about the use of genetically-modified (GM) ingredients in some dog foods. If you are worried about this, contact pet-food manufacturers to find out their stance on GM foods.

SUPPLEMENTS
If you use modern mass-produced foods (dry or canned), there should be no need for you to give additives. Some people do like to give some herbal additives, such as garlic pills or cod-liver oil, but beware of over-supplementing your pup's diet, as this can cause damage and even malformation of joints and/or limbs. It is advisable to discuss the matter with your vet.

CHANGING THE DIET
It will be better if you keep your pup to what he has been used to – at least for some time after you collect him. This is to avoid

upsetting his digestion. A sudden diet change can result in diarrhoea, which is not a good start to his new life.

If you wish to change his diet once he is settled, you can gradually change his diet to what you prefer by mixing the 'new' diet into his existing one until the new has gradually taken over from the old. This should be done slowly, over the course of about a week.

However, do not be tempted to switch diets in order to save money. If you give your pup the best diet you can, you will be providing him with the best start to life. At least you can rest assured that he will reach his full potential if he is fed well – and he is more likely to have a strong constitution should he encounter a health problem in later life. For more information on feeding, see Chapter Six: Diet and Nutrition.

COAT CARE
Good-quality food on the inside is the number-one tool for producing a healthy, shiny coat on the outside. One of the many advantages of owning a Stafford is that grooming is minimal – and because they have such short coats, they have very little 'doggie' smell.

An occasional brush with a strong, bristled brush will help to remove dead hairs – which means fewer to remove from your household furniture. Brush him on a table, where you can handle him easily.

An occasional bath will make sure your pup remains sweet-smelling – especially necessary, of course, if your Stafford happens to like rolling in something unmentionable. It is not a good idea – unless you use a specialist and expensive shampoo – to bath your Stafford too often, as you will be removing the natural oils from the dog's coat.

An alternative to bathing is to use a coat spray (there are many types on the market). As well as making the coat shine, the spray will also enhance the smell of the coat.

While you are grooming him, inspect his ears, check his nails, and brush his teeth. If he gets used to these procedures now, he will not object when he is a strapping adult.

If his nails need trimming (it should never be necessary if the foot is well-constructed and the dog receives adequate exercise), press each toe flat so the nail becomes unsheathed. Only clip the tip of the nail – the dark part that runs the length of the middle of the nail is the 'quick' (the nerves and blood supply).

DENTAL CARE

Puppies get their first set of teeth between four and six weeks of age. Between three and six months, they will gradually lose these first 'milk' teeth and the permanent adult teeth will emerge. While teething, your puppy will be prone to chewing, which relieves the pain of his sore gums. Giving him something solid to chew on will help him.

Some Staffords experience hair loss during this stressful time, particularly on the top of their skull and on the middle of their tails.

Gently check the pup's mouth regularly to ensure that the old teeth are being replaced with the new. If they are not, then the puppy could end up with two rows of teeth. This is unusual in Staffords, except where the canines are concerned. It is not uncommon for Stafford puppies to retain a milk canine while the new one is growing up. Many believe that this is one of the common causes of the converging canine – where the path of the new tooth is diverted by the presence of the old one. If you notice this happening, you should gently try to wiggle the old tooth out. If this proves useless, consult your vet.

Some Staffords never chew anything, but others demolish everything in sight. Keeping the young dog well entertained and exercised, plus giving him safe chews and toys, can minimise this effect. It is important that the family trains itself not to leave anything chewable where the dog can get it. Consider the use of a crate when you need to leave the dog unsupervised for short periods.

It is worth remembering that he must keep his adult teeth all his life, so you must take care of them. If his diet is mainly of soft food, try to give him something to chew, e.g. a nylon-type bone, which may also help to stop him chewing furniture or door jambs.

Regularly cleaning the teeth is also recommended – there are special dog toothbrushes and toothpaste on the market, although, if you cannot afford these, an old brush of yours would do as well (however, do not use toothpaste intended for human use – the meat-flavoured doggie one should be used instead). There are also special finger-brushes that are very easy to use.

HOLIDAY SEASON

Going away is another problem for some families. You may have a member of the family who will take care of your Stafford, but remember to give the dog-sitter all the details necessary for a happy stay. Clear written instructions should be left. Many dogs come to grief because the sitter lets the dog off the lead in an area or in circumstances with which he is not familiar. The dog can then become disorientated and finish up on the road – with tragic results.

If you do not have a friend or family member who can care for your Stafford while you are away, then you must look around for a suitable boarding kennel. Because of their love for humans, Staffords tend to pine when they are in kennels. To minimise this, it is best to start them with a short stay in kennels while they are still young – say, under two years of age.

Inspect all recommended kennels in your area to choose a suitable one. Be sure to meet the people who will be looking after your pet, and look for two things:
1. That they like Staffords and are sensitive to their needs.

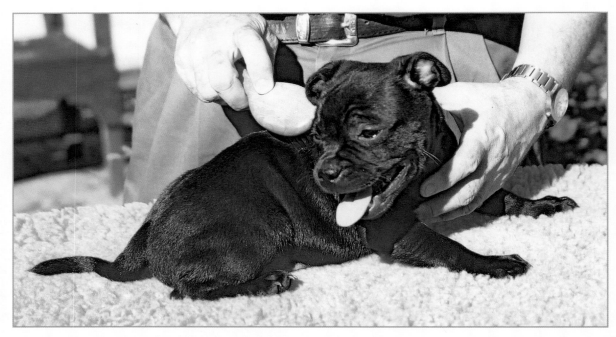

Get your pup accustomed to being groomed from an early age.

After grooming, inspect your puppy all over to get him used to being handled and to ensure that any problems are quickly identified.

Your Stafford's teeth should be checked regularly, particularly during teething.

2. That they do not mix strange dogs together. Remember: a bad experience in a kennel involving other dogs can have long-lasting effects for the rest of the dog's life. An alternative to boarding kennels is the professional dog-sitting agency. These have

several advantages – the dog is in his own home, the sitter can give lots of attention to the dog and is on hand day and night, other pets can be looked after at the same time, your plants can be watered, and they are a burglar deterrent. Obviously, care must be taken in whom you employ. Use personal recommendations, and check all references.

UK FOREIGN TRAVEL

Gradually, the United Kingdom's draconian quarantine laws are being changed, and, thanks to the PETS travel scheme, pets can travel to certain European countries provided they have the necessary jabs, microchip, paperwork, etc.

However, owners cannot just take their pets in and out as they like. It is important to plan ahead. Make sure you understand about all the vaccinations that you will need, plus any laws that might be in operation in the country you plan to visit. Check also on any diseases which might be endemic there, but are not known in the UK.

Finally, be sure you know all the rules and regulations which must be adhered to when you are bringing a pet back into this country. Even if this is his permanent home, he will have to keep to all the regulations, just as if he was a foreign dog!

Contact your vet for more advice, or DEFRA (the Department for the Environment, Farming, and Rural Affairs).

RESCUED DOGS

Having read about all the problems of bringing up a young Stafford, you may feel it is preferable for you to try an adult dog. There are many breed rescue organisations – a list can be obtained from your national kennel club.

A good rescue organisation will want to check on you, your house, and your family, and should insist on neutering – at least in bitches. They will take notes about your family and style of living, and should try to match you with a Stafford who will best fit into your family.

While some of these dogs might have had bad experiences, and a few may well have

An older, rescued dog will prove to be just as faithful and loving a companion as a puppy.

behaviour problems as a result, the vast majority are perfectly normal Staffords who are just victims of modern living – split homes, desire for a trendier, more fashionable breed, etc. Staffords regularly live until 12 to 14 years of age and at any age can give a great deal of love and pleasure, so do consider this option.

VET CHECK

Before you collected the pup, you should have made arrangements to visit your vet (page 61). If you don't have one already, you can look for your nearest surgery in the telephone directory, or, best of all, ask other dog owners for personal recommendations.

The vets' receptionist will tell you about the practice's inoculations regime – probably these jabs will start at eight weeks of age, followed by a second set at around 10 to 12 weeks and with annual boosters thereafter. The inoculations will cover your animal for the major common diseases in your area (distemper, hepatitis, leptospirosis, parainfluenza, parvovirus, and, in some countries, rabies).

In addition, you may want to have some defence against kennel cough – important if you plan to show your dog, attend any training or socialising classes, or put him in boarding kennels when he is older. Not all strains of kennel cough can be covered, but the inoculations on the market at the present time will give protection against the worst form of this disease.

WORMING

It is important that your puppy has been wormed by the breeder. All puppies have worms, because, during pregnancy, worm larvae migrate to the puppies from the bitch via the placenta. It is important that the breeder has tried to eliminate them and that you follow a regime to keep the dog as worm-free as possible. You should ask when the pup was last wormed, and, armed with this information, take the advice of your vet.

The following signs suggest that a pup may be wormy:
• Pot-belly
• Dull coat
• 'Scooting', where the pup rubs his bottom along the floor.

Small rice-like segments around a dog's bottom are signs of tapeworm infestation, which is very rare in a pup. Roundworms are the commonest puppy worms, and are like threads of cotton or thin spaghetti.

Each country will differ as to the worms that it needs to protect against. In warm climates, for example, heartworm and lungworm may pose a problem. Your vet will give you guidance on treating or protecting your dog (see also Chapter Twelve).

IDENTIFICATION

You may have a physically tough, stable, well-adjusted Stafford, but such a dog may tempt the unprincipled. It is amazing how many Staffords are stolen every year. Because of their friendly nature, Staffords will often go off quite happily with absolute strangers. To help identification and ensure a quick return to you should he be found, you might consider permanent identification in the form of either a tattoo or microchip. The microchip is about the size of a grain of rice and is implanted by a vet, quite painlessly, under the dog's skin. It contains a number that is registered with a central bureau. Most dog wardens are now given the equipment to read these, so lost dogs can usually be returned to their owners quickly. Ask your vet for more details.

In any case, you should always make sure you know where your pup is at any time. Don't shut him out in the garden and forget about him for a couple of hours. Make sure your garden is secure – particularly garden gates, garage doors, etc. Be especially vigilant after workmen, refuse collectors, or window cleaners have called – they are adept at leaving gates open, and, hey presto, your pup has wandered away.

NEUTERING

With two dogs of the opposite sex there is always the problem of mismatings. Do not be tempted to keep an unplanned litter. If you don't know what you are doing, the resulting puppies may grow into poor adults. There are too many Stafford litters being bred, and the rescue organisations are grossly overstretched. The majority of the dogs involved come from people who had the litter 'for fun', because they thought it would be 'good for the bitch' or would constitute a good money-maker. These are all the wrong reasons.

Having a bitch spayed should not in any way spoil her quality of life. Strictly, spaying involves the removal of the ovaries (the part that houses the eggs); however, most vets now remove the womb or uterus as well. Most breeders will have this operation done

Neutering should be considered if you have a female (left) and a male (right).

after a bitch has produced a litter because they wish to avoid any complications (such as life-threatening womb infections) that often occur in later life to unspayed bitches.

The more we learn about wild packs of animals, the more we come to understand how nature deals with these problems. It seems that, in wild-dog families, it is often only the dominant bitch who actually produces a litter. If one of her lesser sisters should produce a litter, the 'top bitch' may actually kill all these puppies.

Similarly, with male animals, it is in no way a certainty that every male will be allowed to reproduce himself. It cannot, therefore, be seen as 'unnatural' to stop your pets reproducing. Once upon a time, vets advised people to let a bitch have one season before neutering. Today, however, some vets are suggesting very early neutering.

Castrating a male (i.e. removing his gonads or testicles) is not as popular as spaying a bitch (although there are significant health benefits for both sexes – see Chapter Twelve).

There are many advantages to spaying – you will not be bothered by neighbouring dogs camping on your doorstep, and you will abolish the mess around the house that a season brings.

Some people consider castration for a dog when he shows aggression towards other dogs (especially males). Unfortunately, castration for this reason is not always successful. You should consult your vet – there may be a chemical injection which could test out the possible effect of an operation. The dog cannot reproduce, but if the operation is done later in life, it may not destroy his interest in the opposite sex.

In either case, the animals should not, as is so often rumoured, put on a great deal of weight. If you notice any increase in weight after a neutering operation, don't hesitate to put the dog on a carefully controlled diet.

Note: in the UK, neutered animals cannot be exhibited at shows unless the operation is done for medical reasons. One exception is a bitch who has progeny registered with the Kennel Club. In some countries, e.g. Canada, neutered (or 'altered') animals may be shown, usually in special classes.

For more information on neutering, see Chapter Twelve.

PET INSURANCE

Pet insurance – which pays for accidents and illness (though not prophylactic treatment) is very popular in the UK, but is not as common in the US. It is an option worth considering. Although the Stafford's strong constitution should keep normal vet fees to a minimum, the breed is accident-prone – and injuries (particularly those that require surgery) can be very costly.

5 TRAINING YOUR STAFFORD

Whatever your reason for choosing the Staffordshire Bull Terrier, the most important consideration must be to raise him as a family pet – it is very important that your dog is taught both social and basic obedience skills if he is to live a full and happy life.

The Stafford is not a breed usually associated with Competitive Obedience and other canine sports, but many Staffords are regularly competing in these disciplines and doing very well.

While I, Wendy Clewley, would be the first to agree that not all Staffords could – or should – compete at this level, we owe it to this great breed to teach them social skills. Many people do not understand the Stafford's temperament – that they are second to none with people and yet their interaction with other dogs can leave a lot to be desired. The way forward for our breed is as 'Good Citizens' (see page 94).

Dogs are creatures of habit and learn by repetition and association. Remember that YOU are the main ingredient in the pie – you must understand your dog, know what you want to achieve, and make sure that you get results.

Although not a traditionally working breed, your dog can be taught almost anything. You just need to break each exercise down into small compartments. The Stafford can be very stubborn, but he has a great desire to please. The key to successful training is to channel this energy in the right direction.

BASIC OBEDIENCE TRAINING

The earlier your Staffordshire Bull Terrier puppy commences his training, the better. It is a myth that puppies cannot learn anything until they are six months old – your pup will be learning from the very moment you bring him home. Actually, the younger he is, the more receptive he will be to new experiences.

It is advisable to train the pup on an empty stomach to ensure that you have your Stafford's undivided attention. Initially, keep training sessions short, especially for young puppies, and always end on a good note (finishing with an exercise he can do easily and that you can reward him for). Forget training if you don't feel well or are not in the best of tempers – your despondent mood will quickly rub off on your dog.

Finally, be prepared. Think carefully about what and how you will teach a particular exercise before you start.

In the following exercises, I have given the commands that I use; if you don't like them, use your own words. The most important thing is to choose a command word and stick to it!

WATCH

Teach your puppy that being with you is a nice thing. One of the first things to teach is Watch, which is the basis of all future training.

In this exercise, you are basically encouraging your puppy to give you his attention. It comes in useful in many, many situations, and is very easy to teach.

- Say "Watch" to gain your puppy's attention.
- Hold his attention for just three seconds and then praise and reward him with a treat or a game with a toy.
- With practice, gradually extend the time he watches you.
- Always make it a happy, expectant command, so the puppy looks forward to what might happen next.

COLLAR AND LEAD

Firstly, ensure you have a suitable collar and lead. I find that a standard leather-style collar, with a 6-ft (1.83-m) lead with adjustable clips, is the most appropriate.

Many people think that a short lead gives more control; in fact, you will have far less control and your Stafford will pull more.

A good leather lead may be a little more costly than other types, but it will last you many years. The chain-link type of lead is not suitable for any breed. This style of lead is often short and heavy in construction. Not only do they have a tendency to rust, but they also do not offer the versatility and control of a leather lead. Similarly, choke chains should also be avoided.

- Begin by getting your puppy used to his collar, perhaps initially by introducing it just before a meal.
- Your puppy may well scratch at it, but just ignore the behaviour. Only remove the collar at a moment when he is not scratching at it (or directing any other

Initially, your Stafford will be irritated by his collar, but he will soon get used to the sensation of wearing it.

Distract the pup with a treat while he is wearing his collar and lead.

negative behaviour towards the collar).
• Repeat this exercise little and often.
• Always ensure the collar is removed when you cannot supervise your puppy (for example, if he is in his crate). This is a basic precaution to prevent accidents from occurring.

When your puppy is happy with the collar, you will then need to introduce the lead. This can be traumatic for the puppy, but, handled correctly, any undue stress can be kept to an absolute minimum.

• Again, train your Stafford on an empty stomach.
• Kneeling on the floor, attach the lead, while keeping the puppy's attention with treats or a toy.
• Your pup may back off and sit at the full extent of the lead, acting as if he is suffering a terrible injustice.
• Don't coax or cajole him – instead, play with one of his toys or pretend to eat some of his treat. He will soon relent and his curiosity and sense of fun will get the better of him – remember to praise and reward him as soon as he comes to you.
• This exercise needs to be repeated little and often. Then try shuffling forwards and encouraging the pup to move with you.
• Over time, stand up and encourage the puppy along, a step at a time.
• Once he has settled a little with the lead, you will need to add some resistance to the lead occasionally, as the pup cannot always be allowed to wander wherever and whenever he wants.
• Keep your voice bubbly, and, giving a little tug, call his name, step backwards, and praise him when he comes to you.

WALKING TO HEEL
Although not everyone wants to be able to perform competitive heelwork, with the dog's head glued to the owner's left leg, it is important that your Stafford will walk on-lead in a calm, controlled manner. He should be reasonably close to you, he should ignore any distractions, and he should not pull.

• Begin with your dog on your left-hand side, holding a slack lead in your right hand. Your left hand is used to 'correct' your dog. For example, should you need to check your dog for maybe pulling ahead, your left hand would come down on to the lead half-way along and 'correct' the dog by pulling him back slightly (also backed up by a verbal command). When the correct behaviour is obtained, then the hand can be released.
• You need to gain your dog's attention, using the command "Watch" (above), and then command "Heel" before stepping off on your left leg.

Not everyone wants competition-standard heelwork from their dog; most simply aspire to a dog who walks calmly and confidently on the lead.

Getting your dog's attention before you set off is half the battle.

- Ensure that your enthusiasm spills over to your dog, so say the command in an eager, excited tone of voice.
- Should your dog go wide (i.e. walks too far from your left leg), step away from him, call him to you, and say "Heel" as you do so.
- Remember to talk to your dog – this is often overlooked. You cannot initially expect your dog to know what you want of him.
- Walk a few paces straight ahead at first, then stop, and give lots of praise and a reward.
- With practice, you can walk for longer before stopping, and you can also start to introduce gradual turns. With more practice, the turns can become more pronounced.

- When you want to turn left, use the command "Back" and take your left hand down the length of the lead to pull the dog slightly into place before turning.
- When turning right, use the command "Close" and encourage the dog round with you. Keep it happy.
- Don't walk for too long in the same direction, as your dog will get bored easily.
- Also begin to change your pace from normal to slow and then to fast.
- Do not practise for long periods – have a break after ten minutes, and enjoy a game together before returning to your training once more.
- Eventually, when walking at heel, get your dog to sit when you stop (see below). In time, your dog will do this automatically, which will be invaluable when walking your dog beside a road, stopping to give someone directions, or even buying an ice-cream!

SIT
- Hold a treat in your left hand, get your dog's attention, and raise your hand over the puppy's head.
- He will follow the treat with his eyes, and, if it is held in the correct position above his head, he will need to sit to see it (or try to get at it).
- Just as he goes into the Sit position, say "Sit", then bring your left hand down and reward him with the treat.
- Each time you practise this exercise, the puppy will sit more and more quickly, as he will begin to understand what he has to do to earn the treat.
- If, initially, he does not sit, use your right hand to push his bottom down gently (do not push his back), and repeat the command "Sit". Make sure that your left hand remains above the pup's head. As before, when he sits, say "Sit", and praise and reward him.

SITTING PRETTY
Even tiny pups can be taught to sit by luring with a treat.

The treat is ideally positioned just above and behind the pup's nose: he must lower his bottom in order to focus on the treat.

When his bottom hits the floor, he can be given the reward.

DOWN
- Holding a treat in your left hand, put it in front of the puppy's nose before bringing it down to the floor in front of him.
- As he goes down to investigate, give the command "Down".
- Again, the puppy will probably go down automatically. If he does not, use both hands on either side of his chest and gently push backwards, repeating "Down".
- Reward and praise when successful.

From the Sit, hold a treat in your hand and lure the puppy into the Down position.

COME
Many people do not let their dogs off the lead for fear of them running off in to the horizon. Training your dog to come should be started as early as possible.

STARTING EARLY
- When feeding your puppy, call his name and add the command "Come". This will teach your Stafford to come from a young age, and he will get a great reward into the bargain.
- Keep your voice light and cheerful, and call him to you. Encourage him to come by showing him toys or treats.
- Always make a fuss of him when he comes.
- In the early stages, train him in a confined room, before moving on to an enclosed garden.
- Should he disobey, don't shout – simply go to him, hold him by the collar or attach his lead, take some steps back, repeat the command, and praise him.

ADDING DISTRACTIONS

Gradually, you can set up situations to get your puppy to come while there are distractions. This is important, as training in the confines of your home will be very different to when your puppy is in the park – with all the outdoor smells, sights and sounds that dogs find irresistible.

Until you are certain that your dog will come to you, no matter what is going on around him, do not let him off the lead.

- Use either an extending lead or a 30-ft (9-m) Tracking lead in your Recall training.
- Firstly, use it in your garden, before moving on to a quiet area in your park.
- To start with, get him to sit and wait while you move away from him; and then call him to you.
- Over several practice sessions, use the entire length of the lead.
- You can give your Stafford his 30 ft of freedom to play and sniff; then, after a few minutes, call him to you.
- Vary the time when you call him and how long he is kept with you before being released to play again – but always praise him when he does well.
- If a distraction appears (for example, another dog comes into view), call your dog to you and then give lots and lots of praise (and a treat) when he comes.
- If he ignores you, then gently pull the lead to encourage him to you, and, again, give plenty of reward when he reaches you.

OUT AND ABOUT

Coming back to you (Recall) should always be a pleasurable experience for your Stafford – praise and reward him every time he comes.

- Many dogs associate being called back to their owners with the end of their walk, and are therefore reluctant to return. Calling your Stafford back to you in the middle of his walk prevents this association.
- Call him to you maybe a dozen times on his walk. Each time, praise and treat him, and then send him off for another run or play.

LATE RETURNS

Should your dog decide that the horizon is where he wants to be and he makes a run for it, you must, of course, go after him. However, when he eventually returns, he must be praised.

If he does not return and you feel he needs to be chastised, always go to him – never chastise him if he has returned to you, no matter how belatedly.

Should you feel he needs to be disciplined, then do this as a bitch would do to her puppies – take him by the scruff of the neck and growl a few words. This usually does the trick. However, for a Stafford in particular,

Give lots of positive body language, and your Stafford will return to you with enthusiasm.

when they have done wrong, ignoring them often works as well as anything else because they crave so much attention.

STAY

"Stay" means that you are commanding your dog to remain in one position until you return to him. It is therefore different to "Wait", which means that the dog must pause until the owner calls him to come.

- Begin with your dog in his favourite position – either Sit or Down. You should stand in front of your dog, just a few feet away.
- Say the command "Stay" and put your outstretched hand in front of the dog's face.
- The tone of voice is very important for this exercise. You need to be firm, remembering not to use the dog's name (or he may come to you). Staffords are very clever at reading their owners and working out if they really mean something or not! Should your dog move, say nothing, while you step back to him, put him back where he was. Then repeat the "Stay" command and hand signal, and step back again.
- Keep your voice low – you don't want to sound too excited as the dog will be tempted to join you. Save the excitement for when you have returned to your dog and he gets his well-deserved praise.
- Only do as much as you can, building up slowly. For example, start by being close to the dog and making him stay for just five seconds, and then step forward to him, praise and reward him.
- The main objective is that the dog understands what "Stay" means, even if, initially, you are only working 12 inches (30 cms) away and literally holding the dog in place.
- When he reliably stays at five seconds, take a step back and extend it to ten seconds.

An outstretched hand encourages the dog to stay put.

Sometimes the Stay hand signal elicits a different response! Who's telling whom to stay?

- Gradually work further and further away, and for longer and longer. Do remember to build up slowly, and don't use your dog's name during this exercise (it will encourage him to move to you).
- When returning to your dog, wait a few seconds before you praise – this will stop him anticipating when to move. Additionally, you could return to your dog and then step away again.
- Should your dog move, do not scold – simply step back towards him, put him back in position, repeat the command, and

With practice, your Stafford will learn to stay off-lead at and you can increase the distance you leave him.

step away again. Also, try standing side-on to your dog – this way, he won't confuse it with a Recall.

- Additional options can be brought into the training. Alter the distances you leave your Stafford, add distractions (such as walking round your dog, throwing a toy or having people walk past).
- Remember, never be afraid to go back a stage. My own bitch, Tammy, regularly does 10-minute out-of-sight Stays among many other breeds, but she would soon become stale if that was all we trained for. Use your imagination and vary the exercises.

NOSEWORK

Dogs love to use their noses. Nature has given them a powerful tool but, unfortunately, many do not get to use their noses to their full potential. You will really see your dog 'come alive' when he gets the hang of scent training.

- Kneel on the floor with a favourite toy or a treat hidden in a very easy-to-find place (such as just a few feet away, maybe under a newspaper or slightly sticking out from the paper).
- Ensure the toy is well handled before you hide it, so it will have fresh scent on it.
- The toy should be one that is a particular favourite with the dog, and you should now only bring it out at training sessions so it remains 'special'.
- Let your dog see you hide the treat/toy and then send him to "Find".
- When your Stafford finds the object, give lots of praise and play with him.
- Always ensure that your dog finds the article, so he is always rewarded for his efforts. Should he struggle, help him, and then give lots of praise when he eventually finds it.
- Gradually, you can hide the toy further away, with your dog still watching.

Like all dogs, Staffords love to use their highly-sensitive noses to track a favourite toy or treat.

- Initially, you will need to offer your dog lots of encouragement; as training develops, send him out after the initial command ("Find"), keep quiet and let him work, only offering encouragement when needed.
- Use your imagination with nosework training – try hiding the toy in another room, then progress to hiding it in the garden.
- As your dog gets more confident, hide many different articles – but remember that each one must be well handled before being hidden.

BASIC ROAD TRAINING

Many Staffords do not display a fear of traffic. I remember a story of an accident where the car came off worse when in collision with a Stafford. This said, tragically many Staffords are killed on the road every year. Time spent teaching your dog road manners may well save his life.

- Always put your dog on the lead when near a road or traffic.
- Take your puppy road-walking to accustom him to traffic (it should form part of his early socialisation programme – see Chapter Four).
- Begin by teaching your dog to walk by your side without undue pulling (page 86).
- Then move on to teaching your dog to sit at the kerb before you cross the road (see page 88).
- You will need to ensure that you do this over a period of time. The more you teach your dog, the better he will be.
- Your Stafford needs to be well socialised and taught to ignore pedestrians, cyclists, bins and many other everyday distractions. Should your Stafford respond to any of these distractions, do not make a fuss or reassure him (verbally or physically) – otherwise you will just be reinforcing the

Staffords have little road-sense, and should be taught to behave in a calm and controlled manner near traffic.

message that his reaction was justified.
- Try using the "Watch" command and gaining his attention with your voice and maybe a toy or a treat to help if necessary. Then, walk him. All the time he looks at you, give lots of praise. If he looks at, or objects to, the distraction, then reinforce the "Watch" command again. Give lots of praise when you have his attention once more.

RESPONSIBLE OWNER

Whenever you are out in a public place, remember to carry your 'poo bags'. Picking up after your dog is much easier if you teach him to wait quietly while you do so. When he has finished his business, get his attention, and tell him to sit.

Keep reinforcing the command while you pick up. If you are consistent, it will become second nature to your Stafford to sit after doing his business.

FINDING A TRAINING CLUB

Your breeder or breed club may be able to help; alternatively, most veterinary surgeries hold lists of local clubs. If you still have no luck, contact your national kennel club.

For the first time, go along to the class on your own to see whether it is suitable. You will be able to get a 'feel' for the class and the instructor, and for the training methods used. I would avoid a club that doesn't encourage praise and reward, and that insists on all dogs wearing choke (check) chains. Look at how the instructors deal with difficult dogs. Are the exercises explained properly? Does the instructor have any experience of the bull breeds? Visit a few training clubs and opt for the one you feel happiest with.

AMERICAN AGILITY ORGANISATIONS

USDAA (United States Dog Agility Association)
Dogs under 12 inches (30 cms):
12-inch jumps
Dogs under 16 inches (40 cms):
16-inch jumps
Dogs under 21 inches (52.5 cms):
22-inch jumps (55 cms)
Dogs over 21 inches (52.5 cms):
26-inch jumps (65 cms).

AKC (American Kennel Club)
Under 10 inches (25.5 cms):
8-inch jumps (20 cms)
Under 14 inches (35 cms):
12-inch jumps (30 cms)
Under 18 inches (45 cms):
16-inch jumps (40 cms)
Under 22 inches (55 cms):
20-inch jumps (50 cms)
Over 22 inches:
24-inch jumps (60 cms).

GOOD CITIZEN SCHEME

Several national kennel clubs run 'good citizen' schemes, with the aim of producing well-mannered, well-behaved dogs and of encouraging responsible pet ownership.

The schemes contain many basic commonsense exercises, which vary in difficulty according to the level you are training for. Most of the exercises are based on everyday situations – such as a stranger approaching or handling your dog, testing how your dog behaves in the company of other dogs, his obedience, etc.

Although many of the exercises are straightforward, some will require more training. For example, when greeting someone, it should be in a controlled manner – something that does not come easy to the sociable, enthusiastic Stafford!

Contact your national kennel club to find out if it runs a canine good citizen scheme. If it does, ask for details of your nearest club that supports the scheme. It is important that you learn how to teach your dog correctly.

AGILITY

The objective of Agility is to complete a course of designated obstacles in the fastest time, hopefully without incurring any faults. The equipment is made up of:
• Long jumps
• Hurdles
• Tyres (which the dog should leap through)
• Tunnels (rigid and collapsible, that the dog should run through)
• Weave poles (a line of poles that the dog should weave through at speed)
• Pause table (dogs must jump on to the table and go down for a five-second count).
• Contact equipment: see-saw, dog walk (a ramp leading to a plank and then a ramp back to the ground), and A-frame (an A-shaped obstacle that the dog must climb and descend).

THE AGILE STAFFORD
The energetic Stafford thrives on the challenge of Agility.

Tiny (MACH Shady Grove's Fortunate Son UDex Mex MexJ), bred by Margo Milde, is the first Stafford to become a Master Agility Champion (MACH).
Courtesy: Patti Pentler.

The tyre is tackled with enthusiasm.

The tunnel holds few fears.

Patience is needed to train the weave.

A positive approach to the hurdles.

The contact equipment is so called because the elements have painted areas at their start and finish with which the dog must make contact. They not only test that the dog can be accurate at speed, but also ensure his safety (flying off the A-frame too high up can be dangerous).

FAULTS

Missing a contact, knocking down a pole from a jump, or missing a weave pole will incur faults. You can also be eliminated if your dog takes the wrong course or if he fouls in the ring.

During competition, treats are not allowed and all collars must be removed (as they can get caught on the equipment).

I recently lost 1st place because I had forgotten to remove Tammy's collar and was eliminated, even though she completed the course in the fastest time with an otherwise clear round.

GETTING STARTED

Most Staffords will fit into the Mini (15 ins/37.5 cms or under at the shoulder) or Midi (15-17 ins/37.5-42.5 cms) categories in the UK. In the US, there are two organisations that organise Agility (see panel).

In the UK, Collies dominate the sport; in the US, it is the Golden Retriever.

However, many, many breeds compete in Agility. There are quite a number of Staffords regularly competing, and they generally do very well.

The biggest problem is that they have no respect for the equipment. My own Tammy has broken poles with her head and not even altered her stride!

Your dog needs to be at least 12 months old before beginning Agility training (Tammy was 17 months before she started). The intervening time can be used socialising your dog and training in basic Obedience skills, as your dog will need to be trusted off-lead with other breeds.

I would recommend working through a puppy socialisation class before moving on to a regular basic obedience class. Ideally, your dog should know all the basic commands, such as "Come" and "Sit", "Stay" and "Wait". The more obedient and attentive your dog is, the easier he will cope with the Agility classes. The most important factor is that your dog has a sound temperament and can be trusted off-lead with other dogs.

When your dog is old enough, and you think he is ready for Agility training, join a local club. The sport is so popular it won't be difficult to find a club near you. Contact your national breed club or kennel club if you have trouble locating one.

FUN AT HOME

Should you find that competitive Agility training classes are not for you, why not try making or buying some equipment for your garden? Keep the jumps to a height of 15 inches (37 cms), and invest in a good Agility book to guide you.

US TITLES

Aex (AKC Agility Excellent)
Mex (AKC Master Agility Excellent)
NAJ (AKC Novice Agility Jumpers)
OAJ (Open Agility Jumpers)
AexJ (AKC Agility Excellent Jumpers)
MexJ (AKC Master Agility Jumpers)
AKC CD (Companion Dog)
AKC CDex (Companion Dog Excellent)
AKC UD (Utility Dog)
AKC UDex (Utility Dog Excellent)
MACH (Master Agility Champion)
OTCH (Obedience Trials Champion)
ADCH (USDAA Agility Dog Championship title).

WORKING TRIALS

Working Trials is a mixture of Agility, Obedience and Tracking. In the US, many of the skills in Working Trials are tested in Obedience. Hence, the Trials' titles of CD (Companion Dog) and UD (Utility Dog) are also found in US Obedience. The tracking component of Working Trials is a sport in its own right in the US, with dedicated titles.

Working Trials are split into Stakes. The first two Stakes are CD (Companion Dog) and UD (Utility Dog), and it is from these that it is possible to qualify a 'small' dog, as there are height allowances in the Agility section. To qualify, you have to score 80 per cent or higher; you are not in competition with anyone else – if you achieve the marks, then you qualify. After qualifying your dog, this then entitles you to add letters after the dog's name: CDex, or UDex.

Dogs are not permitted to compete in a trial until 18 months of age. As before, I would suggest using the intervening time to work on good obedience skills.

The exercises are split into sections, from which you have to obtain a minimum amount of points per section to qualify overall.

AGILITY SECTION

- 6-ft (1.83m) long jump (for dogs up to 15 inches (0.38m) at the shoulder – this changes to 9-ft (2.75m) for dogs over 15 inches).
- 2-ft (0.61m) high jump (for dogs up to 15 inches, changing to 3-ft (0.91m) for dogs over 15 inches).
- 4-ft scale (1.22m) (for dogs up to 15 inches, changing to 6-ft (1.83m) for dogs over 15 inches).

These are completed under controlled conditions. Having been sent over an obstacle, the dog has to wait in that position until rejoined by the handler.

Trilby (Libellula Lass of Copyhold CDex UDex) clears the six-foot long jump with ease.

Bertie (Cyclone Sweetheart of Copyhold CDex UDex) returning over the four-foot scale.

The long jump is made up of four elements, which range from 3 ft to 3ft 8 inches wide (0.91m to 1.11m). Each element graduates in height from 4 to 11 inches (10-28 cms).

The long jump at 6 ft is rather punishing for a Stafford. My own bitch is 14.5 inches (37 cms) at the shoulder and is not exactly an athletic build, but, because of her Agility training, she will attempt to jump anything put in front of her. Should she not manage the jump and hit the last element, it is usually because she has taken off too soon and not because she cannot do it. However, with careful training, all the jumps in this section are possible.

The 4-ft scale and 2-ft high jump should cause no major problems for any dog used to jumping. However, care should always be taken to avoid any accidents. I do not think dogs should train for the Agility section before 18 months, as the section is very tough – especially with our breed's construction.

However, before your dog reaches this age, you can lay the groundwork – feeding his enthusiasm and working on his basic training. For example, you can lay the hurdle poles directly on the ground for your dog to walk over. These can gradually be raised, but remember not to overstretch your dog too soon – it must be fun!

CONTROL SECTION
• Heelwork on-lead
• Heelwork off-lead
• Recall
• Sendaway.

The heelwork in Working Trials is very different to Obedience. The dog should walk naturally, reasonably close to the left knee.

The Sendaway is where your dog is sent towards a marker a minimum of 30 yards (27.43m) away, although, in practice, it is

Trilby working a very muddy search square.

normally a much longer distance. The marker could well be a bag tied to a tree or a telegraph pole in the distance.

NOSEWORK SECTION
• Search square
• Retrieve with a dumb-bell.

The search square is a 15-25 yard (13.71-22.85m) square, where a set of small items are hidden. Your dog must find and return all the items in the stipulated time. The ground can be anything from stubble to grass of any length.

STAY SECTION
• 10-minute Down-stay
• 2-minute Sit-stay.

Both these group Stays are done out of sight of the owner. All the dogs competing for the Stake will be in the group, and the dog must remain in position until the steward ends the exercise. Any movement is penalised.

TRACKING SECTION
The UD Stake also includes steadiness to gunfire and a tracking exercise, for which the dog must follow a 30-minute-old track and find two articles. As the stakes get higher, the tracks are longer and older.

WORKING SPIRIT: ADVANCED TRIALS
Marney Wells

Of all the disciplines, Working Trials is probably the most appropriate for Staffords. Good control is essential, but the heelwork does not have to be as precise as in Obedience. Most trials take place at a good distance from the distraction of other dogs, and, best of all, there are exercises where the dog does the brainwork for the team, so Staffords, with their confidence and intelligence, are excellent competitors.

If, at Championship Trial, you manage to achieve 80 per cent or more of the marks available (see above), you can have the distinction of having CDex after the dog's name to prove what a genius he is! It may sound impossible, but there were Staffords in the 1940s and 1950s who competed successfully in Trials – such as Captain Warwick's Bedgebury Chieftain. At present, in the UK, there are two Staffords with CDexs – my own bitches Cyclone Sweetheart of Copyhold CDex UDex (Bertie) and Libellula Lass of Copyhold CDex UDex (Trilby).

To be allowed to have 'UDex' after their names, they had to qualify in the next Stake up in Trials, the UD – Utility Dog – Stake. This is when the very best bit of training comes in, the tracking. Although handler and dog are still very much a partnership, it is the dog who is boss, as only he knows where that track goes. And boy, do Staffords love it when they know best!

Some of the other exercises vary a little in UD: less heelwork and no Sit-stay. In Working Trials, the only concession to the dog's size is the alteration in jump sizes. The Sendaway and tracks are just the same as for the GSD police dogs taking part, so when your Staffordshire Bull Terrier qualifies, you know that you have competed on equal terms with the very best and maybe even beaten them! It can be done!

DUAL CHAMPIONSHIP

OTCH
The Obedience Trial Champion title is the most prestigious title offered by the American Kennel Club, as well as being the most elusive to obtain. Starting in 1997, when the title was first offered, it soon became the pinnacle of achievement aspired to by Obedience enthusiasts across the United States.

OTCH requirements are based upon placements in competitive Obedience Utility B and Open B classes. Since the better OTCH-titled dogs often continue on in competition seeking yearly or lifetime OTCH points totals, an OTCH aspirant must be prepared to enter Obedience classes and win against the very best nationally ranked Obedience dogs in current competition.

MACH
For this title, a dog must earn 20 double qualifiers by scoring perfect 100s and being under the course time in the AKC Excellent B Standard class, and the AKC Excellent B Jumpers with Weaves class on the same day. The dog must also earn 750 MACH points, which are full seconds under time on the AKC Excellent Agility courses.

Only the most gifted and athletic Agility dogs have been able to earn this title, the highest title the AKC offers in Agility.

OBEDIENCE

As I said earlier, Staffords are ideal to train, as they so want to please. This, together with their love of food, can hopefully be channelled into training. The problem with competitive Obedience is not in the breed's lack of ability but in the Stafford's construction. With his broad chest and rather short neck, it is almost impossible for both the dog's head and shoulder to be in contact with your leg.

Some Staffords are doing very well at Obedience and while there aren't any Stafford Obedience Champions in the UK yet – who knows what the future might bring?

In the US, there are three AKC Champions – see Clever Staffords, page 103. One, Moose, is a dual OTCH (Obedience Trial Champion) and MACH (Master Agility Champion).

Basic obedience exercises for beginners involve heelwork (on and off the lead), Recalls, Sit-stays for one minute, and Down-stays for two minutes. The classes then get progressively harder and move on to Scent Discrimination, Sendaways, Retrieves, out-of-sight Stays, and Distance Control.

THERAPY DOGS

The therapeutic value of pets cannot be disputed. They make us feel happier, and can

Gus: rescued from an illegal dog-fighting ring, where he was terribly abused, this remarkable Stafford is now a loving therapy dog.

Therapy work is a Stafford's ideal job – meeting people who want to make a fuss of you!

even speed recovery from illnesses. However, for many people (in hospitals, hospices or care homes, for example), the benefits of pet ownership are denied to them. Fortunately, there are several organisations that run schemes through which volunteers spare a couple of hours a week taking their confident, calm, well-behaved dogs to visit the elderly, the sick, etc.

Pets as Therapy (PAT) is one such organisation. Devised by the late Lesley Scott-Ordish, the charity has hundreds of registered, active dogs (and a handful of cats) that visit establishments all over the UK. Similar organisations can be found all over the world.

There are many Staffords who have successfully registered as therapy dogs, offering unconditional love to make life more bearable and to help speed recovery.

Being a therapy dog is ideal work for the Stafford, who adores human company. Especial care must be taken that the dogs are trained to greet people in a calm, controlled way, however.

Gus, owned by Jean Bond, is a registered PAT dog and is a great ambassador for the breed. Gus was rescued by the RSPCA from a dog-fighting ring, where he was used as a bait

ADVANCED COMPETITIVE OBEDIENCE

Scent discrimination

The cloths are laid out.

Tammy is sent in to investigate them.

She picks up the correct cloth before
returning to her owner.

RETRIEVING A DUMB-BELL

This exercise is used in Competitive Obedience,
but you can also make it into a fun game.

The handler prepares to throw the dumb-bell.

Edith must wait until she is instructed to fetch it.

A clean pick-up is required.

Edith returns with the dumb-bell.

dog. He had had his paws slashed and then been strung up for the other dogs to attack. He spent six months undergoing treatment before being rehomed, and he now lives each day to the full, making daily visits to hospices and hospitals.

CLEVER STAFFORDS

Many Staffordshire Bull Terriers are regularly competing in Agility, Working Trials and Obedience. When thinking of Obedience, Sandra Stredwick's Chelsea (Hadendale Eternal Flame) springs to mind. This little bitch excels at the sport, is regularly placed at Open Shows, and was at Crufts representing the Midlands Obedience team.

Marney Wells's three Staffords have done tremendously well, competing in all three disciplines, and excelling in Working Trials. Both Bertie (Cyclone Sweetheart of Copyhold) and Trilby (Libellula Lass of Copyhold) have their CDex and UDex qualifications. The dogs have also had their 15 minutes of fame appearing in 101 Dalmatians, and all are registered PAT dogs.

Lorraine Walchester with Jess (Jessica Joe Lighly) has regularly competed in Agility finals at Crufts and, in 2000, was placed in the pairs competition at over nine years of age.

Chloe Gardner, who is now 80 years old, still competes in Agility, but was known for Rosie (Roxstaff Helena) who was the Mini-Agility dog of the year in 1987. She was a great ambassadress for the breed and an inspiration for others to follow in her pawprints.

My own bitch, Tammy (Araidh Sweetest Taboo), is a registered PAT dog. She competes in Agility, Obedience and Working Trials, but it is in Agility that she excels – she is reckoned to be among one of the fastest Mini dogs in the UK. She took to the sport with a passion and often beats the fastest Border Collie for speed. She is also an Obedience demonstration dog at a local training club and is a Gold Good Citizen.

In the United States, Moose (AKC OTCH MACH Shady Grove's Enchantment UDex Mex MexJ) is owned and bred by Margo Milde from America. He is the first Stafford to earn an OTCH. Margo also owns Tiny (MACH Shady Grove's Fortunate Son UDex Mex MexJ), the first Stafford to earn this very difficult title – MACH.

MACH Tragob Princess Diva UD, owned by Kathy Prince, became the third Stafford MACH in July 2002. She is also the first Stafford bitch to earn a MACH.

Gus (right), with fellow therapy dog Nippa (left).

Trilby (Libellula Lass of Copyhold CDex UDex) with the Ch. Linksbury Amanda trophy for the Stafford bitch gaining most points in Working Trials.

Bertie (Cyclone Sweetheart of Copyhold CDex UDex) with the CDex certificate and first-place trophy gained at a Championship Working Trial in 1999.

Tammy (Araidh Sweetest Taboo) competing in Mini-Agility at Crufts. One of the fastests Minis in the sport, Tammy regularly beats the fastest Collies!

Brenda Buja from the USA owns Stella (ADCH Quicksilver Winter Stella) who was the USDAA 16-inch National Champion in 2001, unprecedented in the history of the sport. Stella also earned her USDAA Agility Dog Championship (ADCH) which consists of 27 legs in five different Masters level classes: Standard, Jumpers, Gamblers, Snooker, and Pairs Relay. Stella is the second Staffie to earn this title (Uandi Sholtze's Guinness was the first).

Hopefully with Agility Championship status available in the UK, we will soon see our first Agility Champion Staffordshire Bull Terrier.

BEHAVIOUR PROBLEMS

CHEWING

I have never really experienced this problem with my Staffords, since all were crated as young puppies (see page 66). The situation was always monitored and so it was never allowed to happen. However, my German Shepherd did make quite a mess of my three-piece suite, and I have heard stories about Staffords chewing through walls, so they can do a lot of damage.

Firstly, remove temptation. Don't expect your dog to know that chewing his toys is okay, but furniture, shoes etc. is not. Monitor the situation and don't allow him to get hold of anything he shouldn't. If you need to leave the dog for a short time, then invest in a crate. Properly used, they are invaluable as your dog learns the house rules.

Use your common sense and don't give your dog an old shoe to chew – he should have his own toys. Invest in a Kong, which were especially developed for Staffords. These tough, rubber toys can be stuffed with food and are essential when your puppy is teething.

Only scold your dog when caught in the act. There is no use scolding after the event.

The Kong: a tough, safe, enjoyable chew that can withstand even a Stafford's attention!

Think about what has happened – it may well be your own fault.

BARKING

Dogs bark for many reasons. First, you need to ascertain why your dog is barking before you can begin to look at curing the problem. Although barking is a normal means of communication, in excess it can be a nuisance not only for yourself, but also for your neighbours.

Barking to deter people from entering your property is fine, but should the dog bark at every passer-by, then it soon becomes a problem. Unfortunately, owners often attempt to cure the problem by shouting at the dog, but, as your dog does not speak English, he thinks you are joining in the barking. Some dogs discover that barking makes their owners give them attention, if only to shout at them. Often, the dog will bark just to get a response from an owner, in which case your dog needs to have his mind stimulated.

However, most dogs are barking 'territorially' and this is reinforced as every person they bark at goes away. Your dog doesn't realise that they didn't want to come in anyway, so he assumes he has saved the day yet again.

Maybe he barks when left alone – in order to call you back. Then, miraculously, back you come. The dog believes that barking gets results. Maybe your dog barks excessively at visitors, and, in an attempt to stop the behaviour, you put a hand down to stroke your dog – you are simply reinforcing the behaviour.

HOW TO STOP THE BARKING
If, every time your dog barks for attention, you get up and walk out of the room, or turn your back, your dog will eventually learn that barking is counterproductive. However, more ingrained barking problems may require some well-laid plans and several months of hard work to cure.

One of the simplest ways to teach your dog not to bark is to teach your dog to bark on command. Use the command "Speak", for example. The point is that, after your dog associates this command with barking, it is relatively easy then to introduce a word such as "Quiet" while your dog is barking, and then reward him when the barking stops.

Reward is, of course, the best motivation, so it's important to praise the dog at the time he is doing the right thing, not afterwards. This means rewarding him when he stops barking, and also remembering to praise when your dog doesn't bark in a situation in which he normally would.

PULLING ON THE LEAD
All dogs will pull on the lead at some time – such as when they are first going for a walk and are excited. Most Staffords enjoy pulling. I used to put this to good use and get my male Stafford to pull my shopping trolley home!

With Staffords (and their tendency to stubbornness), jerking them back is entirely counterproductive – they just pull harder. Instead, you should communicate with your dog – tell and show him what to do.

While headcollars work for some breeds, they really aren't suitable for Staffords, due to the dog's short muzzle. Body harnesses only

Many Staffords enjoy pulling on the lead, but the behaviour can be rectified easily.

offer a temporary solution – when you revert back to the ordinary collar once more, the problem will recur.

As with any dog, he should be taught to walk at your side without any undue pulling. Taught correctly and with rewards, dog-walking will become a pleasurable experience for both of you. It is, of course, much easier to teach a puppy to walk correctly, thus building the foundations for the rest of his life as to what is and isn't acceptable.

Teaching an older Stafford to walk on the lead is possible – as we know, the breed is intelligent and quick to learn – but you must persevere with your training and be consistent every time you walk him.

- Get your dog's attention (through the Watch exercise, page 86).
- Have your dog on the side you want to walk him (the left side is the usual side).
- Gain his attention. Say "Heel", take a step, and get him to sit. Give lots of praise.
- Repeat this exercise until your Stafford understands what is expected of him.
- Gradually add more steps, remembering always to gain his attention first.
- When he is comfortably walking several paces with you, try walking in different directions, such as left- and right-hand circles and figures of eight.
- Next, change your pace – through slow, normal and fast.

106

- All the time, remember to get your dog's attention first, and praise him when you get it.
- Heelwork doesn't have to be boring – change pace, alter your direction unexpectedly, use toys, treats, and a happy voice so your dog finds it exciting and fun.

I teach my dogs competitive heelwork, where they have to look up at me when they work. To obtain this in the beginning, I give a treat every time the dog looks up at me. Pretty soon, my Staffords learn that looking at me is worth their while! Treats need to be phased out gradually, but simply having your hand near your treat pocket is just as effective!

Depending on your dog, you may have to change other areas of your dog's life. For example, if he frequently barges through doors in front of you, work on this – teach your dog what is and what isn't acceptable behaviour. You need to be consistent, to think about situations and why your dog is not understanding.

AGGRESSION TO OTHER DOGS

Hopefully, you will have done your homework before buying a Stafford, and will realise that, although they have a well-deserved reputation for a great love of people, this doesn't always extend to other canines. The Stafford is not a breed that you should expect to play ball with all the other dogs in the park, although Staffords differ greatly and some are better than others. It is best not to take any risks – if there is a nasty incident, your Stafford will almost certainly get the blame, for which the entire breed is penalised.

Sometimes it is hard for the general public to realise that 'dog-to-dog' aggression is not the same as 'dog-to-human' aggression.

Early socialisation is essential. Most veterinary surgeries hold puppy classes between eight and fourteen weeks; then, after vaccinations, you can move on to puppy classes which include basic obedience and socialisation skills.

Chastise your Stafford if he barks at another dog. Tell him "No!" firmly, and, with a small jerk of the lead, get him to 'Watch' you (page 86), and to concentrate on you alone when another dog approaches. Make sure you shorten the lead, so he cannot reach the other dog, and, if possible, get his attention on you before he objects to the other dog – prevention is the best approach. If your dog is very bad with others, change your walking route or times, to avoid any conflicts. In such circumstances, of course, your Stafford should always be kept on the lead.

JUMPING UP

A puppy jumping up may well be considered cute and often encouraged, but when the dog is older and considerably heavier, the action does tend to lose its 'cute' appeal – and may even knock over children. Plus, there is always the very real danger that an overfriendly Stafford will jump at a passing stranger who is not a dog lover, and this may be misinterpreted as aggression.

Your Stafford should be discouraged from jumping up by utterly ignoring him. Do not respond (do not tell him off or even look at him), as you will be indirectly rewarding him with your attention. Staffords hate to be ignored. They jump up to get your attention. If they learn that jumping up results in being given a cold shoulder, they will realise their behaviour is counterproductive and will stop. You just have to be consistent (and make sure that guests behave in the same way). As soon as your dog sits down and is quiet, then you should give him attention – he'll soon get the message that he doesn't get petted unless all four feet are on the ground!

6 DIET AND NUTRITION

Nutrition has never been the sole domain of the medical practitioner or veterinary surgeon. It is relatively recently that the medical profession has developed clinical nutrition to the point that there are professors in the subject, and that veterinary surgeons in companion-animal practice have realised that they have an expertise to offer in this area of pet health care. This is curious because even the earliest medical and veterinary texts refer to the importance of correct diet, and, for many years, veterinary surgeons working with production animals such as cattle, pigs and sheep have been deluged with information about the most appropriate nutrition for those species.

Traditionally, of course, breeders, neighbours, friends, relatives, pet-shop staff, and even the local supermarket have been a main source of advice on feeding for many pet owners. Over the past few years, there has been a great increase in public awareness about the relationships between diet and disease, thanks mainly to media interest in the subject, but also to education by major pet-food manufacturing companies.

Breeders have always actively debated the 'best way' to feed dogs. Most dog owners are aware of the importance of good bone development and the role of nutrition in achieving optimal skeletal characteristics.

However, as a vet, I am constantly amazed and bewildered at the menus that breeders give to new puppy owners. These all too frequently consist of complex home-made recipes, usually based on large amounts of fresh meat, goat's milk, and a vast array of mineral supplements. These diets are often very imbalanced and could easily result in skeletal and other growth abnormalities.

Domesticated dogs usually have little opportunity to select their own diet – they are solely dependent on their owners to provide all the nourishment they need. In this chapter, I aim to explain what those needs are, dispel a few myths, and hopefully give some guidance as to how to select the most appropriate diet for your dog.

ESSENTIAL NUTRITION

Dogs have a common ancestry with, and are still often classified as, carnivores. However, from a nutritional point of view, they are actually omnivores. This means that they obtain all the essential nutrients they need from dietary sources consisting of either animal or plant material. As far as we know, dogs can survive on food derived solely from plants – that is, they can be fed a vegetarian diet. The same is not true for domesticated cats, who are still obligate carnivores, and whose nutritional needs cannot be met by an exclusively vegetarian diet.

ENERGY

All living cells require energy. The more active they are, the more energy they burn up. Individual dogs have their own energy needs, which can vary even between dogs of the same breed, age, sex and activity level. Breeders will recognise the scenario in which some littermates develop differently, one tending towards obesity, another on the lean side, even when they are fed exactly the same amount of food.

For adult maintenance, a Staffordshire Bull Terrier will need an energy intake of approximately 30kcal per lb of body weight (or 65 kcal/kg body weight). If you know the energy density of the food that you are giving, you can work out how much your dog needs; but you must remember that this is only an approximation – you will need to adjust the amount you feed to suit each individual dog. This is best achieved by regularly weighing your dog and then maintaining an optimum body weight.

An adult Stafford requires 30kcal per lb of body weight.

If you are feeding a commercially prepared food, you should be aware that the feeding guide recommended by the manufacturer is also based on average energy needs, and therefore you may need to increase or decrease the amount you give to meet your own dog's requirements. In some countries (such as those within the European Union), legislation may not allow the energy content to appear on the label of a prepared pet food; however, reputable manufacturing companies can and will provide this information upon request.

When considering different foods, it is important to compare the 'metabolisable energy', which is the amount of energy in the food that is available to a dog. Some companies will provide you with figures for the 'gross energy', which is not as useful because some of that energy (sometimes a substantial amount) will not be digested, absorbed and utilised.

There are many circumstances in which your dog's energy requirement may change from his or her basic adult maintenance energy requirement (MER):

Work

Light	1.1-1.5 x MER
Heavy	2-4 x MER
Inactivity	0.8 x MER

Pregnancy

First 6 weeks	1 x MER
Last 3 weeks	1.1-1.3 x MER
Peak lactation	2-4 x MER
Growth	1.2-2 x MER

Environment

Cold	1.25-1.75 x MER
Heat	Up to 2.5 x MER

VARYING REQUIREMENTS

Light to moderate activity (work) barely increases energy needs, and it is only when dogs are doing heavy work, such as pulling sleds, that energy requirements are significantly increased.

Note that there is no increased energy requirement during pregnancy, except in the last three weeks, and the main need for high energy intake is during the lactation period. If a bitch is getting sufficient energy, she should not lose weight or condition during pregnancy and lactation. Because the energy requirement is so great during lactation (up to 4 x MER), it can sometimes be impossible to meet this need by feeding conventional adult maintenance diets, because the bitch cannot physically eat enough food. As a result, she will lose weight and condition. Switching to a high-energy diet is usually necessary to avoid this. See also page 113, later in this chapter.

As dogs get older their energy needs usually decrease. This is largely due to being less active. This can be caused by a number of issues:

• Perhaps the owner is elderly and the dog is getting less exercise
• Mobility problems (such as arthritis)
• Altered metabolism that occurs with old age.

These factors reduce the amount of energy that older dogs need. The aim should be to maintain body weight throughout old age, and regular exercise can play an important part in this. If there is any tendency to decrease or increase weight, this should be countered by increasing or decreasing energy intake accordingly. If the body weight changes by more than ten per cent from usual, veterinary attention should be sought, in case there is a medical problem causing the weight change.

Changes in environmental conditions and all forms of stress (including showing), which particularly affect dogs with a nervous temperament, can increase energy needs.

Some dogs when kennelled for long periods lose weight due to a stress-related increase in energy requirements which cannot easily be met by a maintenance diet. A high-energy food containing at least 1900 kcal of metabolisable energy/lb dry matter (4.2 kcal/gram) may be needed to maintain body weight under these circumstances. Excessive energy intake, on the other hand, results in obesity that can have very serious health effects.

OBESITY

Orthopaedic problems, such as ruptured cruciate ligaments, are more likely to occur in overweight dogs. This condition, which often requires surgical intervention, may present as a sudden-onset complete lameness or a gradually worsening hind leg lameness. Although the Staffordshire Bull Terrier is not inherently prone to developing a ruptured cruciate (it is a far more common condition in breeds such as the Labrador Retriever and the Poodle), obesity will significantly increase the strain on the joint and ligament and may cause rupture.

The Stafford should be muscular but not fat: obesity can cause numerous health problems.

Dogs frequently develop heart disease in old age, and obesity puts significant extra demands on the cardiovascular system, with potentially serious consequences. Obesity is also a predisposing cause of non-insulin-dependent diabetes mellitus, and has many other detrimental effects on health, including reducing resistance to infection and increasing anaesthetic and surgical risks. Once obesity is present, activity tends to decrease and it becomes even more necessary to decrease energy intake; otherwise more body weight is gained and the situation is made worse.

For obese or obesity-prone dogs, a low-energy intake is indicated, and there are now specially prepared diets that have a very low energy density; those which are most effective have a high fibre content. Recent research has shown that overweight dogs benefit from being fed diets supplemented with the vitamin-like substance L-carnitine. This vitamin is required by the body to metabolise (burn) fat. Dogs on a weight-reduction programme are required to burn more fat and so have a higher demand for L-carnitine. Your veterinary surgeon will advise you about the most appropriate type of diet if you have such a problem dog. Incidentally, if you do have an overweight dog, it is important to seek veterinary advice in case it is associated with some other medical condition.

FAT

Energy is only available from the fat, carbohydrate and protein in a dog's diet. A gram of fat provides $2\frac{1}{4}$ times as much energy as a gram of carbohydrate or protein, and so high energy requirements are best met by feeding a relatively high-fat diet. Dogs rarely develop the cardiovascular conditions, such as atherosclerosis and coronary artery disease, that have been associated with high fat intake in humans.

PROTEIN

Owners may think that protein is the source of energy needed for exercise and performance, but this is not true. Protein is a relatively poor source of energy because a large amount of the energy theoretically available from it is lost in 'meal-induced heat'. Meal-induced heat is the metabolic heat 'wasted' in the digestion, absorption and utilisation of the protein. Fat and carbohydrates are better sources of energy for performance.

CHOOSING A DIET

The first important consideration to make when selecting a maintenance diet is that it should meet the energy requirements of your dog. In some situations, specially formulated high-energy or low-energy diets will be

The diet you choose should reflect your dog's energy requirements.

needed to achieve this. Other nutrients that must be provided in the diet include essential amino acids (from dietary protein), essential fatty acids (from dietary fat), minerals and vitamins. Carbohydrates are not an essential dietary component for dogs, because they can synthesise sufficient glucose from other sources.

Do not fall into the trap of thinking that if a diet is good for a human, it must be good for a dog. There are many differences between a human's nutritional needs and those of the dog. For example, humans need a supply of vitamin C in the diet, but, under normal circumstances, a dog can synthesise his own vitamin C, and so a dietary source is not essential. The amount of nutrients that a dog needs will vary according to his stage of life, environment and activity level. For the rest of this section, life-cycle feeding will be discussed.

FEEDING FOR GROWTH
Growing animals have tissues that are actively developing and growing in size, and so it isn't surprising that they have a relatively higher requirement for energy, protein, vitamins and minerals than their adult counterparts (based on the daily intake of these nutrients per lb/kg of body weight).

Birth weight usually doubles in seven to ten days, and puppies should gain 1-2 oz per day per lb (2-4 grams/day/kg) of anticipated adult weight. An important key to the successful rearing of neonates is to reduce the puppies' energy loss by maintaining their environmental temperature, as well as by ensuring sufficient energy intake.

Bitch's milk is of particular importance to the puppy during the first few hours of life, as this early milk (called colostrum) provides some passive immunity to the puppy because of the maternal antibodies it contains. These will help to protect the puppy until he can produce his own immune response to any

Ad-lib feeding can encourage overeating, particularly if there is competition between littermates.

challenge from infectious agents.

Survival rate is greatly decreased in puppies that do not get colostrum from their mother. Orphaned puppies are best fed a proprietary milk replacer, according to the manufacturer's recommendations, unless a foster mother can be found. Your veterinary surgeon will be able to help if you find yourself in such a situation.

Obesity must be avoided during puppyhood, as so-called 'juvenile obesity' will increase the number of fat cells in the body, and so predispose the animal to obesity for the rest of his life. Overeating is most likely to occur when puppies are fed with the free choice method (ad lib) throughout the day, particularly if there is competition between littermates. A better method is to feed a puppy a daily ration based on his body weight, divided into two to four meals per day – the number decreasing as he gets older. Any food remaining after 20 minutes should be removed.

HIP DYSPLASIA
Hip dysplasia is affected not only by genetics but also by environmental factors in the early weeks of life (such as the condition of the

113

flooring the puppies are reared on) and food intake.

Studies have shown that feeding large-breed puppies ad lib increases the risk of the dog developing hip dysplasia later in life. Many pet food manufacturers now produce special growth diets indicated for larger-breed puppies (puppies that will weigh more than 25 kgs/55 lbs when mature adult dogs). These are beneficial in helping to reduce developmental bone disease, if fed according to the manufacturer's recommendations. They contain a lower level of energy and a reduced calcium content.

It may at first seem odd that breeds that have to develop a lot of bone during the period of growth would actually benefit from a reduced level of calcium. However, studies have now shown the dangers of excessive calcium intake in the development of optimal skeletal structure. The larger and heavier the dog, the greater the risk.

DIETARY DEFICIENCIES
Proper growth and development is dependent upon a sufficient intake of essential nutrients, and if you consider how rapidly a puppy grows, usually achieving half his adult weight by four months of age, it is not surprising that nutritional deficiencies, excesses, or imbalances can have disastrous results.

Deficiency diseases are rarely seen in veterinary practice nowadays, mainly because proprietary pet foods contain more than sufficient amounts of the essential nutrients. When a deficiency disease is diagnosed, it is usually associated with an unbalanced home-made diet. A classical example of this is dogs fed on an all-meat diet. Meat is very low in calcium but high in phosphorus, and demineralisation of bones occurs on this type of diet. This leads to very thin bones that fracture easily, frequently resulting in folding fractures caused simply by weight-bearing.

Development of a good skeleton results

from an interaction of genetic, environmental, and nutritional influences. The genetic component can be influenced by the breeder in a desire to improve the breed. Environmental influences, including housing and activity level, can be controlled by the new puppy owner with good advice from the breeder. However, nutrition is one of the most important factors influencing correct development of the puppy's bones and muscles.

In growing puppies, it is particularly important to provide minerals – but in the correct proportions to each other. The calcium:phosphorus ratio should ideally be

Excessive calcium intake in puppyhood can result in skeletal deformities.

1.2-1.4:1, and certainly within the wider range of 1-2:1. If there is more phosphorus than calcium in the diet (i.e. an inverse calcium:phosphorus ratio), normal bone development may be affected.

Care also has to be taken to avoid feeding too much mineral content. Excessive calcium intake actually causes stunting of growth, and an intake of 3.3 per cent calcium has been shown to result in serious skeletal deformities, including deformities of the carpus ('wrist'), osteochondritis dissecans (OCD), wobbler syndrome, and hip dysplasia (see Chapter Thirteen). These are common diseases, and while other factors such as genetic inheritance may also be involved, excessive mineral intake should be considered a risk factor in all cases.

Staffordshire Bull Terriers can sometimes develop a form of OCD known as Ununited Anconeal Process (also called elbow dysplasia), in which a small bone within the elbow joint fails to develop correctly. This leads to arthritis at a very young age. If diagnosed early enough, the condition can be surgically treated, however normal joint function may not be possible in all cases.

If a diet already contains sufficient calcium, it is dangerously easy to increase the calcium content to well over three per cent if you give mineral supplements as well. Some commercially available treats and snacks are very high in salt, protein and calories. They can significantly upset a carefully balanced diet, and it is advisable to ask your veterinary surgeon's opinion of the various treats available and to use them only very occasionally.

A growing puppy is best fed a proprietary pet food that has been specifically formulated to meet his nutritional needs. Those that are available as both tinned and dry are especially suitable to rear even the youngest of puppies. Home-made diets may theoretically be adequate, but it is difficult to ensure that all

the nutrients are provided in an available form. The only way to be sure about the adequacy of a diet is to have it analysed for its nutritional content and to put it through controlled feeding trials.

Supplements should only be used with rations that are known to be deficient, in order to provide whatever is missing from the diet. With a complete balanced diet, nothing should be missing. If you use supplements with an already balanced diet, you could create an imbalance, and/or provide excessive amounts of nutrients, particularly minerals.

Nutritional management alone is not sufficient to prevent developmental bone disease. However, we can prevent some skeletal disease by feeding appropriate amounts of a good-quality, balanced diet. Dietary deficiencies are of minimal concern with the ever-increasing range of commercial diets specifically prepared for young growing dogs. The potential for harm is in overnutrition from excess consumption and supplementation.

PREGNANCY AND LACTATION

There is no need to increase the amount of food being fed to a bitch during early and mid-pregnancy, but there will be an increased demand for energy (i.e. carbohydrates and fats collectively), protein, minerals and vitamins during the last three weeks. A bitch's nutritional requirements will be maximum during lactation, particularly if she has a large litter to feed. Avoid giving calcium supplementation during pregnancy, as a high intake can frustrate calcium availability during milk production, and can increase the chances of eclampsia (also called 'milk fever' or 'puerperal tetany') occurring – see also Chapter Ten.

During pregnancy, a bitch should maintain her body weight and condition. If she loses weight, her energy intake needs to be

A bitch's nutritional requirements are at a maximum during lactation.

increased. A specifically formulated growth-type diet is recommended to meet her nutritional needs at this time. If a bitch is on a diet formulated for this stage of her life, and she develops eclampsia or has had previous episodes of the disease, your veterinary surgeon may advise calcium supplementation. If given during pregnancy, this is only advisable during the very last few days of pregnancy when milk let-down is occurring, and preferably is given only during lactation (i.e. after whelping).

It should be noted that, due to their reduced calcium and energy content, the special larger-breed growth diets mentioned earlier are contraindicated for pregnancy and lactation, regardless of the size of the dam.

MAINTENANCE AND OLD AGE
The objective of good nutrition is to provide all the energy and essential nutrients that a dog needs in sufficient amounts to avoid deficiency, and at the same time to limit their supply so as not to cause overnutrition or

toxicity. Some nutrients are known to play a role in disease processes, and it is prudent to avoid unnecessarily high intakes of these whenever possible. The veterinary surgeons at Hill's Science and Technology Centre in Topeka, Kansas, are specialists in canine clinical nutrition and they are particularly concerned about the potential health risks associated with too high an intake of the following nutrients during a dog's adult life:
• Protein
• Sodium (salt)
• Phosphorus.

These nutrients are thought to have an important and serious impact once disease is present, particularly in heart and kidney diseases. Kidney failure and heart failure are very common in older dogs and it is believed to be important to avoid feeding diets high in these nutrients to this at-risk group of dogs.

Furthermore, these nutrients may be detrimental to dogs even before there is any evidence of disease. It is known that salt, for example, can be retained in dogs with subclinical heart disease, before there is any outward evidence of illness. Salt retention is an important contributing factor in the development of fluid retention (congestion), swelling of the limbs (oedema) and dropsy (ascites).

A leading veterinary cardiologist in the USA has claimed that 40 per cent of dogs over five years of age, and 80 per cent of dogs over ten years, have some change in the heart – either endocardiosis and myocardial fibrosis (or both). Both of these lesions may reduce heart function.

Phosphorus retention is an important consequence of advancing kidney disease, which encourages mineral deposition in the soft tissues of the body, including the kidneys themselves, a condition known as 'nephrocalcinosis'. Such deposits damage the

Exercising a dog around mealtimes increases the chances of developing bloat.

kidneys even more, and hasten the onset of kidney failure.

As a dog ages, there are two major factors that determine his nutritional needs:

1. His changing nutritional requirements due to the effects of age on organ function and metabolism
2. The increased likelihood of the presence of subclinical diseases.

Many Staffordshire Bull Terrier owners are aware of a condition called gastric dilatation and torsion, commonly known as 'bloat'. This potentially life-threatening condition was previously thought to be due to the ingestion of a high-fat or carbohydrate meal. Current thinking is that bloat is due to aerophagia (the intake of large amounts of air with a meal), common in greedy individuals, and the predisposing factors may be:

• Genetic make-up
• Competitive feeding
• Strenuous exercise around mealtimes
• Excitement at feeding time.

(The last three factors encourage rapid eating.) Special highly digestible diets are available from veterinary surgeons that can be given to at-risk individuals.

Energy requirements usually decrease with increasing age, and food intake should be adjusted accordingly. Also the dietary intake of some nutrients needs to be minimised – in particular, protein, phosphorus, sodium and total energy intake. Dietary intake of other nutrients may need to be increased to meet the needs of some older dogs, notably essential fatty acids, some vitamins, some specific amino acids and zinc. Unlike humans, calcium and phosphorus do not need to be supplemented in ageing dogs – indeed to do so may prove detrimental.

FOOD LABELLING

Labelling laws differ from one country to the next. For example, pet foods sold in the USA must carry a Guaranteed Analysis, which states a maximum or a minimum amount for the various nutrients in the food. Pet foods sold in Europe must carry a Typical (as fed) Analysis, which is a declaration of the average amount of nutrients found from analysis of the product.

'COMPLETE' VERSUS 'COMPLEMENTARY'

In the UK, a pet food must declare whether it is 'complete' or 'complementary'. A complete pet food must provide all the nutrients required to satisfy the needs of the group of pet animals for which it is recommended. At the time of writing, there is no obligation for a manufacturer to submit such a diet to feeding trials to ensure that it is adequate.

In the USA, some manufacturers submit their pet foods to the feeding trials approved by the Association of American Feed Control Officials (AAFCO) to ensure that they meet the nutritional requirements of the National Research Council (e.g. the Hill's Pet Nutrition range of Science Plan products).

A complementary pet food needs to be fed with some other foodstuff in order to meet the needs of the animal. Anyone feeding a complementary food as a substantial part of a dog's ration is obliged to find out what it should be fed with, in order to balance the ration. Failure to do so could result in serious deficiency or imbalance of nutrients.

DRY MATTER

The water content of pet foods varies greatly, particularly in canned products. In the USA, there is a legal maximum limit (78 per cent) which cannot be exceeded, but no such limit is in force in Europe, and some European canned pet foods contain as much as 86 per cent water. Legislation now makes it compulsory for the water content to be declared on the label and this is important, because to compare one pet food with another, one should consider the percentage of a nutrient in the dry matter of food.

For example, two pet foods may declare the protein content to be 10 per cent in the Typical Analysis printed on the label. If one product contains 75 per cent water, it has 25 per cent dry matter, so the protein content is actually $10/25 \times 100 = 40$ per cent. If the other product contains 85 per cent water, the protein content is $10/15 \times 100 = 66.6$ per cent. This type of calculation (called Dry Weight Analysis) becomes even more important when comparing canned with dry products, as the water content of dry food is usually only 7.5 to 12 per cent.

You can only effectively compare pet foods if you know:

1. The food's energy density
2. The dry weight analysis of the individual nutrients.

COST

The only valid way to compare the cost of one food against another is to compare the daily feeding costs to meet all the needs of your dog. A high-energy, nutritionally concentrated type of diet might cost more to buy per kilogram of food, but it could be cheaper to feed on a cost per day basis. Conversely, a poor-quality, poorly digestible diet may be cheaper per pound/kilogram to buy, but actually cost more per day to feed, because you need to feed much more food to meet the dog's requirements.

The only valid reason for feeding a food is that it meets the nutritional requirements of your dog. To do that, you need to read between the marketing strategies of the manufacturers and select a diet that you know provides your dog with what he needs.

HOME-MADE DIETS

What about home-made recipes? Well, theoretically it is possible to make a home-made diet that will meet all the nutritional requirements of a dog. However, not all published recipes may actually achieve what they claim. The reason is that there is no strict quality control of ingredients, and the availability of nutrients may vary from one ingredient source to another. If you feed a correctly balanced home-made diet, meals are often time-consuming to prepare, usually need the addition of a vitamin/mineral supplement, and, if prepared accurately, can be expensive. Variations in raw ingredients will cause fluctuations in nutritional value.

The only way to be absolutely sure that a home-made diet has the nutritional profile that you want is to mix all the food ingredients plus supplements, treats, snacks, scraps, etc. in a large pot, homogenise them, and have a sample analysed chemically (this costs well over £100/US$160) for a partial analysis). Compare this analytical content with the published levels for nutrient requirements.

You may feel that feeding an existing home-made recipe passed on to you or developed over a number of years is adequate. But how do you know? What is the phosphorus level of the diet that you are feeding? An undesirably high level of intake may take a long time before it results in obvious problems.

Sometimes the condition of your dog will give you an idea that all is not well with the diet you are feeding. One of the most common questions asked by breeders at dog shows is "Can you recommend a diet that will keep weight on my dogs?". Unless there is a medical problem (and in such cases you should always seek veterinary attention first), the only reason dogs usually have difficulty maintaining their weight is simply that they have an inadequate energy intake. This does not mean that they are not eating well – they could be eating like a horse – but if the food is relatively low in energy content, and if it is poorly digestible, your dog may be unable to eat sufficient food to meet his energy needs.

Large, bulky faeces are an indicator of low digestibility. A poor-looking, dull, dry or scurfy coat, poor skin, and other external signs of unthriftiness may also be an indicator of poor nutrition. How many 'poor-doers' and dogs with recurrent infections are on a diet with a marginal nutritional level of adequacy?

SUMMARY

The importance of nutrition has been known for many years and yet, sadly, it is still surrounded by too many old wives' tales, myths and unsubstantiated claims. The emergence of clinical nutrition as a subject in its own right has set the stage for the future. Hopefully, in the years to come, we shall hear about the benefits and dangers of different feeding practices from scientists who can base their statements on fact, not merely opinion.

Already we know that an ill dog has different nutritional requirements to a healthy dog. In some cases, dietary management can even offer an alternative way to manage clinical cases. For example, we currently have the ability to dissolve struvite stones in the urinary bladder simply by manipulating dietary intake instead of resorting to surgery.

But please note, dietary management is not 'alternative medicine'. Proper nutrition is key to everything that a living animal has to do, be it work or repairing tissues after an injury. It is not an option; it is a crucial part of looking after an animal properly. If you own a dog, then you should at least ensure that the food you give supplies all his needs, and avoids the excessive intake of energy or nutrients that may play a role in the development of disease.

Bright eyes, a muscular, sleek physique, and a shiny coat – the hallmarks of a good diet.

7 THE BREED STANDARD

Every breed of dog has a Breed Standard. This document sets out the distinguishing features of the breed concerned, differentiating it from any other breed. It is a truism that there can be no breed without a Standard, and it is often described as the 'bible' of the breed.

Breed Standards are comparatively recent innovations. In centuries past, dogs were given generic names associated, in general, with their use for man, e.g. retrievers (who fetched game); sheepdogs (who controlled flocks); and terriers (who were sent to ground for sport). Within these main groups, various types evolved dependent on the exact nature of the work or even the terrain in which they carried out this work.

It is really with the introduction of dog shows and the organisation of these that it was found desirable to have a Standard for each breed and the emphasis at this point changed from producing a dog who could fulfil a special job to one who came nearest to a desired picture – a creature of beauty rather than one of function. It remains the show breeder's task to balance these two things – to produce a good-looking dog who is also a physically and mentally sound animal.

The Standard should be an instrument for the continued improvement of the breed it describes, and the blueprint to which breeders should aspire. It gives judges the specifications – the standard – by which the breed can be recognised and within the limits of which judges should operate. It must therefore contain enough detail to enable breeders, judges and purchasers to form a picture of an ideal specimen with which they can compare the reality of any dog being examined.

SETTING THE STANDARD

The Staffordshire Bull Terrier was accepted as a pure breed of dog by the Kennel Club in April 1935, and its supporters then formed a club – the Staffordshire Bull Terrier Club. Only in June 1935 did fanciers draw up a Standard, which was published as a 'Description of the Staffordshire Bull Terrier'. At this time, all Breed Standards were owned by the relevant breed clubs.

Some 30 enthusiasts met at the Old Cross Guns Inn at Cradley Heath, West Midlands, to draw up this document. There is a popular myth that the whole thing was based on just one dog – Jim the Dandy. Originally known as Shaw's Jim, he was owned by Jack Barnard, the first president of the Staffordshire Bull Terrier Club and a great publicist for the breed and his own stock. The epithet 'The dog on which the Standard was based' first appeared in one of Jack's adverts for Jim the Dandy.

Jim the Dandy (left) and Fearless Joe (right): the basis of the original Breed Standard.

Joseph Dunn, first secretary of the club, writes in his book that two dogs were, in fact, present at this meeting – Jim the Dandy and Peg's Joe, later registered as Fearless Joe (a dog, who, in the first books on the breed, was given much more prominence than Jim).

Mr H.N. Beilby, the author of one of the very first books on the breed, goes one step further. He writes that the Standard was made as wide as possible in order to bring in as many animals as possible. He gives a very reasonable account of the method used to arrive at this description of the breed. Those concerned, he claims, had dogs, sketches, and photographs to study, and where they found a characteristic appeared in several animals they, rather naturally, assumed that that characteristic was typical for the breed. So, for example, having found that most of the animals studied were broad in the skull, it was concluded that this was a typical characteristic for this breed they had now recognised as the Staffordshire Bull Terrier.

Trying to accommodate both these aims, namely to describe the typical but not to eliminate too many specimens, led to some compromises. For example, with the ears, they could agree the full drop was undesirable, but they had to include all three of the other types of ear carriage – rose, half-prick and prick – because, presumably, there was no overwhelming evidence that any one

of these predominated.

There are many other examples of where one might wish the originators could have been more exact in their descriptions! They did, however leave us one remarkable thing – a scale of points, dropped from the present Standard, but giving us a clear idea of what they considered to be the most important parts of the Staffordshire Bull Terrier.

THE ORIGINAL 1935 STANDARD

GENERAL APPEARANCE: The Staffordshire Bull Terrier is a smooth-coated dog, standing about 15-18 inches high at the shoulder. He should give the impression of great strength for his size, and, although muscular, should be active and agile.

HEAD: Short, deep through, broad skull, very pronounced cheek muscles, distinct stop, short foreface, mouth level.

EARS: Rose, half-prick and prick; these three to be preferred, full drop to be penalized.

EYES: Dark.

NECK: Should be muscular and rather short.

BODY: Short back, deep brisket, light in loins with forelegs set rather wide apart to permit chest development.

FRONT LEGS: Straight, feet well padded, to turn out a little and showing no weakness at the pasterns.

HIND LEGS: Hindquarters well muscled, let down at hocks like a terrier.

COAT: Short, smooth, and close to the skin.

TAIL: The tail should be of medium length, tapering to a point and carried rather low; it should not curl much and may be compared with an old-fashioned pump handle.

WEIGHT: Dogs 28-38 lbs. Bitches 4 lbs less.

COLOUR: May be any shade of brindle, black, white, fawn or red, or any of these colours with white. Black and tan and liver not to be encouraged.

FAULTS TO BE PENALIZED: Dudley nose, light or pink eyes (rims), tail too long or badly curled, badly undershot or overshot mouths.

SCALE OF POINTS

General appearance, coat and condition	15
Head	30
Neck	10
Body	25
Legs and feet	15
Tail	5
Total	100

THE 1948 REVISION

In 1948, the Kennel Club decided to take over all Breed Standards and contacted all clubs asking them to submit their Standards. Evidently, some breeds had more than one Standard! The Kennel Club also issued a list of clauses to be included, so as to bring a degree of uniformity into the Standards' composition.

At this time in the UK, there were only five breed clubs set up purely for Staffords, and these were each able to send four representatives to the meeting in October 1948. In fact, the north of the country was very badly represented.

- Northern Counties sent only one representative (Mr Woodhead).
- The Scottish Club used four people from the Midlands to represent them (Mr Dudley, Mr Jack Dunn, Mr Priest, and Mr Amos Smith).
- The North West Club sent four delegates (Mr Hargreaves, Mr Gregson, Mr Rawnsley and Mr Thomas).
- Southern Counties sent four (Mr Cairns, Mr Gordon, Mr Russ and Mr Servat).
- The Staffordshire Bull Terrier Club also sent four (Mr Holden, Mr Brooks, Mr Davenport, and Mr Hatton).

Mr Beilby was unanimously elected to chair the meeting. Surprisingly enough, the whole thing was wrapped up in three and a quarter hours. Commencing at 2.30pm, the Standard proper was finished by 5.45pm. There was an evening session, but this was taken up with considering setting up a central discussion body – a forerunner of what, much later, became the Breed Council.

1948 STANDARD

CHARACTERISTIC: From the past history of the Staffordshire Bull Terrier, the modern dog draws his character of indomitable courage, high intelligence and tenacity. This, coupled with his affection for his friends, and children in particular, his off-duty quietness and trustworthy stability, makes him the foremost all-purpose dog.

GENERAL APPEARANCE: The Staffordshire Bull Terrier is a smooth-coated dog. He should be of great strength for his size, and, although muscular, should be active and agile.

HEAD AND SKULL: Short, deep through, broad skull, very pronounced cheek muscles, distinct stop, short foreface, black nose.

EYES: Dark preferable, but may bear some relation to coat colour. Round, of medium size, and set to look straight ahead.

EARS: Rose or half-pricked and not large. Full drop or prick to be penalised.

MOUTH: The mouth should be level, i.e. the incisors of the bottom jaw should fit closely inside the incisors of the top jaw, and the lips should be tight and clean. The badly undershot or overshot mouth to be heavily penalised.

NECK: Muscular, rather short, clean in outline, and gradually widening towards the shoulders.

FOREQUARTERS: Legs straight and well boned, set rather wide apart, without looseness at the shoulders, and showing no weakness at the pasterns, from which the feet turn out a little.

BODY: The body should be close-coupled, with a level topline, wide front, deep brisket, well-sprung ribs, and rather light loins.

HINDQUARTERS: The hindquarters should be well muscled, hocks let down with stifles well bent. Legs should be parallel when viewed from behind.

FEET: The feet should be well padded, strong, and of medium size.

TAIL: The tail should be of medium length, low set, tapering to a point and carried rather low. It should not curl much, and may be likened to an old-fashioned pump handle.

COAT: Smooth, short and close to the skin.

COLOUR: Red, fawn, white, black or blue, or any of these colours with white. Any shade of brindle or any shade of brindle with white. Black-and-tan or liver colour may not be encouraged.

WEIGHT AND SIZE: Weight: dogs 28 to 38 lbs, bitches 24-34 lbs. Height (at shoulder) 14-16 inches, these heights being related to weight.

FAULTS: To be penalised in accordance with the severity of fault: Light eyes or pink eye-rims. Tail too long or badly curled. Non-conformation to the limits of weight or height. Full drop and prick ears. Undershot or overshot mouths. The following faults should debar a dog from winning any prize: Pink (Dudley) nose. Badly undershot or overshot mouth. Badly undershot – where the lower jaw protrudes to such an extent that the incisors of the lower jaw do not touch those of the upper jaw. Badly overshot – where the upper jaw protrudes to such an extent that the incisors of the upper jaw do not touch those of the lower jaw.

- As you can see, the basic 1935 description (see page 122) was largely left unchanged, with only a few exceptions. They were confident enough now to think that the Bull Terrier blood had been eliminated and so they dropped the 'prick ear'.
- The term 'short-coupled' replaced the previous description of 'short back'.

- 'Well-bent stifles' was introduced into the hindquarters clause.
- The colour blue was introduced for the first time. Today, it is popular to speak about the historic dog called a 'Blue Paul' as being a Stafford, so it is strange that the colour was not included in the 1935 Standard. The breed or type of dog known as the Blue Paul was a fighting dog found in Scotland (especially around Glasgow), which became extinct in the middle of the 19th century. From what little has been written and illustrated about the dog, it would appear that it was some sort of Bull and Terrier cross. Its head shape (particularly the formation of the deep-set eyes), and its size (around 20 inches/50 cms) and weighing in the region of 60 lbs mark it out as a different type of fighting dog from that developed in the Black Country. Because the colour blue occasionally crops up in Stafford litters, it has been suggested that Blue Paul blood went into the making of the Stafford. However, any breed carrying brindle can produce a dilute blue or blue-brindle coloured coat. Furthermore, the presence of so many Whippets in areas where many Staffords were popular make it much more likely that crosses with this breed, who often carry the colour blue in their genes, produced the blue colouring in Staffords.
- The scale of points had to be dropped later, at the behest of the Kennel Club – the meeting had wanted it to be kept and indeed had extended it to include movement and balance.
- The top limit of the height was lowered to 16 ins (40.5 cms) and the bottom end reduced to 14 ins (35.5 cms) for both dogs and bitches, but the weights remained unchanged, with a 4 lbs (1.81 kgs) differential between the sexes. The Kennel Club would have preferred one, simple, desired height and weight. There was no unanimity between the clubs, however, and so the present sliding scale with 'heights being related to weights' was introduced.

THE THIRD STANDARD

In 1987, the Kennel Club asked for a revamp of all Standards, and changed the title of the clauses somewhat, and, most importantly for our breed, at last insisted upon a movement clause. All clubs were now asked, independently, for their input. This resulted in some small changes – even some amplification of various fanciers' points.

- Because of the alteration in titles for the various clauses, the old Characteristics clause, for example, has been spread between the first three clauses of: General Appearance, Characteristics and Temperament.
- The term 'light in loins' was replaced with a description of what this term means.
- The word 'desirable' was inserted into the size clause.

This Standard is the only one in operation throughout the world, with one or two minor differences in some countries overseas, mainly where they still use the 1948 version and terminology. These differences are noted below.

The Fédération Cynologique Internationale (FCI), the canine governing body of European countries, traditionally takes the Standard for any breed from its country of origin, although it must be said that a few minor differences occur in translation. In 2000, a few adjustments to the height/weight clause had to be made when the United Kingdom changed to the metric system. Originally, when the UK turned to metric measurements, a straight conversion was made for the height-/weight of individual breeds. In order to hold standardisation worldwide, in 2000 the Kennel Club decided to round up or down these measurements to the nearest centimetre or half-inch, and half-kilo or pound. Thus, for the Stafford, the height of 35.5-40.5 cms became, more simply, 36-41 cms. The weight for dogs is now stated as 13-17 kgs and for bitches as 11-15.4 kgs.

Below each clause for the current Stafford Standard is an analysis, explaining exactly what the descriptions mean, and giving national variations.

1987 BREED STANDARD

GENERAL APPEARANCE
UK: Smooth coated, well balanced, of great strength for his size. Muscular, active and agile.

The Stafford is an impressive dog "of great strength for his size".

A close, smooth coat is characteristic of all healthy, fit Staffords, and care with his diet and plenty of hand massage (stroking!) can enhance this.

'Balance' is often quoted as the one thing that marks out an excellent dog from a merely good dog. In the simplest terms, a balanced dog will look as though all his parts belong together – that all his measurements are in harmony. If you look at a Stafford and one characteristic stands out – maybe his head looks big, or his legs appear long – then chances are he is out of balance. A well-balanced Stafford will be able to jump, spin, and 'turn on a sixpence' quickly and more efficiently than almost any other breed.

A Stafford must have great power in a comparatively small package – and yet be active and agile. Some people talk about a Stafford being able to 'run all day'. In fact, he is not required to be a running dog but an agile one – a swift-moving, turning, twisting dog.

CHARACTERISTICS
UK: Traditionally of indomitable courage and tenacity. Highly intelligent and affectionate, especially with children.

The Stafford is virtually unique in having a Standard which demands him to be affectionate with all people and especially children. All old-time breeders valued the courage of the dog – accepting that, in past generations, this was what breeders aimed for in dogs that would be pitted against each other. They did not breed for aggression. Most dogs bite from fear or lack of stability. A brave Stafford is bomb-proof. All the rules of old-time dog-fighting meant that a handler had to go and break up the dogs at the end of each round. Because of this, the Stafford had to be able to tell the difference between 'two' and 'four' legs – it would have been of no use if the dogs had turned on the handlers as soon as they were taken off their opponent!

In the fighting ring, the dog had to think for himself if he was going to survive – this is the basis for the high intelligence that a good Stafford possesses. Finally, whatever further use other fighting breeds may have been put to, the Stafford has never had any other job than that of family pet, who might clear the barn of rats. Pure-bred Staffords have proved completely inept as guard dogs – they simply love people too much.

TEMPERAMENT
UK: Bold, fearless and totally reliable.

Again, these attributes – so useful for a trustworthy pet in today's busy, stressful modern society – were forged in the breed's history. We cannot deny his past, and we should not apologise for it, but we must understand it – aggression was not the key and never has the breed been used to attack people.

Canada, New Zealand, and the USA retained the following two clauses of the 1948 Standard in place of the above:

CHARACTERISTICS
(TEMPERAMENT for USA)
From the past history of the Staffordshire Bull Terrier, the modern dog draws his character of indomitable courage, high intelligence and tenacity. This, coupled with his affection for his friends and children in particular, his off-duty quietness and trustworthy stability, makes him the foremost all-purpose dog.

The big advantage of setting out this clause in this way is that it states where the positive virtues of the Stafford come from – his past history!

GENERAL APPEARANCE
The Staffordshire Bull Terrier is a smooth-coated dog. He should be of great strength for his size, and, although muscular, should be active and agile.

This clause is very much in the spirit of the UK, but unfortunately does not mention 'balance'.

HEAD AND SKULL
UK: Short, deep through with broad skull. Very pronounced cheek muscles, distinct stop, short foreface, nose black.

It is worth noting that in the original Description of the Staffordshire Bull Terrier of 1935 (see page 122), the scale of points gave 30 out of 100 to this one characteristic, which shows how important it has always been to a typical Stafford. It is the most distinctive of attributes and one that should clearly mark the dog as being a Stafford and no other breed.

A vestige from his days as a baiting dog, the head is broad, with pronounced cheek muscles.

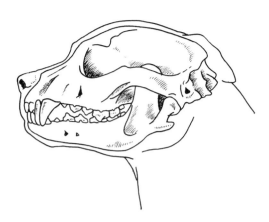

Correct skull.

The head must be strong and powerful with no impression of narrowness in any part. Although the skull must be broad, it must not be massive in girth – it should balance the overall size of the dog. Looking down on the head, the skull is wide and has an indentation medially, running from before the eyes and finishing just in front of the ears. This shape is best suited to the muscular development around the areas of the jaw, and these muscles can be seen protruding outside the bony structure from the ears to the underjaw. These, acting in conjunction with the short foreface, impart maximum biting power. The short, strong foreface, or muzzle, tapers gradually and slightly to the nose, and is blunt at the end, showing no pointedness (snipiness).

There is a distinct stop or step up from the muzzle to the skull, and this 'stop' is the fulcrum point of the head. Looking at other breeds of dog, we can best understand the importance of the stop in the overall picture of the Stafford's head. Some breeds, e.g. the Bull Terrier, Borzoi etc., have no stop, are long-headed, down-faced and have small eyes, set to the side of the head. At the other end of the spectrum, such breeds as the Bulldog or Boxer have very deep stops, ultra-short forefaces, are dish-faced and have bulbous, very full eyes. The Stafford head is

The Head

A correct head, with a good stop.

Incorrect: a short ('dish-faced') foreface, bulbous eyes, and an overly pronounced stop.

Incorrect: too 'lippy'. The lips should be tight and clean.

Incorrect: snipy. The foreface is too long, there is a poor stop, a weak underjaw and an almond eye shape.

bang in between these two alternatives, having enough stop to allow for the skull and muzzle to be roughly on the same plane – neither down-faced nor dish-faced – having a short foreface and medium-sized, round (but not bulbous) eyes, which are set to look straight ahead.

The ratio of foreface to skull is approximately one-third to two-thirds, that is the distance from the end of the nose to the stop is one-third whereas the distance from the stop to the occiput (the rather prominent bone at the end of the skull between the ears) is two-thirds. There is no definite measurements for these lengths, only that if the muzzle is, say, two and a half inches from the nose to the stop, then the skull should be five inches from stop to the occiput. All these measurements are done in straight lines.

The most important part of the muzzle is that it is wide and deep; snipiness or distinct tapering of the foreface is a fault in a Stafford. The underjaw should be deep enough to be clearly visible when the head is viewed from the front. The whole head should be clean with no loose skin, sponginess around the muzzle or wrinkling anywhere on the head. Such a head is firm to the touch, even in old age when much of the muscle tone may be wasted.

The nose should be black, whatever the coat colour of the animal. A brownish-pink nose – often termed a 'Dudley' nose – is a fault in the Stafford. This term would appear to come from the Bulldog fraternity where it describes a whole colouring of the dog and not just the nose. In the early 1935 Description of a Staffordshire Bull Terrier, a Dudley nose precluded the dog from winning a prize.

Occasionally a brownish nose is seen and a careful look at other parts of the dog (e.g. lips, nails) may show further dilution of pigment. Blue-coloured puppies sometimes lose their colour and acquire slate-coloured noses on maturity. It should be noted that pied puppies, whether brindle or red pied, are sometimes born with partially coloured black and pink noses. The nose will, or should, become completely black within the first few weeks of life. If it persists into an adult animal, such a marking is termed a 'butterfly' nose and is a fault.

The USA puts the whole of head, eyes, ears, and mouth into one composite clause. For the purpose of this study, we will break these up into individual parts. So: USA head is as above, with the addition that: Pink (Dudley) nose to be considered a serious fault.

EYES

UK: Dark preferred but may bear some relation to coat colour. Round, of medium size, and set to look straight ahead. Eye rims dark.

As previously stated, the correct eye is dependent upon the dog having a correct stop – too little and the eye will tend to an almond shape and be at the side of the head rather than set to look straight ahead. Where the dog is dish-faced, the eye is likely to be bulbous and overly large. A correct round eye rim, set rather wide and not too high in the skull is what gives the Stafford his very special expression.

An eye set to look straight ahead is also important in helping the dog to judge distances of things in front of him – one reason why the Stafford is so adept at catching treats thrown at him, compared with an almond-eyed breed where the eyes are set at the side of the head. A dark eye is desirable in all Staffords.

The codicil that the eye "may bear some relation to coat colour" can cause confusion, as people will ask "Does that mean a white dog may have white eyes?". But the reasoning behind this statement is sensible, as

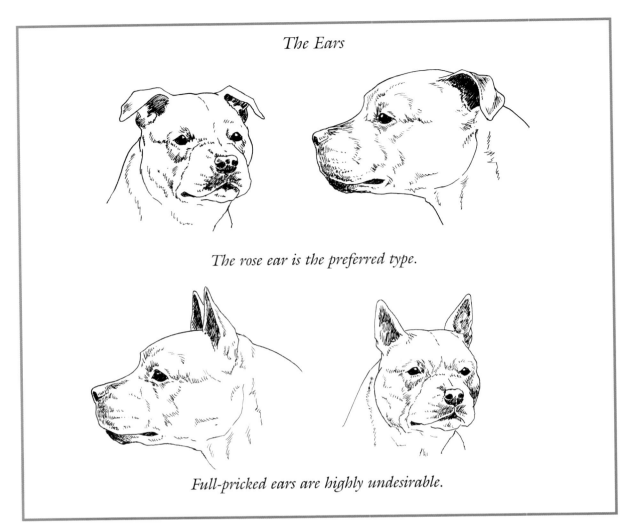

The rose ear is the preferred type.

Full-pricked ears are highly undesirable.

a fairly dark-brown eye will look fine in a red dog, whereas, in a black brindle, it may look light. One therefore has to use some common sense in applying this part of the Standard.

The really objectionable colour is pale yellow, in whatever colour coat. In general, if you notice the colour of a dog's eyes, you should look again to see if they are really dark. In a white dog, or a pied dog with a white patch (or patches) over the eye, a pink eye rim is permissible, otherwise the rims must be dark.

CANADA & NEW ZEALAND as above, but without 'eye rims dark'.
USA: as above with a good amplification: "pink eye rims to be considered a fault except that, where the coat surrounding the eye is white, the eye rim may be pink."

EARS
UK: Rose or half-pricked, not large or heavy. Full-drop or pricked ears highly undesirable.

As previously stated, at first the fanciers allowed the prick ear – the preponderance of half Bull Terriers in the general pool of so-called Staffordshire Bull Terriers made this inevitable. Even today, an occasional full-prick ear is seen in a Stafford.

The really desirable ear is the rose – this is the one that breeders aim for. All ears should be thin, small and tidy – in other words, very unobtrusive. They should be set at the side of the skull, the top line of the ear showing just above the top line of the skull.

In a rose ear, the strong crease holds the ear in the desired shape and runs straight across the ear, starting at the base of the ear taking it in a backwards direction which then folds forward to the top edge of the ear.

In the half-prick ear, this crease is not clearly defined and the tip of the ear turns over and the flap is carried forward. Unfortunately, most half-prick ears are set too far on the top of the head. Correctly placed, small, thin rose ears complement the dog's expression and can make a fairly mediocre head look better than it is.

CANADA & NEW ZEALAND: Rose or half-pricked and not large. Full-drop or prick to be penalised.
Note – no mention of the ear not being heavy.

USA: Ears – rose or half-prick and not large. Full-drop or full-prick to be considered a serious fault.

MOUTH
UK: Lips tight and clean. Jaws strong, teeth large, with a perfect, regular and complete scissor bite, i.e. upper teeth closely overlapping the lower teeth and set square to the jaws.

Strong, wide jaws allow the dog to have big, strong teeth. In a perfect scissor bite, the lower incisors touch the inner side of the upper incisors and the lower canines are visible between the upper canines and incisors, when the mouth is viewed from the side. The lips should be close to the teeth with the upper lip slightly overlapping but never long or pendulous.

Because of the Bulldog ancestry, mouth faults – particularly the undershot mouth, where the lower jaw protrudes in front of the upper – are not uncommon.

Some breeders attempt to avoid this fault by deliberately breeding for a weak underjaw which is simply 'throwing the baby out with the bath water'.

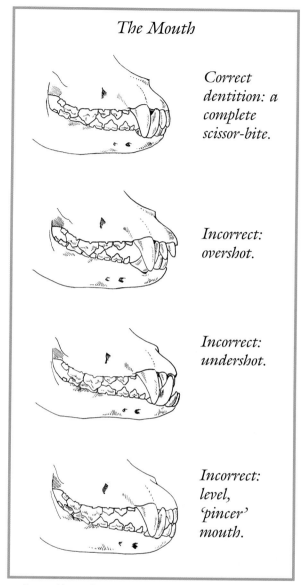

The Mouth

Correct dentition: a complete scissor-bite.

Incorrect: overshot.

Incorrect: undershot.

Incorrect: level, 'pincer' mouth.

Actually, a far more serious fault in a dog which must have strong jaws is the overshot mouth – where the upper jaw protrudes in front of the lower. Such a fault is almost always accompanied by a weak underjaw. Where the dog has a really strong underjaw, it will be noted that the lower incisors are in a straight line. The teeth should neither slant backwards nor forwards but be set at right angles to the jaw. Some modern animals have short but narrow forefaces, and their teeth are consequently very small.

CANADA & NEW ZEALAND: The mouth should be level, i.e. the incisors of the bottom jaw should fit closely inside the incisors of the top jaw, and the lips should be tight and clean. The badly undershot or overshot mouth to be heavily penalized.

Strictly speaking a 'level mouth' is where the top teeth are sitting on top of the bottom, and this is not the same as the desired scissor bite. Nor does this description cover the canines. However, this wording does lay down clearly that it is the badly undershot or overshot mouth that is the real one to penalise. There is, of course, a grey area where there is a minor fault in dentition – the jaw being correct and maybe one or two teeth misplaced. If the dog is the best in the class barring this minor blemish, it would be inept of a judge to refuse such a dog the place his virtues deserve.

USA: Mouth – a bite in which the outer side of the lower incisors touches the inner side of the upper incisors. The lips should be tight and clean. The badly undershot or overshot bite is a serious fault.

It is unfortunate that none of these three versions makes any mention of the very important characteristic – strong jaws and large teeth.

NECK
UK: Muscular, rather short, clean in outline, gradually widening towards the shoulders.

The Stafford's neck, especially in the male, has a crest of muscle over the top. There should be no loose skin around the neck. A tight jacket throughout the Stafford is a highly desired characteristic.

Unlike most of the terrier breeds, the Standard does not ask for the Stafford to have 'reach' of neck. Indeed, the term 'short' is once again mentioned. The neck, if too long, was considered a weakness.

The Stafford holds his head low, or should do if allowed by the handler. The top angle of the neck should rise gradually from the shoulders to the head. This angle is related to a well-laid shoulder since a steep shoulder gives an upright or 'ewe' neck. Thus there is a gentle rise from the body, and, viewed from the side, the neck widens to the brisket. The neck must not be so short as to sit the head straight on the shoulders – yet again, the Stafford lies between two extremes.

USA: Again, has a composite clause for neck, topline and body. Where these differ from the UK Standard, the points will be noted.

FOREQUARTERS
UK: Legs straight and well boned, set rather wide apart, showing no weakness at the pasterns, from which point feet turn out a little. Shoulders well laid back with no looseness at the elbow.

The front legs should be straight from the elbow to the pasterns with discernible muscles, and, looked at from the front, should be straight and parallel. They must have substantial bone – round and not flat or coarse. The front is wide – this point being reinforced in the next clause. This characteristic sets it apart from most other breeds that have their root in a fighting dog. But then historians such as Idstone maintain that the Stafford is descended from a breed of fighting dog who were relatively low and wide and were therefore difficult to knock off their feet.

The correct width of the front is dependent upon the correct lay-back of the shoulders. It

Correct: the legs are set wide apart and the feet turn out a little.

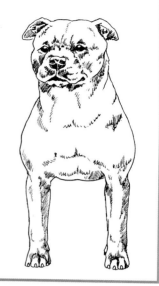

Incorrect: the legs face forward and there is no lay-back of pastern.

is popular today to measure every angle on a dog's body, and the shoulders are an example in mind. It is generally stated that the 'ideal' angle would be 90 degrees; that is that the scapula (shoulder blade) is at about a right angle to the humerus (the bone of the upper arm). Stated another way, it should slope from the lowest point where it articulates with the humerus upwards to the withers at about 45 degrees. In fact, it is not an easy matter with a dog as well muscled as the Stafford to actually feel the bones with any real degree of accuracy, certainly not enough to make some of the bold statements we read in show critiques.

In layman's terms, a Bulldog has its body virtually 'slung' between its two front legs. A running dog, e.g. the Lurcher, has its front legs situated underneath its body (as if the body is sitting on top of the legs). Both these extremes are incorrect for the Stafford who, like the sensible dog he is, has a middle-of-the-road stance with his legs at either corner, giving him a neat but very stable base from which to move.

It is important to hold a picture of a correct Stafford in your head and then to be able to pinpoint where a dog diverges from the ideal. Understanding the assembly of parts which make this picture is fascinating but we must be careful not to get carried

away. Again, I repeat that, in a dog as heavily muscled as a Stafford, it is almost impossible to 'measure' these bones without an X-ray facility.

Sometimes there are two explanations as to why a dog may appear as he does. For example, a dog may appear short and 'cloddy' because he has too short an upper arm (humerus) but then again it may be because he has too deep a brisket. The essential thing to recognise is that the dog is unbalanced, for whatever reason.

The points of the elbows should go straight backwards – pointing neither inwards nor outwards. The correct placement for these is dependent upon the correct lay-back of the shoulder. Too much can cause a looseness of the elbows, too steep can cause a 'tied' look to the front quarters.

It is a very important characteristic that the front feet should turn out slightly and not look straight ahead or point inwards. In order to do this, there is a slight backwards slope from the foot to the wrist that allows the feet their slight turn-out. This is best seen when viewed from the side and should not be confused with a weakness of the pasterns when the whole foot looks flat. Correctly formed with the slight lay-back, this type of pastern is very resilient and springy – important in a dog who should be active and agile.

Elbow Placement

Correct width and placement of the shoulder and elbow.

Incorrect: tied.

Incorrect: loose.

CANADA & NEW ZEALAND: as above, but without the sentence 'Shoulders well laid back'.

USA: FOREQUARTERS – Legs straight and well boned, set rather far apart, without looseness at the shoulders and showing no weakness at the pasterns, from which point the feet turn out a little. Dewclaws on the forelegs may be removed.

In the UK, dewclaws are not usually removed from the forelegs since it is considered unnecessary in a comparatively wide-fronted breed.

BODY
UK: Close-coupled, with level topline, wide front, deep brisket, well-sprung ribs; muscular and well defined.

The Stafford has a fairly long rib cage and his 'shortness' must be at the couplings (the belly part of the dog from the end of the last (floating) rib to the leading edge of the thigh). There is no exact measurement for this – quite obviously, it will vary according to the height and overall balance of each individual dog.

An ultra-shortbacked Stafford is not as agile or flexible as a slightly longer-backed one and often has to compensate in his movement by swinging his back legs because there is not enough room for his hind legs to 'follow through'.

The level topline is another addition to the 1948 Standard and is sometimes misinterpreted because a well-muscled Stafford usually has a crest of muscle just over the hindquarters. The main purpose of this statement 'level topline' is to avoid both the dipped-back animal and also the roached back. Interestingly, the former weakness most often comes in over-heavy animals and the latter when the animal is too light or

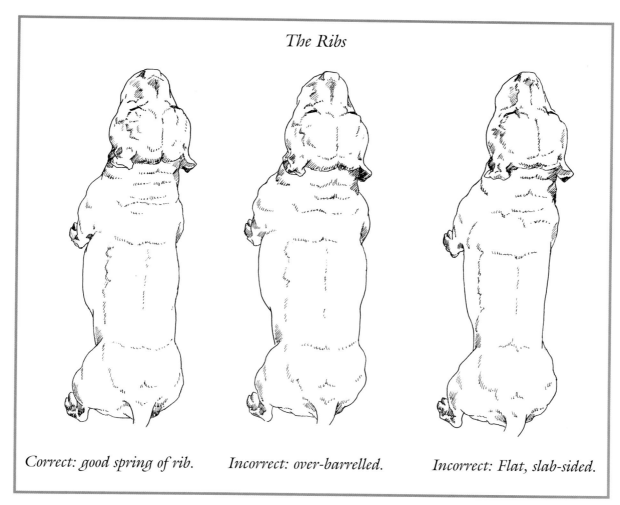

The Ribs

Correct: good spring of rib.   *Incorrect: over-barrelled.*   *Incorrect: Flat, slab-sided.*

'Whippety' in bone. Sometimes a distinct fall-away over the hindquarters may be discerned, which is undesirable.

All these extremes are incorrect for the Stafford. All can be minimised by a good handler, but will be obvious once the animal is moving.

Once more, the wide front is stressed, so we cannot accept the 'two feet in one Wellie' type of front on our Staffords. The brisket should reach to just below the elbow. Further down than this and the front of the dog looks foreshortened and cloddy. Higher than this and the dog looks light and 'shelly' (the body is shallow, narrow, and generally lacks substance). Once again, the Stafford must stand between two extremes.

A good spring of rib is deemed necessary, but this should not be over-barrelled. Equally, a dog with no spring of rib will appear slab-sided (flat-sided) and lacking in the body definition so desirable in a Stafford. A good spring of rib along with the depth of brisket gives adequate lung and heart room. Behind the rib there must be a well-defined waist, followed by his well-muscled hindquarters. This definition of the body is an essential ingredient in making the Stafford look active and agile.

CANADA, NEW ZEALAND & USA: The body should be close-coupled with a level topline, wide front, deep brisket, well-sprung ribs, and rather light in the loins.

The Body

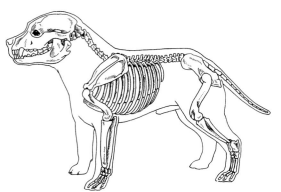

Correct: level topline, close-coupled, wide front, deep brisket, and well-sprung ribs.

Incorrect: cloddy – the brisket is too far below the point of the elbow.

Incorrect: shelly – the brisket is too far above the point of the elbow.

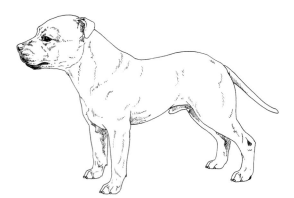

Incorrect: sway-backed.

Incorrect: roached topline.

The term 'rather light in the loins' was in the UK Standard until 1987, when it was replaced by a definition of what this term actually means. This followed numerous debates and arguments – firstly because the term is meaningless to the novice and secondly because, to purists, the area of the spine called the loin should be very strong in a dog such as the Stafford. This clause is in fact referring to the area of the belly, below the spine.

HINDQUARTERS
UK: Well muscled, hocks well let down with stifles well bent. Legs parallel when viewed from behind.

The hindquarters are the powerhouse of the Stafford – with a strong head and good propulsion from behind, he is a strong force. He must be well muscled and feel firm to the touch in the thighs. The hocks should turn downwards towards the ground and this can only be achieved where the stifles are well bent. Where the stifle is not bent but straight, the stifle and hock will be in a straight line and the hocks will not point towards the ground.

Staffords can also be over-bent in the stifle. With this fault, the dog will usually stand with his legs far behind him. A Stafford, being a dog of action, should be ready to jump off at any time. To achieve this, he must have his feet underneath him. In this stance, the hock is most likely to point towards the ground. The hock is the equivalent of the human 'heel' (with the metatarsals being, as with us, the toes). In the Stafford, the metatarsals are rather short and should be carried – if allowed freedom by the handlers – under the stifles and not directly under the point of the hocks. Standing, he is almost like a coiled spring.

Looking at the dog from behind, his back legs should be parallel. This means that the

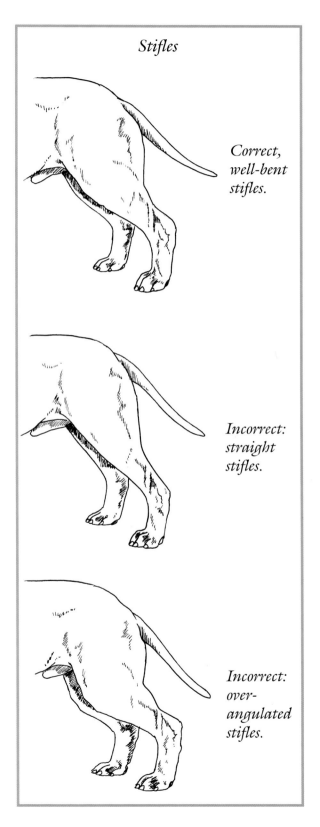

Stifles

Correct, well-bent stifles.

Incorrect: straight stifles.

Incorrect: over-angulated stifles.

point of the stifle (the patella) must face straight forward. If it turns out, the hocks will turn in towards each other, and the dog is 'cow-hocked'. Equally undesirable is when hocks turn out and away from each other, thus causing the back feet to pin in towards each other and the thighs to appear 'bow-legged'.

CANADA & NEW ZEALAND. The hindquarters should be well muscled, hocks let down with stifles well bent. Legs parallel when viewed from behind.

USA: The hindquarters should be well muscled, hocks let down with stifles well bent. Legs parallel when viewed from behind. Dewclaws, if any, on the hind legs are generally removed.

The hocks are only to be 'let down' not 'well let down' in these versions – perhaps this is splitting hairs. I, personally, have never seen dewclaws on the back legs of a Stafford, although I have seen them on other breeds. Certainly, if they are present at birth, they should be removed.

FEET
UK: Well padded, strong and of medium size. Nails black in solid colour dogs.

The shape of the Stafford's foot is halfway between the cat and the hare – that is, it must be larger than the tiny cat foot but shorter than the long-toed hare foot. The pads must be deep and feel positively bouncy when gently squeezed. The toes should be fairly close together and the deep pads, together

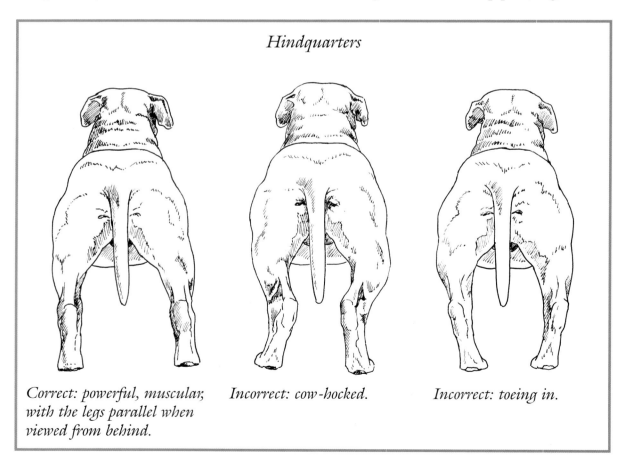

Hindquarters

Correct: powerful, muscular, with the legs parallel when viewed from behind.

Incorrect: cow-hocked.

Incorrect: toeing in.

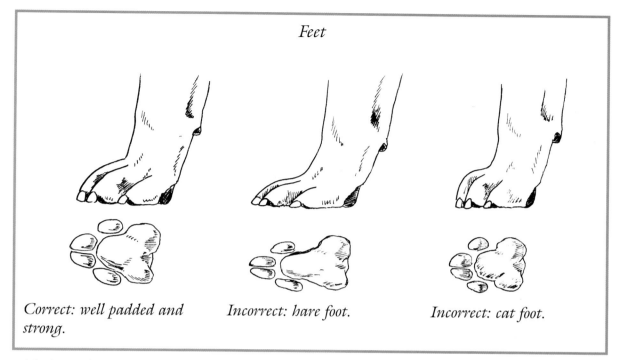

Feet

Correct: well padded and strong. *Incorrect: hare foot.* *Incorrect: cat foot.*

with the springy, laid-back pasterns, all help to give the dog activity and stability.

The shape of the hind feet is the same, although they are a little longer and smaller than those on the front. The front feet are more knuckled up than the rear. Nails must be black, but, where the foot is white, it is permissible for the nails to be pink. In a properly constructed foot, the nails on the front will be short, and, given exercise on hard surfaces, should never need to be cut. The pronounced knuckles bring the nails into strong contact with the ground. A foot that does not show the knuckles is thin and poorly padded and is usually accompanied by long nails and splayed toes.

CANADA & NEW ZEALAND: As above but without mention of the nail colouring.

USA: As above, but stating that hind feet are 'as in front'.

TAIL
UK: Medium length, low-set, tapering to
a point and carried rather low. Should not curl much and may be likened to an old-fashioned pump handle.

An ideal length for the tail is generally accepted as coming to or just below the point of the hock. It should be thick at the root – indicative of good bone – and tapering to a point. It emerges just below the distal end of the hip bones and is carried low, covering the anus and then sloping down in a gentle curve.

Incidentally, 'low-set' is a 1948 addition to the original description which merely asked for the tail to be carried low. It must be said that too long or too short a tail or one set too high can spoil the balance of the silhouette.

USA: The tail is undocked, of medium length, low set, tapering to a point, and carried rather low. It should not curl much and may be likened to an old-fashioned pump handle. A tail that is too long or badly curled is a fault.

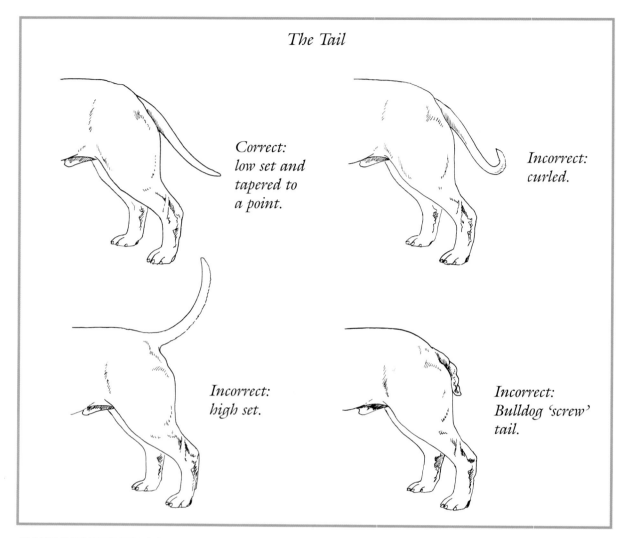

The Tail

Correct:
low set and
tapered to
a point.

Incorrect:
curled.

Incorrect:
high set.

Incorrect:
Bulldog 'screw'
tail.

GAIT/MOVEMENT

UK: Free, powerful and agile with economy of effort. Legs moving parallel when viewed from the front or rear. Discernible drive from hind legs.

Free and purposeful is the keynote for correct movement of the Staffordshire Bull Terrier. At the front, his action should be low, and contrary hind leg movement goes straight into the tracks of the front feet.

Front and rear feet are only lifted sufficiently to clear the ground – economy of effort. Going away, his hind legs obscure the front legs; on the return, his front legs obscure the hind legs.

Standing, the feet should be under the dog and ready to go into action. When stationary, it is difficult to judge whether a dog is completely sound, but, once on the move, a defect becomes more apparent. If, for example, the dog has loose shoulders, then the forelegs will tend to cross. If the shoulder is too tight (tied), the front legs will tend to be thrown wider apart as he moves. If the stifle is turned out (everted) then the hocks turn inwards and the rear pasterns turn out (cow-hocked) – this means a loss of propulsion and a general lack of strength in the hindquarters.

When the hocks are bowed outwards, the

The Gait

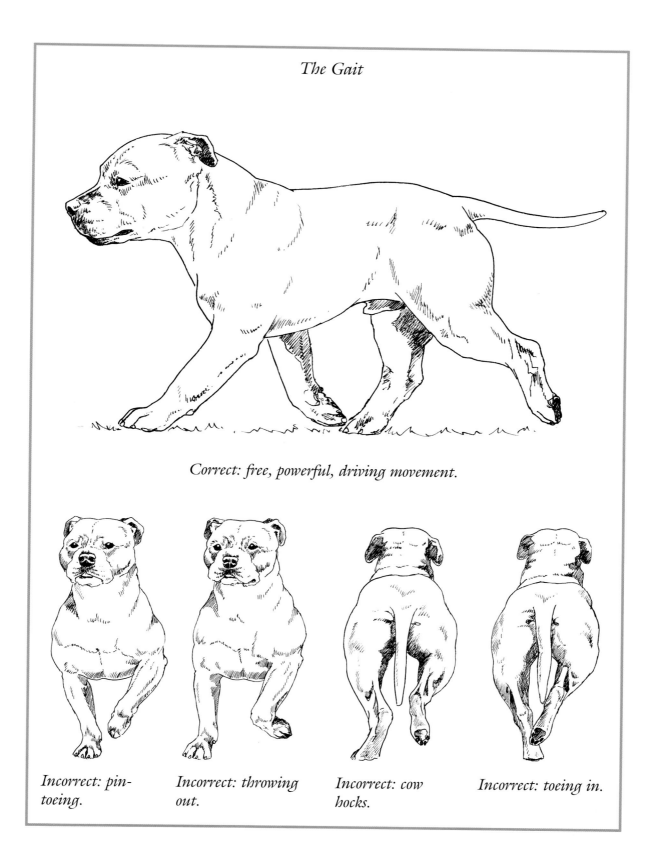

Correct: free, powerful, driving movement.

Incorrect: pin-toeing.

Incorrect: throwing out.

Incorrect: cow hocks.

Incorrect: toeing in.

hind feet tend to move too close together and you will see them between the front legs as the dog moves towards you. Correct shoulder placement will prevent poor movement – circling, hackney action, and in-toeing at the front.

Correct bend of stifle with good musculation (especially in the upper thigh), is the key to good back movement – that with discernible drive.

Some Staffords can be seen moving their hind feet in a circular, rotating type motion. Others pick up their hind feet and put them down nearly where they started, in a piston-like fashion – this is putting more pressure on the front for propulsion rather than the rear. When correct, the Stafford gives the impression of great strength when he moves, while at the same time he conserves his energy because he lifts his feet only barely off the ground. With his head held low, he looks purposeful rather than graceful when he moves.

Handlers should be sure to check that they are moving their dog at the correct pace to get this determined, driving movement.

CANADA: No gait clause.

COAT
UK: Smooth, short and close.

A good coat shows off the contours of a dog's muscle and the sheen denotes health and fitness. A dog may be trim, but, if his coat doesn't shine, you can fairly safely say that he has been slimmed by cutting his rations rather than by working off the extra calories. The coat should fit the dog closely without wrinkle or fold. The hairs are short, and lie close to the skin, giving a very smooth feel.

USA: Smooth, short and close to the skin, not to be trimmed or de-whiskered.

It is not normal practice to cut the whiskers of a Stafford, although, in the past, this practice was fairly common in the UK – it was believed that cutting them gave a cleaner outline of the muzzle.

COLOUR
UK: Red, fawn, white, black or blue, or any one of these colours with white. Any shade of brindle with white. Black and tan, or liver colours highly undesirable.

Red, fawn, white, black or blue should appear as definite colours and not as dilutions. Blue is not often seen, although some slate-grey colours or mushroom brindle colours are, wrongly, described as blue. Stafford puppies who are blue in the nest often turn out to be these dilute colours on maturity, and sometimes lose the blackness of their noses. Confusion sometimes arises because a red dog may have a white chest and a black mask to his face. As long as this black coloration is confined to the muzzle of the animal, it is not considered to be proscribed coloration.

Brindle is a pattern made from black and tan. Several attractive tones of brindle can be seen – from silver to deep mahogany. Liver is generally accepted as a deep – almost blood-red – colour, and such animals invariably have miscoloured noses and green eyes. Black and tan is often a cause for argument – in the dog world, 'black and tan' is a set pattern, as seen in the Dobermann, for example. Sometimes Staffords appear with this patterning and this is definitely considered a fault.

More problematical is the dog that has black with tan patches. Generally speaking, a Stafford with black and tan coloration should have these arranged in a brindling pattern. Some of the clearest red adults may have carried a lot of black hairs in the nest, which gradually clear in the first weeks of life.

The Stafford coat has many colour and pattern variations.

Fawn is a very pale colour of red. It is the original colour for Staffords, and the deep red as seen most commonly today, although very attractive, was rarely seen in the early days of recognition.

USA: Red, fawn, white, black or blue, or any one of these colours with white. Any shade of brindle with white. Black and tan, or liver colour to be disqualified.

SIZE

UK: Desirable height at withers 36-41 cms (14-16 ins), these heights being related to the weights. Weight: dogs 13-17 kgs (28-38 lbs); bitches 11-15.4 kgs (24-34 lbs).

There have been more arguments about this clause than any other, and yet it should be appreciated that a good Stafford does not depend on pounds and inches for his excellence, but rather on his close approximation to all the other requirements. By and large, it is impossible, without the use of weights and measures, to apply this clause with real accuracy.

Much nonsense is written about the change made to the Standard in 1948, as if, at a stroke, all the Staffords who were supposedly at least 18 inches tall had to lose 2 inches. In fact, there was little argument about these changes (the meeting was so short, there couldn't have been much debate – see page 123), and the drop of size reflected the dogs as they were.

I have a 'Suggested Standard for the Staffordshire Bull Terrier' typed and signed by H.N. Beilby and dated June 12th 1935.

BEILBY'S SUGGESTED STANDARD

GENERAL: The Staffordshire Bull Terrier is a smooth-coated dog standing about 15 to 16 inches high at the shoulder (rather less for bitches). He should give the impression of great strength for his size, and, although muscular, should be active and agile.

HEAD: The skull is of moderate length but wide and slightly domed – with the cheek muscles well developed. Measuring round the widest part, it should not be less than the height of the dog at the shoulder. There is a pronounced 'stop' in front of the skull, and from the stop to the nose, the head is short and wedge-shaped. The jaws are tight and clean-lipped – there should be no 'flew'. The ears should be half-prick or rose – but prick ears will not disqualify. Drop ears are undesirable. The jaws should be level – neither overshot nor undershot. The nose should be black – cherry or liver colour will be penalised. The eye should be brown or dark brown.

BODY: The neck should be muscular and rather short. The ribs are deep and well sprung, with forelegs set rather wide apart to permit chest development.

LEGS AND FEET: The forelegs should be well boned and fairly straight, with no weakness showing at the pastern. The hindlegs should be well muscled on the thighs, and well bent at stifle – anything approaching a 'stilted' action is most undesirable. Feet should be hard and close and of fair size.

TAIL: The tail should be from 8 to 10 inches long, tapering to a point and carried rather low. It should not curl much, and may be compared to an old-fashioned pump handle.

COLOUR: May be any shade of brindle, black, white, fawn or red, or any of these colours with white. Black and tan, and liver, not to be encouraged.

WEIGHT: 28/30 lbs when in hard condition. About 5 lbs less for bitches.
Probably it was in preparation for the meeting that drew up the final Description in the same year (see page 122), since it contains several of the points included in the final versions. Some of his ideas were not included – as, for example, his idea for measuring the tail, which he records as from 8 to 10 inches (20-25.5 cms) long.

More interesting for us is the fact that he

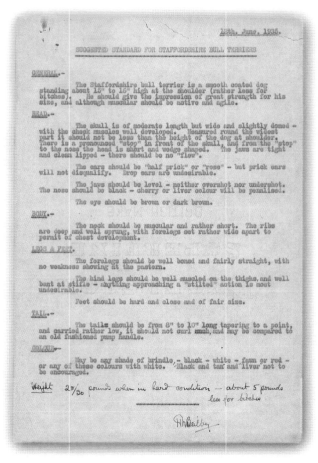

gives the height range as 15 to 16 inches (38-40.5 cms) high at the shoulder (rather less for bitches). The weights he gives are: "28/30 pounds when in hard condition – about 5 pounds less for bitches".

More controversial than reducing the upper limits in 1948 was including the 14-inch (35-cm) male Stafford – now this really was a novelty. However, research shows that even this was a further reflection of what already existed – one of the biggest winners of his day was Int. Ch. Head Lad of Vilmar, born in 1945, and advertised as 14 1/2 ins and 38 lbs.

But what can we learn from this clause today? Firstly, that the Breed Standard allows us to have a good big one and a good little one. Secondly, that there is no difference drawn between the height of a bitch and a dog – the difference lies in the weight. Indeed, this is the only time in all the

Standards that any difference is made between the sexes – the head, ears, front, etc. are all supposed to be the same, only the weight is expected to be different.

As far as weight goes, again this may vary widely – the early UK stud books register Bulldogs of enormously different weight – 20 to 70 lbs! (9.07-31.7 kgs).

Weight, of course, is a more variable measurement than height, and anyone reading old material about dog-fighting days will appreciate the enormous amount of weight that can be taken off a dog if one really sets one's mind to it.

The Kennel Club has historically never been in favour of this involved size clause, and have now included the word 'desired'. The pity is that we could not have had just one 'desired' height and weight. If this had been done, it is almost certain that 16 inches would be the most popular choice, and, with modern feeding and improved husbandry methods, I would expect the average dog to weigh in at 40 lbs (18.1 kgs) at this height.

Debate has also ranged over the term 'at the withers'. We can do no better than quote the Kennel Club's definition of 'withers': "The highest point of the body, immediately behind the neck".

It is fairly obvious that the weights and heights have to correlate – there would be no point in the tallest animal weighing the least, and the shortest the most; the general effect, however, is to further complicate the situation with involved mathematical calculations coming into play if we are going to be strictly accurate.

USA: Height at shoulder: 14 to 16 inches. Weight: dogs 28 to 38 pounds; bitches 24 to 34 pounds, these heights being related to weight. Non-conformity with these limits is a fault. In proportion, the length of back, from withers to tail set, is equal to the distance from withers to ground.

Int. Ch. Head Lad of Vilmar: a top winner in the 1940s, advertised at a height of 14.5 ins (35 cms) some years before the 1948 Standard change.

At first, reading this description of a square dog appears attractive and one can imagine this gives us the secret of the squarely-built, balanced animal we all aim for. Actually doing the measurements, however, we find that, once again, our mania for laying down hard-and-fast rules about measurements lets us down. Following these measurements creates a dog that is far, far too long for his length of leg – in other words, it completely unbalances the animal.

FAULTS
UK: Any departure from the foregoing points should be considered a fault and the seriousness with which the fault should be regarded should be in exact proportion to its degree and its effect upon the health and welfare of the dog.

The Kennel Club's decision to drop the old faults clause and to replace it with this, is, in my opinion, one of their more far-sighted decisions. The whole emphasis now is on the positive – previously one could learn the faults clause, look out for the faults, and judge the dogs accordingly. Now one is encouraged to think positively and to train oneself to weigh up virtues and to compare these against the others in his class. This is all one can do as a judge. We may not always have Champion stock in a class, in the whole of the show we may not have a 'world beater', but, thinking positively, we can hope to pick the best of the bunch.

CANADA & NEW ZEALAND: To be penalized in accordance with the severity of the fault: Light eyes or pink eyerims. Tail too long or badly curled. Non-conformation to the limits of weight or height. Full drop and prick ears. Undershot or overshot mouths. The following faults should debar a dog from winning any prize: Pink (Dudley) nose. Badly undershot or overshot mouth. Badly unershot – where the lower jaw protrudes to such an extent that the incisors of the lower jaw do not touch those of the upper jaw. Badly overshot –

where the upper jaw protrudes to such an extent that the incisors of the upper jaw do not touch those of the lower jaw.

USA: Faults are described in each clause.

DISQUALIFICATION: Black-and-tan, or liver colour.

NOTE
UK: Male animals should have two apparently normal testicles fully descended into the scrotum

That the testicles are *apparently* normal has to be stated in this way, as, of course, without veterinary examination and maybe even X-rays, we cannot, with any certainty, say that the testicles are absolutely normal.

As will be fairly obvious from the need to amplify the Standard, there is room for interpretation, and, to some extent, the personal preference of a judge.

The 'art' of judging lies in the ability to weigh up a dog's virtues against his faults and, with this balance in mind, to compare him with the others in his class. Whatever our personal preference, however, we must act within the limitations of the Breed Standard.

8 *ALL-TIME GREATS*

Staffordshire Bull Terriers were recognised by the UK Kennel Club in 1935. Since that time, there have been several benchmarks in the progress of the breed, including the formation of the first breed club, known as the Parent Club. This club was dedicated to furthering the interests of the dogs, sponsoring dog shows, and running shows specifically for Staffords. Once a club had been formed and the Kennel Club had granted the breed Championship status in 1938, Staffords became more well known throughout the country, and the breed's popularity has increased steadily over the years.

Described in this chapter are some of the all-time greats – dogs and breeders – that have emerged in the years since the Parent Club was formed. In a chapter such as this, it is impossible to include all dogs worthy of mention. Consequently, entries have been restricted to dogs that have sired five or more Champions, won a considerable number of Challenge Certificates (CCs), or achieved a landmark win.

1930s AND 1940s

CH. GENTLEMAN JIM
Once Staffords had gained recognition from the Kennel Club, they became eligible to compete for CCs. The Parent Club organised

Ch. Gentleman Jim: The breed's first Champion, made up in 1939.

Ch. Jim's Double Of Wychbury: A son of Ch. Gentleman Jim.

shows so that, for the first time, this newly recognised breed could compete against each other in 'beauty' (conformation) classes. It was from these shows that the first Champion of the breed was born, Ch. Gentleman Jim. He achieved his Championship title at the Bath Show in 1939.

Ch. Gentleman Jim sired four Champions – Ch. Widneyland Kim, Ch. Fearless Red of Bandits, Ch. Jim's Double of Wychbury and the bitch Ch. Eastbury Lass, grand-dam of Ch. Eastaff Danom.

PREFIXES AND AFFIXES

During the 1940s, with so few Stafford enthusiasts competing in the show ring, it was not necessary to register a prefix with the Kennel Club. Consequently, many of the well-known kennel names were recognised through use rather than right. Later, the Kennel Club disallowed the practice and passed new rules about registering prefixes and ownership. For an owner to attach a kennel name as a prefix, he or she had to own the dam of that kennel. If the dam was not owned, the owner of the dog with the prefix attached must have bred the sire and dam of that prefix, even if ownership changed hands subsequently.

At present, owners purchasing a dog may add their affix at the end of the dog's registered name. In this way it is possible to have two kennel names attached to a dog's name, that of the breeder (appearing as a prefix), and that of the new owner (appearing as a suffix at the end).

CH. WIDNEYLAND KIM

Ch. Widneyland Kim was the first Champion son of Ch. Gentleman Jim. Kim carried the prefix of Mr A. Payton-Smith, although he was owned by well-known breeders Gerald and Gwen Dudley.

Kim was a top-sized, dark-brindled dog,

Ch. Widneyland Kim: A top-sized, brindle dog, he was the sire of eight Champions.

Ch. Godfrey's Pride: This handsome Stafford was a son of Ch. Widneyland Kim.

Ch. Rellim A'boy: A grandson of Ch. Widneyland Kim, out of his daughter, Ch. Wychbury Midly Girl.

with a broad, white flash on his chest. His head was wedge-shaped, broad and tapered, and his muzzle was longer than deemed desirable today, but typical of dogs from that era. His stop was not as defined as that of the modern Stafford. Kim was upright in stance, with a broad, straight front, nice legs and good feet. He had a well-shaped rib and was relatively short-coupled, with strong hindquarters and a lovely whip tail.

Ch. Widneyland Kim sired eight Champions – five dogs and three bitches, the best known being Ch. Wychbury Kimbo. In addition to Kimbo, Kim's Champion progeny included the dog Ch. Godfrey's Pride, the bitch Ch. Della of Impkin, and Ch. Wychbury Sportsman, a lively tiger brindle. Another of Kim's Champion daughters, the bitch Ch. Wychbury Midly Girl, joined the kennel of Therese Miller in the North East, where she became the dam of Ch. Rellim A'boy and great grand-dam of Ch. Rellim Saratoga Skiddy. The white dog, Ch. Subtle Difference, was owned by a Mr Gittings, although he was bred by Mr Worrall from a Family 58 bitch. Mr Gittings worked as a foreman on railway maintenance and owned a smallholding where he was able to indulge

his interest in all sorts of animals. This included turkeys, and woe betide foxes attempting easy pickings, for Mr Gitting's dogs wasted no time in seeing them off!

CH. WYCHBURY KIMBO

Kim's most well-known son, Ch. Wychbury Kimbo, was a dog of high quality. A clear, red-fawn, he was, as I recall, without white markings. He conformed to the Standard extremely well, standing four-square with plenty of bone. He had a deep brisket, a straight front, well-laid-back shoulders, and a short, level topline. However, it was his head that caught the eye – broad skull, deep through with a short, strong muzzle and good cheek bumps. Above all, he handed down these excellent features to his progeny through successive generations.

Kimbo was one of Ch. Widneyland Kim's finest sons, being a very worthy Champion and sire of a further five Champions. Three of these were bitches – Ch. Tessa's Gem, Ch. Williamwood Golden Lass, and Ch. Eastaff Nicola. The two dogs were Ch. Widneyland Little Gent of Pynedale and Ch. Wychbury Red Riband (see overleaf).

Ch. Wychbury Kimbo: A clear red fawn of high quality. He is the most famous son of Ch. Widneyland Kim.

CH. BELLEROPHON BILLY BOY

Ch. Bellerophon Billy Boy was sired by Ch. Quiz of Wyncroft and came from Family 2 stock. His dam, Honest Martha Le Loup, was a very game bitch. Billy Boy was a well-marked, tiger brindle. He was very typical of the stock descended from the breeders living in the Yorkshire area – solid and well built, with a strong head carrying a longer muzzle and a slightly flatter head than stock from the south of the UK. These physical characteristics (referred to as Yorkshire-headed in this book) were typical of stock in Yorkshire, and can be traced back to Bob Salisbury and the Guests's Blandonas.

Billy Boy sired five Champions, three dogs and two bitches. The three dogs were Ch. Son of Billy Boy, Ch. Buster Bill, and Ch. Top Hat, while the two bitches were Ch. Judy of Brunaburgh and Ch. Marjorie's Choice.

ALAN GREENWOOD

Alan Greenwood is one of the real characters of the breed, well known and highly respected for his terrific handling abilities. He moved to Scotland and nursed his wife (who was confined to a wheelchair) for several years, but he is best known 'down South' for the extraordinary effort he made in 1990 to raise money for 'rescue', walking all the way from Dundee to the North East Staffordshire Bull Terrier Club Championship Show held at Newton Aycliffe near Bishop Auckland in County Durham.

1950s AND 1960s

CH. WYCHBURY RED RIBAND

Ch. Wychbury Red Riband was born in 1952. Sired by Ch. Wychbury Kimbo, from a lovely brindle-and-white bitch named Regnant Show Lady, Red Riband inherited a great many of his father's good points. He was a clear, red-fawn with white markings and plenty of substance. He had an excellent head

with a good bite, carrying dark pigmentation and neat ears. Throughout his show career, he was managed by pigeon fancier Horace Priest, a superb handler and one of the most knowledgeable Stafford men I have ever met. He managed several of breeder Gerald Dudley's dogs – six or seven well-known stud dogs being in his yard at any given time.

Later, Ch. Wychbury Red Riband joined Therese Miller's household, where a mating with Ch. Wychbury Midly Girl produced the white dog Ch. Rellim A'boy. In addition to Ch. Rellim A'boy, Ch. Wychbury Red Riband sired three Champion bitches and another Champion male. Ch. Little Diamond Tiara was owned by Daisy Hoggarth, the Scottish Ch. Williamwood Fawn Lass belonged to Mr Judge, and Ch. Towan's Merry Maid belonged to George Smith, a man who worked very hard for the East Midlands Staffordshire Bull Terrier Club and whose wife, Mabel, is president of the club today. The other male Champion sired by Red Riband was Batham's Ch. The Red Brickmaker, who stood at stud in the Midlands.

Ch. Major In Command At Wychbury: A top-sized dog with lots of substance. He sired five Champions.

Ch. Fredanita Of Wychbury: A daughter of Ch. Major In Command At Wychbury.

CH. MAJOR IN COMMAND OF WYCHBURY

Produced by a granddaughter of Ch. Wychbury Kimbo in 1954, Ch. Major in Command of Wychbury (pictured page 150) was acquired by Horace Priest for Gerald Dudley. This top-sized, attractively marked, brindle-and-white dog had lots of substance. He sired five Champions, four of them bitches – Ch. Gay Moment, Ch. Brindle Ballerina, Ch. Fredanita of Wychbury, and Ch. Fredenzella. Fredanita and Fredenzella were produced by the same dam, Fredansante, and breeders Fred Holden and Dan Potter used the prefix Fredan with considerable success. The one dog sired by Ch. Major in Command of Wychbury was Ch. The Prince of Diamonds.

He was bred by G.W. Bass, who owned some lovely red-fawn bitches, notably Ch. Lady Cherie of Uddffa. Bass was very much a loner, although this did not hinder his success. His stock was descended from Family 2 bitches, as was Ch. Gay Moment.

CH. GOLDWYN'S LEADING LAD

Born in 1948, Ch. Goldwyn's Leading Lad won 13 Challenge Certificates in his exhibition career, rising to fame in the 1950s. However, despite his success, his potential as a stud was never fully recognised. Leading Lad was bred and campaigned by Jack Altoft, who lived well off the beaten track in Lincolnshire. In the 1950s, Stafford enthusiasts tended to be concentrated in regional pockets, each group working separately with perhaps one or two dedicated breeders dominant in each group. Public transport was the main way to travel in those days. Championship shows were geared up for exhibitors arriving by rail, with special buses connecting the shows to railway links. Few breeders travelled to Lincolnshire to use Ch. Goldwyn's Leading Lad at stud, even though his pedigree and potential were superb.

Jack Altoft pictured with Ch. Goldwyn's Leading Lad, Ch. Goldwyn's Gracious Lady, and Ch. Goldwyn's Lucky Lad.

Ch. Goldwyn's Leading Lad was the result of breeding two brothers to the same bitch and then mating the best dog and bitch from the resulting litters. This breeding plan is known to produce dominant sires, providing the original stock is sound. Certainly, the plan seemed to work for Jack Altoft as Leading Lad sired a further four Champions (a bitch, Ch. Trenton Tiger Lily, and three dogs – Ch. Golden Boy of Essira, Ch. Goldwyn's Lucky Lad, and Ch. Eastaff Danom).

Despite his limited use at stud, Leading Lad was highly successful in the show ring. Along with the bitch, Ch. Tawny of Dugarde (one of the best Stafford bitches I have ever seen), Ch. Goldwyn's Leading Lad dominated the exhibition world. When these two Staffords were in the ring together they created a picture of true excellence.

CH. GOLDEN BOY OF ESSIRA
The son of Ch. Goldwyn's Leading Lad, Ch. Golden Boy of Essira, was a high-quality, red-fawn dog in the higher size bracket. Owned by Mr and Mrs Weller, he was well balanced with good bone and a punishing head, Golden Boy was the product of combining two breeding lines – that of Ch.

Goldwyn's Leading Lad and Titian of Dugarde. Titian of Dugarde was sired by Ch. Little Gent of Pynedale, a dog that not only carried the genes of Ch. Wychbury Kimbo, but also those of his grand-dam, the marvellous Ch. Tawny of Dugarde.

Another of Ch. Goldwyn's Leading Lad's progeny, Weycombe Judy. The Downs are highly respected Championship show judges, awarding Challenge Certificates in many breeds, but Staffords have always been very close to their hearts. Ch. Golden Boy of Essira sired three Champions in one litter for George Down.

CH. WEYCOMBE CHERRY
The dam of the litter sired by Ch. Golden Boy of Essira (bred by George Down) was Ch. Weycombe Cherry. She was the product of a mating between Weycombe Judy and a son of Ch. Fearless Red of Bandits. The three Champions produced by the mating were Ch. Weycombe Julie, Ch. Weycombe Melody of Senkrah, and Ch. Weycombe Dandy. Ch. Weycombe Cherry has been a great influence on both Abe Harkness's (Senkrah) breeding and Walter Watson's (Sanville) stock. By judicious breeding back to Ch. Goldwyn's Leading Lad, through his two sons (Ch. Eastaff Danom and Ch. Golden Boy of Essira), a host of first-class stock emerged, establishing Ch. Weycombe Cherry as one of the great foundation bitches of all time.

Ch. Golden Boy Of Essira pictured with his dam, Titian Of Dugarde.

Ch. Fearless Red Of Bandits: His son was the sire of Ch. Weycombe Cherry.

ABE HARKNESS (SENKRAH)

Abe Harkness was secretary of the Scottish Staffordshire Bull Terrier Club, and the well-respected breeder of Staffords with the Senkrah prefix. In the late 1960s, he mated his bitch, Senkrah Sabelle, to Ch. Weycombe Dandy, the son of Ch. Golden Boy of Essira and Weycombe Cherry. This produced three Champion bitches – Ch. Senkrah Saffron, Ch. Senkrah Sabeau, and Ch. Senkrah Sapphire.

Sabeau went to Mr McEvoy in Ireland. Traditionally, exhibitors from Ireland (both north and south of the border) find it very difficult to campaign a dog in mainland Britain, and it is much to Billy McKnight's credit that he achieved so much. Saffron was sold to Sid Craik and became a foundation bitch for the Badgerlea prefix.

SID CRAIK (BADGERLEA)

Ch. Senkrah Saffron was produced by a mating between Ch. Weycombe Dandy and Senkrah Sabelle. Owned by Sid Craik (Badgerlea), in one litter she produced two Champions under the Badgerlea prefix – Ch. Badgerlea Biddy and Ch. Badgerlea Rascal.

Ch. Buninyong Caesar, sired by Ch. Weycombe Dandy.

Sid Craik's house was situated in the grounds of Stormont Castle, Belfast, where he was in charge of the gardens and of those in Belfast town, where he was well known for giving talks and advice on the radio. Sid often travelled to mainland Britain to exhibit his Staffords, and it was during one of these visits (for the Richmond Championship show in the early 1960s) that Ch. Senkrah Saffron went missing. She escaped from her travelling box on the aircraft when the plane landed at Heathrow. She was missing for ten days before being found on Christmas Eve by a 'posse' from the Southern Counties Staffordshire Bull Terrier Society, just on the south-west perimeter of the airport.

CH. LINDA OF KILLYGLEN

A descendent of Ch. Gentleman Jim, Ch. Linda of Killyglen was my first bitch. She was the dam of the great Ch. Eastaff Danom, from whom many of the great Staffords are descended. Linda was originally designated as a Family 58 bitch (by Mr H.N. Beilby), but she was later redesignated as Family 2 (by Alf Tittle) after perusal of some papers supplied by Mrs Westwood of 'Nethertonian' fame.

Linda was a well-marked, fawn bitch with a white collar and bib. Well balanced, about 15 inches (39 cms) at the shoulder, and not so strong in the head as present-day stock, she was quite a handful, being afraid of nothing. One of her major wins was Best Bitch in Show at the Suffolk Kennel Association show.

Linda was mated to Ch. Goldwyn's Leading Lad, and the mating was quite an experience! Due to a postal strike, which resulted in Jack Altoft never receiving my letter of confirmation, we arrived 'out of the blue'. Furthermore, I had passed my driving test only a week previously, so the journey to Lincoln and through the city was my first long drive and extremely nerve-wracking. However, despite the less than auspicious start, Linda proved herself to be an excellent brood bitch, being the dam of Ch. Eastaff Nicola as well as Ch. Eastaff Danom. Unfortunately, she later became ill with pyometra (see page 241) and had to be spayed.

CH. EASTAFF DANOM

Ch. Eastaff Danom was one of the pillars of the breed. He was born on August 7th 1955 from Ch. Linda of Killyglen and Ch. Goldwyn's Leading Lad. Danom was a well-marked, fawn-and-white dog with a dark mask. His well-shaped head carried the correct proportions, with a broad skull and a short, strong muzzle. He had a good, level bite, the darkest of eyes, and small, rose ears, no doubt gained from his grandsire, Pat the Boy, who had the neatest ears I ever saw.

Danom had a wide chest, but not overly so, and this was complemented by good, round bone, a deep brisket, and sound hindquarters with well-let-down hocks.

Danom was a great showman. He adored being in the show ring, being quite a handful for Jack McNeill. In his show career he won

Ch. Eastaff Danom: A great showman, who went on to sire 11 Champions.

Ch. Badgerlea Rascal: A son of Ch. Eastaff Danom.

11 Challenge Certificates and sired 11 Champions. He was remarkable in that he imprinted his balance and breed type on the breed for several generations. Of his Champion progeny, six were bitches and five were dogs. The bitches were Ch. Pitbul Lindy Lou, Ch. Stonnards Nell, Ch. Dennybeck Dani of Belsevore, Ch. Pitbul Coleen, Ch. Curfews White Orchid, and Ch. Badgerlea Biddy. The five dogs were Ch. Badgerlea Rascal, Ch. Hyndland Jaunty Jock, Ch. Jasper of Witts, Ch. Jolihem Dreadnought, and Ch. Sahib of Senkrah.

JOLIHEM

Danom's son, Ch. Jolihem Dreadnought, was born in 1964. He sired several wonderful Staffords, including the bitches Ch. Jolihem Gallant Bess and Ch. Rapparee Roulette, and the two dogs, Ch. Pitbul Jeff's Pal and Ch. Jolihem Ringmaster. Jeff's Pal sired Ch. Kinderdijk Petite Cherie, a lovely brindle-and-white bitch owned by Ron Astley, whose other breed of interest was Chows. In turn, Petite Cherie was dam to Ch. Yankeestaff Bolivar. Ch. Jolihem Ringmaster was an attractively marked, fawn-and-white dog. He carried on the family tradition of siring Champions, being the sire of Ch. Frolbecca Fire Raiser and Ch. Jokartan Royal Tan.

154

YANKEESTAFF

Yankeestaff was the prefix registered by Major and Mrs Malec when they came to England on a tour of duty with the American Air Force. Having bred Ch. Yankeestaff Bolivar from Astaff Clares Cassandra, a daughter of Ch. Kinderdijk Petite Cherie, they later returned to their homeland and established some strong breeding lines there.

CH. RELLIM FERRYVALE VICTOR

Ch. Rellim Ferryvale Victor was born on October 8th 1960. He was shown quite fearlessly, under both specialist and all-breed judges, and became a Champion in 1962. He had a very successful show career, in the course of which he was awarded seven Challenge Certificates.

Victor was sired by Ch. Rellim A'boy, linebred to Ch. Widneyland Kim – bred by Therese Miller from the two Midland Champions Wychbury Red Riband and Wychbury Midly Girl (see above). Therese was a very knowledgeable breeder, but it was her husband, Jack Miller, who handled all the Rellims in the show ring, and, between them, the Millers had considerable influence on the development of the breed in the North East.

Unfortunately, Victor's sire, A'boy, died young (this strongly built, very typical pied dog would surely have been more successful at stud had he lived longer). Victor's dam was Chestonian Chimes, not particularly linebred. After the mating of A'boy to Chestonian Chimes, the Millers planned to view the litter together, but eventually, Jack went on his own. He came back and excitedly announced "I think you had better come and see this pup". Victor grew to be a very clean-cut dog, compared with his sire. He had an excellent-shaped head with good, round, dark eyes and a well-defined stop. He passed on this attribute to many of his progeny, and the correctly shaped head can be traced over many generations from this

Ch. Rellim Ferryvale Victor: Sire of five Champions.

dog and his sire. Body-wise, Victor was strongly but cleanly built, standing well up on his toes, with excellent quality of bone and fine spring of rib. It was not always possible to evaluate his movement, as he was very erratic – sometimes covering the ring on two legs, as opposed to four!

Victor won seven Challenge Certificates between 1962 and 1964, and he sired five Champions. The two bitches were Ch. Lydes Cygnet and Ch. Rellim Saratoga Skiddy (the only Champion bitch bred by Therese and Jack Miller). Of the male Champions, George Down owned Ch. Rellim Warpaint, while Ch. Camdonian Contender was based in the South. The influence of the excellent Ch. Knight Templar can be traced through such animals as Ch. Topcroft Toreador, Ch. Hurricane of Judael, and Ch. Black Tusker.

CH. TOPCROFT TOREADOR

Descended from Ch. Rellim Ferryvale Victor, Ch. Topcroft Toreador gained his title in the late 1960s, while still a youngster. Homebred and owned by Harry and Flo Latham, he was a black brindle of standard size. He was a well-boned and muscular dog of quality, with a punishing head of correct proportions. He had round, dark eyes and ears set wide apart, giving an excellent expression. He had correct dentition, good depth of brisket, and well-sprung ribs.

Ch. Topcroft Toreador improved the northern bloodlines significantly before he was withdrawn from stud. He passed on his many sterling qualities to his offspring, including two bitch Champions, Ch. Kinderlee Critique and Ch. Jumping Bean of Grenoside. He also produced no less than five Champion dogs – Ch. Satan's Master, Ch. Staffshaven Artificer, Ch. Wawocan Kinsman, Ch. Westpoint Warrior, and Ch. Buccaneer Shoemaker.

Shoemaker was exported to Australia where he was used considerably at stud. Artificer was never offered at stud, but both Kinsman and Westpoint Warrior were well used in the north west area. Westpoint Warrior was the sire of some very typical stock; his name appears in the pedigrees of many well-known winners, and includes the Champions St Simons Argonaut, Dark Rose of Topcroft, Reetuns Aristocrat, and Glenrhondda Sombre Bell of Dogan.

NANCY AND JIM BOLTON

The Boltons came to prominence in the early 1960s. They acquired Rapparee Ashfield Star and campaigned her to win her title. She had breeding lines going back to Ch. Eastaff Danom, and was the dam of Ch. Rapparee Roulette. Later, Rapparee Renegade was added to the Boltons' kennels, gaining his title in 1967. He was used considerably at stud, being the sire of the homebred bitch Rapparee Razzle Dazzle; she, in turn, was the dam of litter brother and sister Ch. Rapparee Grand Slam and Ch. Rapparee the Gladiator. Owned by Alan Sparks, Gladiator went on to sire three Champions.

Nancy and Jim Bolton owned or bred eight Champions, with Ch. Rapparee Threapwood Handyman deserving of special mention. Bred by Mrs Banks, sired by Ch. Rapparee Renegade out of a Betchgreen bitch, he was a lively dog in the show ring, possibly most well known for being the sire of Ch. Rapparee Rothersyke Vow (see below).

THE RISE OF THE STAFFORD

By the mid-1960s, Stafford registrations with the Kennel Club had risen sharply, although it remained unusual to find large groups of Staffords housed in one home, unlike hound and toy breeds (where large kennels are the norm). Competition in the show ring became much more popular, as it was realised that the breed was not controlled by professional handlers and even a novice could win. Keen newcomers were welcome, providing they had plenty of enthusiasm and basic handling skills.

Meanwhile, rising costs for show secretaries and the steady decline of the trimmed breeds in terriers, caused show committees to consider means of increasing their entries to help balance the books. Until this time, Staffords had been regarded rather as pariahs in the show world. Exhibition rings were often draughty, poky areas, away from other breeds. It was typical for Staffords to be judged by an all-rounder with little interest in the breed, and this gave scant encouragement to the novice.

Fortunately, there were one or two judges in the Midlands who had more than a passing interest in Staffords. In addition, there were a couple of specialists in other breeds who helped to bring Staffords into the mainstream of the show world, including Bull Terrier man Tom Horner (who always judged in plus-fours), and Ben Johnson, a leading Bull Terrier judge. Furthermore, leading breeder George Down (of Weycombe fame) was a great support, being a member of several

Kennel Club committees and a judge of considerable experience. He could always be relied upon to go that extra mile on the breed's behalf.

As the breed's popularity grew, it became increasingly difficult for the existing clubs to deal with all the enquiries and problems caused by such rapidly growing interest. The North West Staffordshire Bull Terrier Club acted on Arnold Thomas and Ernie Bywater's suggestion that the breed would benefit if its enthusiasts were to speak with one voice, and invited the other clubs to a meeting, to discussed the founding of a Breed Council. The North West hosted the first two meetings, and it would be fair to say that most enthusiasm could be found in the North. Shortly afterwards, research showed that a considerable number of juvenile Staffords were being affected by PHPV and Hereditary Juvenile Cataracts (see page 251), which resulted in the various clubs instructing the Breed Council to research the depth of the problem. The bonding together of the various clubs in an effort to deal with the situation greatly added to the strength of the Breed Council.

With Stafford popularity at an all-time high by the late 1960s, the stage was set for the breed's continued rise in the 1970s and later.

EARLY 1970s

CH. RAPPAREE ROTHERSYKE VOW
Ch. Rapparee Rothersyke Vow was born in June 1969, bred by Dr Davidson. An early developer, he was a Champion by the time he was two years old (1971) and went on to win six Challenge Certificates in all. An impressive black brindle dog of standard size, Vow was well balanced with a good, straight front, nicely rounded bone, deep brisket, and well-padded feet. His beautifully shaped head had a broad skull, short, strong foreface, a good, level bite, and neat, rose ears. His dam,

Rothersyke Gem, was bred from mainly northern stock.

Vow was extremely successful at stud, being the sire of nine Champions (four dogs and five bitches). Breeders Alec and Eileen Waters mated Vow to their superb bitch Ch. Ashstock Artful Bess, a match that produced Ch. Ashstock Lucky Jim and Ch. Ashstock Black Maria – the latter being one of the youngest bitches to be awarded a Challenge Certificate. Another of Vow's Champion progeny was Ch. Moi Daredevil, a Midlands-based dog. When mated to a bitch descended from Ch. The Black Monarch, Vow sired quality brindle-and-white bitch Ch. Meaduns Polly Flinders. The owner, Horace Dunn, was a quiet, unassuming man, with some definite ideas about breeding, but unfortunately, he died rather early in life. His bitch, Polly Flinders, was the dam of Ch. Meaduns Emma Peel.

Ch. Ashstock Artful Bess: Her mating to Ch. Rapparee Rothersyke Vow produced two Champions.

LATE 1970s AND EARLY 1980s

CH. HURRICANE OF JUDAEL
Ch. Hurricane of Judael was a very compact, black-brindled dog with white markings on his chest. Eddie Pringle, his owner, always stated that he was "bang up" to the Standard, being 16 inches (41 cms) at the withers and no more than 38 lbs (17 kgs) in weight. Soundly constructed throughout, Hurricane had a very short back, with a good width of chest and depth of brisket, solid, round bone on the front quarters, well-sprung ribs, and a good skull – very typical of 'Yorkshire' breeding with dark eyes, good pigmentation and a strong underjaw. He was awarded seven Challenge Certificates before retiring from the show ring.

Hurricane sired seven Champions, of which it is interesting to note that only Ch. Little Miss Kek carried breeding lines back to Black King, the grand-sire of Hurricane and the sire of Ch. Black Tusker. Hurricane was a most successful sire, being dominant enough to stamp his mark on a varied range of bitches. He had a typical Stafford temperament. At home he lived harmoniously with several Staffords and Pomeranians. However, in the show ring he was every inch the showman; he was alert all the time. When used at stud, he could always be relied upon to behave as a perfect gentleman.

Of the two dog Champions he sired, Ch. Pegs Bolton Trip is the best known. The other, Ch. MacSchiehallion, was used at stud in the North. One of Hurricane's daughters, Ch. Acid Queen, owned by M.J. Green, won all her four Challenge Certificates in the North of England, while another daughter, Ch. Baroness of Brittandy, won five Challenge Certificates. A further two of the bitch Champions, Ch. Rendorn Deadly Nightshade and Ch. Rendorn Delta Dawn, were bred by Norman and Dorothy Berry.

NORMAN AND DOROTHY BERRY (RENDORN)
Under the prefix Vencristo, Norman Berry and Norman Entwhistle produced a number of first-class Staffords from Family 7 bitches. Later, Norman and Dorothy Berry registered the prefix Rendorn, and bred some of the best bitches of the breed. Their list of Challenge Certificate winners is impressive, including, as it does, nine Champions to date. Both Norman and Dorothy are international judges of repute and have been very active in the North West Staffordshire Bull Terrier Club. Dorothy is also well known for serving succulent meat-and-'tattie' (meat-and-potato) pies.

CH. BLACK TUSKER
Born in 1975, and owned by Malcolm Boam and Bryan Bates, Ch. Black Tusker started his show career in 1976. By this time, Stafford registrations had reached the 2,000 mark, several more breed clubs had been formed, and entries at major shows had risen beyond expectations. The popularity of this enigmatic breed had risen to an all-time high, and Ch. Black Tusker did much to keep that trend strong; this black-brindle dog became a legend in his own lifetime.

SHOW SUCCESS
In 1978 and 1979, Ch. Black Tusker was Top Show Stafford. In total, he won 14 Challenge Certificates and eight Reserves, all under different judges. Furthermore, he won two reserve Terrier group awards at a time when there was very little recognition of the breed in that group. It was a surprise to many people when he was retired from the show ring at four years of age, for it was generally thought that, if he continued to exhibit, he would break the record for Challenge Certificates won. However, his owners felt that this would not have proved anything more – he was already the top-winning

Ch. Black Tusker: Highly successful in the ring, Tusker made breed history by siring 16 Champions.

Stafford of his time, with many admirers in and out of the breed.

In 1989, the Kennel Club published an article called *The Judges' Choice*. A number of top breed judges were asked to select their all-time, greatest Staffordshire Bull Terrier, which resulted in Ch. Black Tusker being the dog most frequently selected. His close conformity to the Breed Standard, combined with an exceptional balance of breed type, substance and soundness, simply oozed quality while not being overdone in any department. He was a great showman, always on his toes but very well behaved in the ring.

PERFORMANCE AT STUD
After his retirement, Ch. Black Tusker's next test was to see how he would perform as a stud dog – being a top winner is of little use if a dog cannot pass on his attributes for the future prosperity of the breed. Ch. Black Tusker more than acquitted himself in this department, however. In total, he sired 16 UK Champions – a breed record that still stands. He is particularly noted for three reasons – tidying up certain structural faults in the breed, being the most admired dog in the breed's history, and founding a strong line for others to build on. If a study is made of many present-day winning black brindles, it will be found that Ch. Black Tusker's name appears somewhere in most of their pedigrees. He was used by many of the top-winning kennels of that time, and a number of his sons went on to prove themselves as producers of quality stock. Like any outstanding dog, he had his critics, but his admirers far outweighed them. He is still talked about today and will go down in Stafford history as one of the breed greats.

CH. SKEAN DHU
Of the 16 Champions sired by Ch. Black Tusker, one of the best known was Ch. Skean Dhu. This dog was the product of mating Ch. Black Tusker to Constones Paragon. Constones Paragon was a full litter sister to Constones Posie, dam of Ch. Lydes Cleopatra and Ch. Lydes Hermoine.

Born in 1978, Ch. Skean Dhu was one of Ch. Black Tusker's better-known Champion offspring, and, like his sire, he was a top-winning dog. He was a top-sized, black-brindled dog, with a grand head. He had an excellent front, nicely short. This was coupled with a level topline, held when moving. His hindquarters were well constructed, immediately confirmed in his movement, which was first class.

Ch. Skean Dhu was awarded his first Challenge Certificate at the Scottish Kennel Club in 1980. He went on to add a further eight Challenge Certificates, being withdrawn from the show ring at the end of 1981. His owner, Mr Carter, worked offshore, which

Ch. Allendale King: The best-known son of Ch. Skean Dhu.

Ch. Staffmaster Pure Opium: A daughter of Ch. Lancstaff Kjells Namsos Noble.

rather restricted the amount of studwork his dog undertook. As a stud force, he sired six UK Champions, including Ch. Allendale King (probably the best known) and Ch. Spartan Victor.

CH. LANCSTAFF KJELLS NAMSOS NOBLE

Ch. Lancstaff Kjells Namsos Noble, or 'Spike' as he was otherwise known, was sired by Ch. Jolihem Ringmaster, and his ancestry can be traced directly to Ch. Eastaff Danom. Born in 1983, from a bitch carrying both Ch. Jolihem Ringmaster and Ch. Hurricane of Judael breeding, he had all the potential to be a useful stud dog. Standard-sized, red-fawn and white, with a black mask and dark pigmentation, Spike was an athletic dog, balanced with a well-shaped head, small, rose ears, very dark, round eyes, well-filled cheek bumps, a correct bite, and plenty of underjaw. His front was straight with round bone on the forequarters, all finished with

well-padded feet. Moving, he was a joy to watch, nicely let down at the stifle with a level topline. Above all, he had a marvellous temperament. He was so laid-back in the show ring he often failed to show himself to full advantage, and, after some considerable winning as a youngster – he won 58 points to his Junior Warrant – he was withdrawn from the show ring so that his owner, Mrs Carole Atherton, could concentrate on breeding from him. Carole is a well-known figure on the North West Committee, as well as a respected Championship show judge. She also bred Spike's brother, Ch. Lancstaff Sparbu Saga.

Spike was a super stud dog; he could charm even the most difficult bitches. He loved having bitches around him, putting on splendid displays of his masculinity for their benefit. Based in the North West, he was mated to some quality bitches and sired five Champions and three other Challenge Certificate winners. Two of his Champion daughters produced Champions. Ch. Staffmaster Pure Opium is the dam of Ch. Staffmaster Flashpoint, and Ch. Jackstaff Heaven Sent is the dam of both Ch. Jackstaff Fatal Attraction and Ch. Jackstaff Forget Me Not.

One of the three Champion dogs sired by Spike, Ch. Eilder Red Shadow, was an attractively marked red-fawn dog with a striking white bib and four white feet – in fact, the white went right up to his chest. Owned by Jaci McLauchlan, he went on to win six Challenge Certificates. Ch. Barcud Silver Machine won four Challenge Certificates, as did his brother, Ch. Yorkstaff Crackerjack.

CH. TEUTONIC WARRIOR
Ch. Teutonic Warrior was a top-sized, red-fawn dog who came into my care when his breeder, David Rivenberg, emigrated to the US. He had an outstanding presence, a lovely, well-shaped head, very deep through, a strong muzzle with a good, clean bite, and he was well boned with a straight front and adequate rib development. A born showman, he moved freely and kept an excellent muscle tone throughout his life. With an excellent temperament, he hated cats and never backed off a challenge.

Warrior's legacy was his relative success as a stud force. Living some way off the beaten track near Glasgow, he sired five Champions – Ch. Wallace the Wizard, Ch. Jackstaff Prima Donna, Ch. Ramblix Roberto, Ch. Jodels Box of Delights, and Ch. Mad Max of Hazeldean. His best-known son, Ch. Wallace the Wizard, was a very impressive dog.

ALAN HEDGES
Both Ch. Teutonic Warrior and Ch. Wallace the Wizard were handled by Alan Hedges, as were all the Eastaff dogs, including Ch. Eastaff Guardian (see below). At the time of print, Alan has piloted more than 28 dogs to

Ch. Teutonic Warrior: A dog with outstanding presence in the ring.

achieve their titles, winning 72 Challenge Certificates between them, under 59 different judges, and his list of achievements is still growing!

CH. WALLACE THE WIZARD
The son of Ch. Teutonic Warrior, Wallace was owned by Sue and Donald Wood. A fairly unruly dog – making it difficult to get the best from him in the show ring – he had a good head, although it was not as clean and well defined as that of his sire. However, this was compensated for by a straight front and a level topline. Wallace possessed a lot of class.

Wallace won five Challenge Certificates before being retired from the show ring. After his retirement, he proved most successful at stud, handing down his good qualities to five Champions – Ch. Parkstaff Witch of the North, Ch. Bonzaries Keliboy, Ch. Caballero Fire Fighter, Ch. Mistress McGrath of Boldmore, and Ch. Rocellio Rip Van Winkle – winner of 10 Challenge

Ch. Wallace The Wizard: A son of Ch. Teutonic Warrior, he became the sire of five Champions.

Certificates and owned by Roger and Doreen Pugh, both of whom are Championship show judges and export some very typical stock all over the world.

CH. SPARTAN VICTOR
Ch. Spartan Victor was bred by a local vet, Jackie Molyneux, and owned by Rob and Yvonne Drummond of the Sparstaff prefix. Zak, as Victor was affectionately known, was from a litter of four bitches and two dogs, and was acquired primarily as a companion. However, having won his class first time out at a small open show, followed by another first at the North East Staffordshire Bull Terrier Club primary show, Zak went on to be Best Puppy at Driffield Championship Show under Norman Berry. Following a string of wins across the country, he gained three Challenge Certificates and one Reserve before he was retired from the show ring in the early 1980s.

Following Zak's retirement, the Drummonds began to show his double granddaughter, Ch. Spartan Wild Thyme. Zak was used sparingly at stud, but at 10 years of age he sired Ch. Szondu Ulster Maddy – a standard-sized bitch standing 15 inches (37.5 cms) at the withers and weighing 37 lbs (16.5 kgs), soundly constructed, with excellent movement and an extremely level topline.

Rob Drummond says of Zak, *"As a companion, you could not have found a more trustworthy dog. Very intelligent and loyal, he had great affection for his family and friends, but was also very protective towards us. With other dogs he was quite tolerant, never starting any skirmishes, but finishing quite a few! On being confronted by an aggressive dog of similar or larger stature, he always stood his ground and rarely had to progress past the dominating stare and four-square stance he would adopt, usually ending the confrontation with the other dog lowering his head and turning to slink off – he didn't feel the need to chase or retaliate further.*

"He was a great playmate for our children – who were toddlers when we bought him – joining in with their games when he could, or, if he was excluded, happy to just lie nearby and watch what was going on. The highlight of his day was going on the walk to and from the school, where he looked forward to all the fussing he would get from the kids at the school gate – even some of the teachers joined in. All our present Staffords have come through Zak in one way or another."

JAN AND BILL HUNTER (SPADILLE)
Ch. Spadille Midnight Lace and Ch. Spadille Spare the Rod were half sisters, being daughters of Black Magic of Spadille. Jan and Bill Hunter kept very few dogs, preferring to give each as much attention as possible. They bred a grand-headed dog called Spadille Sammy Spade, and, when mated to Ch. Spadille Spare the Rod (a half-brother x half-sister mating), a very nice, black-brindled dog

Ch. Bowtman's Razel Dazel: She was awarded a CC by Brian Grattidge at the Crufts Millennium Show.

called Spadille Sandawana Satan was produced. Spadille Sandawana Satan was exported to South Africa, where he was a popular stud. His owner, David Harrison, is a well-known judge in his own country and in England, where he last judged at Bournemouth in 1998.

Spadille Sammy Spade passed on his best attributes to several dogs, including Wyrefare Billy Ruffian, owned by Barbara and Jim Beaufoy. This standard black brindle, with a strong, well-defined head, inherited Sammy Spade's excellent head through his sire, Spadille Netherdale Pride of Barons, with the features strengthened by Nethertonian breeding.

WYREFARE BILLY RUFFIAN

Wyrefare Billy Ruffian was an excellent dog, possessed of the ability to pass on his good points to his progeny. He sired five Champions. The four bitches were Ch.

Nethertonian Rose, Ch. Timgold Rita the Raver, Ch. Fromestaff Nettle of Wyrefare, and Ch. Fromestaff Abracadabra of Wyrefare. Both Fromestaff bitches were bred from the same dam, Black Mash of Frome. Only one Champion dog was sired by Billy Ruffian, this being Ch. Boldbull Black Jack, who has himself sired Champion bitch Spirestaff Avenging Angel of Tikkurilan, and her litter brother, Ch. Spirestaff Jimmy Jazz.

CH. KARJOBRI BLACK PEPPER

Ch. Karjobri Black Pepper was born late in 1977 and gained his title in 1981. He was sired by Ch. Black Tusker, from a bitch carrying genes inherited from Ch. Rapparee Threapwood Handyman, and, from way back, Ch. Eastaff Danom. Black Pepper's breeder was Brian Grattidge, the well-known, ever-helpful, long-term secretary of the Notts and Derby District Staffordshire Bull Terrier Club.

Brian's interests included not only Staffordshire Bull Terriers, but also Fox Terriers, about which he was very knowledgeable, and, as a change, he had some success growing and showing chrysanthemums – those beautiful, large-headed blooms were really spectacular in his garden.

BRIAN GRATTIDGE

Ch. Karjobri Black Pepper was bred by Brian Grattidge. Brian last took the centre of the ring at Crufts in the Millennium year, where he drew a top-quality entry of bitches, making Ch. Bowtman's Razel Dazel his Challenge Certificate winner.

KARJOBRI MISS VANITY

With the dearth of high-quality, fawn stud dogs, breeders began to use black-brindled dogs on their red bitches. Consequently, black-brindle Staffords became very prominent, somewhat superseding the red-fawns that had been dominant previously. It was at this time that Karjobri Miss Vanity joined the Eastaffs.

Brian Grattidge bred a litter containing two bitches, and wanted to use one as a brood bitch. In terms of quality, there was very little difference between the two bitches, so it was purely personal taste that resulted in Miss Vanity becoming the main brood bitch.

Sheba, as she was known, was quite a character. She hated cats and ruled the roost from day one, soon impressing her dominance on all the other dogs at Weston Hall.

Sheba proved to be a very useful brood bitch. When mated to Ch. Skean Dhu, she produced Australian Champion Eastaff Bruiser. Bred to Ashstock Wild Colonial Boy, she was the dam of Eastaff Yoshka. Taken to her grandsire Ch. Black Tusker, she produced Ch. Eastaff Ironsides.

Ironsides was a strongly built, tiger brindle. He was well balanced, with plenty of bone, a good rib cage, a deep chest, and an impressive head. With his broad skull, deep through so that he had a strong underjaw, he was typical of stock that came through from the old Yorkshire breeding.

He had a will of his own, being quite a handful in the show ring. However, his physical attributes earned him four Challenge Certificates.

Ashstock Wild Colonial Boy had a classic pear-shaped head, a wide skull, a deep stop, plenty of depth, and a strong underjaw. Sadly, Oscar was lost in a car accident before he achieved his title, which he surely would have done.

Combining the classic definition of Wild Colonial Boy's head with the many good qualities of Ch. Black Tusker worked very well. The mating of Miss Vanity to Colonial Boy gave us Eastaff Yoshka, who, when mated back to Ch. Black Tusker, gave us Ch. Eastaff Guardian (see below).

LATE 1980s ONWARDS

RELLIM CHAMPIONS TASK FORCE AND BLACK ACE

Jack Miller brought the bitch Rellim Deed I Do to a motel on the night of the Potteries Championship show. She was the last of the Rellim bitches that he owned, and from this mating he produced two male Champions, Rellim Task Force and Rellim Black Ace. Steve Eltinge bought Task Force after he was made a Champion, exporting him to the US where his bloodlines can be traced to this day. Task Force was a really sound, black-brindled dog of very high quality.

Ch. Rellim Black Ace was used extensively at stud in the North East. Owned by Clive and Audrey Hubery, he won four Challenge Certificates under Audrey's handling. He was used extensively at stud, still producing stock in his eleventh year. Recently, one of his best-known sons, Ch. Judael Both Barrels At Nozac (Gus), has been placed in the top ten stud dogs, alongside Eastaff Tally's Man, and Tally's son, Ch. Brystaff Simply the Best.

Ch. Brystaff Simply The Best: Rated among the top ten stud dogs.

Ch. Judael Both Barrels At Nozac: Selected in the nest, 'Gus' won 19 CCs, and has sired six UK Champions to date.

CH. JUDAEL BOTH BARRELS AT NOZAC

Audrey and Clive fell in love with Gus while he was a puppy in the nest. He stood out in a litter of five and his pedigree fitted in nicely with their own breeding programme. Although he had a reputation for being a handful in the show ring, he was a brilliant stud dog and a perfect gentleman at home. He was always full of himself and had a hatred of cats and white dogs! Gus was campaigned fearlessly over a period of three years, totting up a total of 19 Challenge Certificates, and, to date, he has sired six UK Champions and six overseas Champions.

JUDAEL

George Earle and Morris Searle owned the Judael prefix jointly until the latter's death. Their first interest was in Bob Salisbury's breeding, although their first brood bitch came directly from Mrs Cassel's Stonnards stock. She had some lovely Family 22 red-fawn bitches having very cleverly used Ch. Goldwyn's Leading Lad, and both his

Champion sons (Ch. Golden Boy of Essira and Ch. Eastaff Danom) in her breeding plan. Ch. Judael Both Barrels At Nozac was the result of very strong linebreeding, using the bitch Limelight of Judael as the lynchpin.

In total, George and Betty Earle bred 11 Challenge Certificate winners, nine of which were full Champions. In addition, 20 of the progeny exported from the Judael kennels have won their titles in their new homes.

CH EASTAFF GUARDIAN

Ch. Eastaff Guardian (Tunne) was an outstanding puppy. First shown at just over six months of age, he won his class under Abe Harkness at Richmond Championship Show. Alan Hedges handled him throughout his entire show career, winning his first Challenge Certificate in 1985, at the South Wales Staffordshire Bull Terrier Club under Nap Cairns (see below). The bitch CC winner was Ch. Tondoo Miss Moonshine, and it was agreed that they would be paired on her next season. Regretfully, Tunne drowned in a swimming pool not long after he had achieved his title, at just over 18 months of age. Obviously, he had not been used very much at stud by this age, but offspring from three matings he made have had some influence on the breed.

Ch. Eastaff Guardian and Ch. Tondoo Miss Moonshine, with judge Gerald Westwood.

165

The mating of Ch. Eastaff Guardian to Ch. Tondoo Miss Moonshine (a granddaughter of Ch. Black Tusker through Ch. Ginnels Black Tuskyanna) produced two dogs and two bitches. Mr Jones kept the two bitch puppies and one of the dog pups, Tondoo Tallyman, came home to join the Eastaffs at Weston Hall.

TONDOO TALLYMAN AND DEVIL'S BREW OF EASTAFF

Tondoo Tallyman grew up to be a hefty lad – powerfully built, but every inch a Stafford. He had a 20-inch (50-cm) skull. His head was a lovely pear shape, very deep through with a strong underjaw and a good bite. He had tidy, rose ears but his eye placement was not good. Overall, there was too much of him to take into the show ring.

Devil's Brew of Eastaff was the result of a mating between Ch. Eastaff Guardian and a bitch of Ashstock breeding, owned by a Mr Devlin. Mick Clarke, of Boldmore fame, drew my attention to a little black bitch in the litter, which we purchased and registered as Devil's Brew of Eastaff. She was a beautiful bitch, but she absolutely refused to behave in the show ring – she hated shows. She won a Challenge Certificate under Bill Hunter and then took on family duties.

THEIR PROGENY

Tondoo Tallyman and Devil's Brew were the parents of Ch. Eastaff Lil' Stotter, Ch. Eastaff Noire Fille, Ch. Eastaff Trefoil, and Eastaff Tally's Man. In addition, Tondoo Tallyman sired Ch. Sparstaff Dominator, while the Championship show winners Ch. Fromestaff the Minstrel, Ch. Sparstaff Dodgy Docker, Surestaff Intrepid, Karmedy Indestructable, and Ch. Belsevore Ross n Co all trace directly back to him.

Ch. Eastaff Lil' Stotter was christened 'The Wee Stotter' by Mrs June Bennett early in the nest. He sired Ch. Indiana Jet Setter and Ch.

Barda the Bushranger. His full litter brother, Eastaff Likely Lad, was exported to Mr and Mrs Jenks in Queensland, Australia. There, he sired one of the most influential stud dogs of his day, Ch. Southpark Pot Black – a lovely Stafford that I judged in Sydney in 1990, who has sired nearly 30 Champions.

EASTAFF TALLY'S MAN

While Eastaff Tally's Man is a very bad showman, refusing to behave in the show ring, at home he is a different dog – a perfect gentleman, marvellous with children, and the very best of stud dogs. Of the seven Champions he has sired to date, five have been bitches. Of these, Ch. Mistletoe Magic and Ch. Araidh Dot to Dot have both produced Champion daughters. Of the other three bitches, Ch. Brystaff Mindern Rose at Obmarstaff, Ch. Bethane Moonlight Madonna, and Ch. Canny Bairn for Jayneze, the last two have proved successful as brood bitches.

Eastaff Tally's Man: This dog refused to behave in the ring, but he proved his worth at stud, siring seven Champions to date.

Ch. Mistletoe Magic (above) and Ch. Araidh Dot To Dot (below): Champion daughters of Eastaff Tally's Man, who have both produced Champion daughters. Courtesy: Raymond.

NAP CAIRNS (CONSTONES)

A.W.A. (Nap) Cairns was, for many years, secretary of the Southern Counties Club. He was responsible for the first Southern-bred male Champion, Ch. Constones Cadet. Nap founded the first breed-specific magazine, *The Stafford*, which he edited for more than 20 years and which is still produced and distributed worldwide. No one has written more, with more authority on the breed, than he, and very few have done more to promote the positive aspects of the Stafford as a family companion as well as a show dog. Nap was joined in the prefix by his daughter and son-in-law, Clare and Tony Lee, and Constones is now the oldest affix of the breed, with nine Champions carrying this name.

CH. CONSTONES YER MAN

The last son of Ch. Black Tusker, and by far the best known, Ch. Constones Yer Man has placed Staffords firmly in the canine history books. The winner of 20 Challenge Certificates, and the sire of 11 Champions, he has set a record that will be extremely difficult to match. It will prove most interesting to see the next generation carrying this bloodline.

Manny – as Ch. Constones Yer Man is known to his friends – was born on April 12th 1987. He came from a litter of seven, and the remarkable thing about the litter was that his sire, Ch. Black Tusker, was 11 years old at the time of his conception. In the event, it proved to be Tusker's last litter and it produced in Yer Man his 16th Champion – a record for the breed. Yer Man's dam, Jonunas Celtic Caper at Constones, was from Spadille Desperado, a dog who traced one side of his pedigree back to Ch. Skean Dhu, a son of Ch. Black Tusker. On the dam's side, Celtic Caper went back to Constones Overlord, so the circle was complete. Manny was not inbred, but he was linebred quite strongly. Furthermore, his pedigree traces back directly to the first Stafford bought in 1942 by the founder of the Constones kennels, Nap Cairns.

Clare Lee, Nap's daughter, writes, *"Yer Man's show career gives evidence that even the most experienced have to make plans to include the various quirks of individual dogs. He started his show career at the Ladies Kennel Association Championship Show, where he won Best Puppy under the husband-and-wife team of June and David Horsfall. He went on to collect many* accolades, but, when he went into Junior, he seemed to come to a standstill and was not always happy with himself in the ring.

"All his ring training had been conducted by Gerry Holmes, and we had to have a conference to decide whether we would bother to go on showing him at all. In the event, on the advice of the oldest member of the 'committee' (Nap Cairns), it was agreed to withdraw him from serious competition but take him to 'fun' events – such as miners' galas in Gerry's home village, and exemption shows the length and breadth of Yorkshire. We just let him enjoy himself and have time to look around at all the other dogs without any attempt being made to stack him or put any pressure on him to behave in a proper show-ring way. We often had to suffer the indignity of being told 'You've got a good dog there, you should get it to some handling classes!'

"Eventually he returned to the ring in Special Yearling at Crufts under Jim Bolton in 1989,

where he won the Reserve CC. This was the year that Ch. Belnite Dark Huntsman won the Terrier Group, but nothing could have outweighed the joy we felt at our win. From then on, things got much easier; I suppose we all relaxed.

"In March, he won his first CC under Nancy Bolton at the North West Championship Show. Eight months later, at the end of 1989, he had 13 Challenge Certificates. By the end of 1990, he had passed the Breed Record of Ch. Benext Beau that had stood for some 25 years. The 'committee' decided he should go for one more show, the Centenary Crufts 1991, when he won Best of Breed. He was retired that day and never competed at a show again.

"The big laugh between the cognoscenti had always been that the record breaker couldn't produce anything. It was with quiet satisfaction, therefore, that we watched his young stock coming into the ring and beginning to make their mark. Unfortunately, Manny died young,

Ch. Constones Yer Man: The last, and most famous, son of Ch. Black Tusker.

Leading lights in the Stafford world, pictured at the East Midland Staffordshire Bull Terrier Championship Show, 1991: Top row (left to right): Gerald Westwood (Nethertonion), Albert Wood (Reetuns), Jo Hemstock (Jolihem), Derek Smart (Wardrum), Mrs Vera Westwood (Nethertonion), Harry Robinson (Hamason), Ken Fensom (Pitbul), Malcolm Boam (Fulfin), George Walton (Walstaf). Bottom row (left to right): Major John Turner (Jonunas), Clare and Tony Lee (Constones), Joyce Shorrock (Eastaff).

but had, to his credit, the fact that, from 68 litters, he produced eleven Champions.

"What made this dog so special? First and foremost was his balance. Reams have been written about this particular attribute, but if you saw Yer Man you would understand it at once. Every part of him – the length of his legs, the size of his head, the width of his chest, the length of his back – was in complete harmony. Furthermore, these parts were properly put together. The stifle just bent enough, the shoulders properly laid back, and the feet just turning out enough so that it was virtually impossible for the dog to 'stand wrong'. His speed on the turn, and his ability to jump and twist was unsurpassed. In fact, to show him at his best it was necessary only to leave him at the end of a free lead; he moved extremely well. By this, I mean that he didn't glide across the room – that is not the correct way for a Stafford to move – he moved with drive and

determination, but so smoothly, and with such economy of motion, you could almost hear his front nails click on the floor. Once you and he got into step at the correct pace, it was a positive thrill to 'feel him go'. His skull was perfectly proportioned for his body, and his neat rose ears were ideally placed at the side of his head. He had a very good stop and a foreface of the correct ratio, although to be perfect he could have done with more strength in foreface – a deeper muzzle. He was also one of those unfortunate black brindles who had a darkish-brown eye that would have gone unnoticed in a red, but set in the deep black of his coat tended to look a bit light. He had a perfect mouth and correct pigmentation of lips and nails. When young he looked a bit slab-sided, but, as he matured, the rib sprung to give a correct definition to his body. We will probably never own as good a Staffordshire Bull Terrier again."

169

Ch. Belnite Dark Huntsman: Winner of the Terrier Group at Crufts.

A ROSY FUTURE

In recent years, Staffordshire Bull Terriers have truly come of age. As well as being much-loved, popular family pets, Staffords have more than made their mark in the show ring. Ch. Brystaff Simply the Best has been in the list of top ten stud dogs for the last two years, while Ch. Ladarna Birthday Boy won Terrier Group 2 at Crufts in 2001. These accolades, combined with a Crufts Terrier Group win by Ch. Belnite Dark Huntsman a few years earlier, have helped to bring the breed into prominence with some of the best UK judges.

Ch. Belnite Dark Huntsman was bred by Billy McKnight, one of the stalwarts of the breed. He first became interested in the breed while living in Stafford. Later, he returned to Northern Ireland and took on a number of varying committee posts during his years of membership of the Northern Ireland Staffordshire Bull Terrier Club.

Ch. Vanoric Voo Doo: Winner of 26 CCs to date.

Ch. Domino Flashy Lad: Winner of 28 CCs.
Photo: Raymond

As the breeder of Ch. Belnite Dark Huntsman, he was naturally thrilled with the publicity given to the breed, knowing that the presence of such a top-winning dog would raise the profile of Staffords in South Africa – his destination after obtaining his title.

As a breed, Staffords have had their fair share of major awards over the last 20 years. Both Ch. Wystaff Warfare (bred by Mrs Gwen Gallimore) and Ch. Springsteen Boy have been declared Best in Show at major General Canine Championship Shows. The owner of Warfare, Mr Armitage, commemorated the win with a trophy awarded at the East Midlands Staffordshire Bull Terrier Show.

More recently, Ch. Baysend Mystical Secret, a daughter of Ch. Mistletoe Magic, was among the final eight in the Terrier Group at Crufts. Ch. Vanoric Voo Doo, Ch. Black Tusker, and Ch. Eastaff Guardian have all won or stood Reserve in Terrier groups at general Championship Shows.

Of the previous multiple Challenge Certificate winners, Ch. Vanoric Voo Doo has, up to the present, been awarded 26 Challenge Certificates. Ch. Domino Flashy Lad won 28 Challenge Certificates before retiring and looked just as good as a veteran. As a breed, the Staffordshire Bull Terrier has never been so strong.

9 BREEDING STAFFORDS

While a litter of puppies can seem like an irresistible attraction, there should be only one reason for breeding Staffords – to improve the overall standard of the breed, both in body and in temperament.

It is, therefore, essential that the prospective breeder has a clear understanding of what they intend to achieve, and how they intend to achieve it. This involves not only a detailed knowledge of the breed, but also an understanding of the principles behind heredity.

MATCHING THE STANDARD

Breeders frequently use the phrase 'breeding to type'. Although 'type' is extremely difficult to define, it roughly translates as breeding a dog that conforms as closely as possible to the Breed Standard (a 'blueprint' of what the ideal Stafford should look like).

The original Standard for the Staffordshire Bull Terrier was drawn up in the Black Country – the home of the breed. At that time, there was considerable variation in size and type. To reach a consensus of opinion among those present, the wording of the Standard was fairly loose.

By being flexible, the Standard allowed breeders to call on a larger gene pool, which encouraged the breeding of healthy, high-quality stock. As time passed, the breed became more uniform in size and type. When the Standard was revised in 1948, it was felt that height and weight had stabilised, so the revised Standard quoted a desirable height of 14 to 16 inches (35 to 40 cms).

However, although height and weight had stabilised, regional variations in type remained. As well as the different colours, there were big-boned, coarse dogs; finer-boned, more refined types; long-legged and deep-chested dogs; and short-legged, rather squat types.

However, with the development of the UK's road network in the latter half of the 20th century and the post-war economic boom, exhibitors began to visit shows outside their area and breeders began to look further afield in their quest for incorporating better stock into their breeding plans.

Type in present-day stock is far more uniform, although some lesser variation remains. The modern Standard for the Staffordshire Bull Terrier can be found on page 126.

PEDIGREES

All breeders need to understand the pattern of genetic inheritance in their quest for quality stock. A whole host of traits are hidden in a dog's genetic make-up. Although they may not be visible on the outside, it is not uncommon for some of these traits to resurface in later generations.

A breeding programme will need to incorporate dogs and bitches that are excellent examples of type, as well as taking into account the less-desirable traits that may be carried on the back of 'the perfect head', etc. To produce healthy, high-quality puppies consistently, a breeder needs to know the visible and hidden traits contained in his breeding stock. This is why pedigrees are so important.

Each name that appears on a pedigree represents a part of the dog's genetic construction. It follows that, where a name or series of names appear more than once in a pedigree, the greater must be the influence of those animals.

A long pedigree with lots of names in red (for Champions) may look impressive, but to the serious breeder it contains a wealth of information about a dog's genetic make-up. A dog with a pedigree containing several dogs from the same kennel could be expected to exhibit similar traits to the dogs named in his pedigree. The discerning breeder can look at a dog's pedigree to see how that dog conforms to the Breed Standard.

PRINCIPLES OF HEREDITY

Charles Darwin is well known for his theory of evolution, presented in *The Origin of Species,* published in 1859. However, while Darwin concentrated on the wider picture, examining how different species evolved, other scientists were more interested in the variation within species.

A contemporary of Darwin, Augustine monk Gregor Johann Mendel, conducted a series of experiments at a monastery in Brunn, Austria. He examined the common garden pea and how each successive generation of peas varied.

Mendel found, as is well known today, that the 'parents' each provided 50 per cent of the genes that made up their offspring, but that those genes did not have the same value. In other words, while all the offspring inherit 50 per cent of their genes from each parent, the resulting combination is not the same for each offspring – some peas would be yellow, some would be green, some would be smooth, while others would be rough.

This occurs because the joining together of genes at the time of fertilisation is entirely random. Genes are contained in DNA (deoxyribose nucleic acid), the building blocks of life.

A chromosome is formed from a single DNA molecule. Dogs have 78 chromosomes, grouped together in 39 pairs. A dog inherits 39 chromosomes from his father, and 39 chromosomes from his mother. However, the 39 chromosomes contained in the mother's ova (eggs) and the father's sperm are chosen randomly, which is why each puppy is unique.

Each chromosome carries many genes, and each gene has dominant (DD) and recessive (rr) characteristics. The recessive or dominant characteristics of the genes determine the dog's physical appearance.

DOMINANT AND RECESSIVE TRAITS

Breeding for colour is a simple illustration of how recessive and dominant traits work. The coat colour black (B) is a dominant trait, whereas the coat colour fawn (f) is recessive. If a black dog (BB) is mated to a fawn bitch (ff), the first generation of puppies will all be black, because the black gene dominates the recessive fawn. However, although all the pups will appear black, some of them will carry the recessive fawn gene, as shown below.

	B	B
f	Bf (black)	Bf (black)
f	Bf (black)	Bf (black)

Black is a dominant trait, an important factor to consider when planning a breeding programme.

If two of the dogs from that litter were to be mated, the resulting litter may include a fawn-coloured dog among the black puppies, as shown.

	B	**f**
B	BB (black)	Bf (black)
f	Bf (black)	ff (fawn)

Colour is a visible example, but the same principles apply to eye colour, height, and the set of the tail, etc.

BREEDING FOR COLOUR

The Stafford comes in a variety of colours. In the Breed Standard these are described as red, fawn, white, black, or blue, or any of these colours with white. Any shade of brindle, with or without areas of white, is also acceptable. Liver-coloured or black-and-tan dogs are considered highly undesirable, and will be penalised by show judges.

Unfortunately, as the above example shows, breeding for colour is not as straightforward as mating a black-coloured dog to a black-coloured bitch to produce black-coloured puppies.

Anyone attempting to breed a distinct colour needs to do a great deal of research, especially if attempting to improve the richness of the colour at the same time. It is possible for three distinct colour patterns to appear in one litter, and so colour breeding is best left to those who know what they are doing.

WHITE

There are very few pure-white dogs – most have a little colour somewhere on the body (the tip of the ear, the base of the tail, etc). True albinos – those with no pigmentation whatsoever – are very rare indeed. A true albino will have a pink nose and pink or red eyes, known as 'wall eyes'. However, many

Staffords have white patches somewhere on their body. Mating two animals with a large amount of white on their bodies should produce whelps of a similar pattern, but such puppies should have black eye rims, black eyes, and black nails – indeed, these contrasting areas greatly enhance the look of a pied.

White is a partial dominant. This means that it produces different results depending on the colours it is mixed with. For example, white acts as a dominant to fawn (so there may be large patches of white on a fawn dog) but it is recessive to black. However, it is not unknown for a white-marked dog to appear in a litter of black puppies, if there is some fawn ancestry involved.

BLACK
Black dogs should have good pigmentation, with a black nose, dark eyes, and dark toenails. Some black dogs will have patches of white on their body, but others will not. Black is a dominant colour, so, when mated to any other colour, the resultant puppies will be mainly black (see above).

FAWN
Sadly, fawn-coloured dogs have become less evident, the exhibitors' choice being the darker, red-fawn colour.

The Standard allows for a lighter eye colour in fawn dogs, but the nose must be dark pigmented. Generally, toenails must be dark, but, in dogs that have white feet, white toenails are allowed.

Fawn-and-white puppies are often born with pink noses, but as the pups grow older, their noses will darken to the desired black. In some dogs, small, pink areas may remain on the nose, and this is known as a 'butterfly' nose. Fawn is a recessive colour, so, to produce fawn puppies, it is necessary for both parents to be fawn in colour (see above).

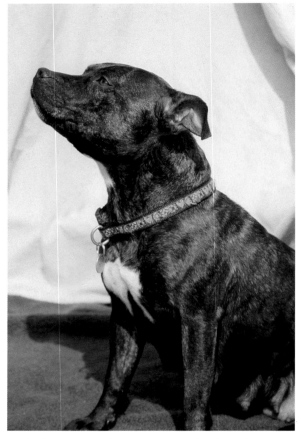

Brindle: a popular colour in the breed.

BRINDLE
The distinctive brindle pattern is overlaid on top of the coat colour. By running the hands through the coat, all three primary colours (black, brown, and fawn) can be seen on one hair.

The brindle pattern, which is a dominant gene, can be found in the glorious mahogany brindle, black or grizzle. The mahogany brindle combines the red or fawn colour with the brindling pattern. On black dogs, the brindling is somewhat hidden, but it is most obvious when the dog grows a new coat in the spring and sheds the old coat across the front and on the hindquarters. Grizzle is a dilute form of black, so the effect is much as black, but with lighter-coloured fur in which the patterning is more obvious.

BLUE
It is possible that the Kerry Blue Terrier, known for his feisty character, was one of the breeds used to create the fighting dog that later became known as the Staffordshire Bull Terrier. In Scotland, there was a group of Staffords known as Blue Pauls. However the genes for the colour blue were incorporated into the breed, this colour is normally evident as a slate-grey or grizzle colour.

The gene responsible for the blue coat is recessive, making it extremely difficult to predict when it will appear. Breeders wishing to improve or specialise in this colour would need to conduct an enormous amount of research. I am aware of a black-brindled stud dog, mated to a considerable number of bitches and producing mainly black stock, who suddenly produced a couple of blue whelps with otherwise good pigmentation. Bob Salisbury, a well-known breeder from the early days of the breed, tried to fix this colour without much success.

RED
Red Staffords are born with black muzzles, and many puppies have a dark line down their spine, often to the tip of the tail. In the first few weeks of life, the pup's colour can appear quite muted. However, by the time the pups go to their new owners (at about eight weeks), the coat will have cleared to show the lovely clear, red coat so distinctive in the breed. Presented in the show ring, with the coat glowing with health, a red is a very eye-catching dog.

ESTABLISHING A BREEDING PROGRAMME
Before discussing how to begin a breeding programme, it is essential that the reader considers the overall health of the breed to which he or she will be contributing. Only sound, healthy stock should be included in a breeding programme. Tests for PHPV, Hereditary Juvenile Cataracts, Hip Dysplasia and skin problems (see chapters 12 and 13)

Red: a rich, eye-catching colour.

Careful breeding soon establishes a recognisable 'line'. Pictured: father (right) and daughter (left).

should be carried out *before* any mating is planned.

This chapter is not intended as a step-by-step guide to breeding Staffordshire Bull Terriers, nor will it explain all of the complexities involved in the study of genetics. Rather, it aims to demonstrate that, through observation and knowledge of the pedigrees of your stock, as well as a thorough understanding of genetic inheritance, it is possible to breed for desired characteristics and to eliminate unwanted faults.

So, how does one go about establishing a breeding programme to put these principles into practice? Inbreeding, linebreeding and outcrossing are all types of breeding programme. Occasionally, breeders may use more than one method, but this can be fraught with danger and only the truly knowledgeable and experienced should attempt it.

INBREEDING

Inbreeding refers to the mating of close relations – mother to son, brother to sister, father to daughter, etc. It helps to perpetuate certain distinct traits, preventing their disappearance. However, this applies to undesirable traits as well, so it is not recommended for the novice breeder.

Inbreeding is frequently blamed for all sorts of genetic faults, but it should be remembered that wild animals have no such reluctance to mate with near relatives. Practised with care, inbreeding can produce dogs of a very distinct type with no detrimental effects on the genetic health of each individual.

LINEBREEDING

Linebreeding refers to the mating of related animals, commonly granddaughter to grandfather, grandson to grandmother, nephew to aunt, uncle to niece, cousin to cousin, and half-brother to half-sister. The main criterion is that both specimens must have similar good points. The old saying 'like breeds like' is a sound practical theory to follow in linebreeding, providing that dam and sire both carry the points you wish to perpetuate in your stock.

OUTCROSSING
Outcrossing refers to the mating of two unrelated animals. On the whole, this method is best avoided unless it is essential to incorporate a special factor, such as colour. Outcrossing can result in the loss of many good points developed through years of linebreeding or inbreeding. It can also result in undesirable genetic traits appearing in the breeding stock.

THE PET MARKET
Without a strong 'pet market' it would not be possible for breeders to implement any type of breeding programme. Not all dogs are suitable for breeding, and, for every dog bred from, many more are not. Dogs are rehomed as pets when they fall slightly short of the

Standard, which may mean nothing more than having a nose of the wrong colour. This in no way detracts from the dog's value as a companion, only his suitability as breeding stock. Good breeders like to forge strong links with the pet market, taking steps to ensure that their dogs are homed with owners who will rear and manage their dogs so they are a credit to the breed.

BREEDING STOCK
The object of a serious breeder is to establish a strain that is not only consistently good, but also better than that already produced. Each successive generation of dogs should be an improvement on the previous generation. It costs the same to rear a poor litter as a good litter – veterinary fees, food and bedding cost the same whether your puppies are of show quality or not. With this in mind, it stands to reason that much depends on the quality of the original breeding pair.

CHOOSING A BROOD BITCH
To the serious breeder, ownership of a high-quality brood bitch is essential. Most breeders will attribute the success of their kennels to a

The skill of a breeder is to choose a stud dog that will complement the bitch as well as bringing his own virtues to the resulting offspring.

main brood bitch. A thorough inspection of pedigrees will soon reveal several bitches as 'pillars of the breed'.

The brood bitch should be sound and healthy, carrying a great many good points without exaggeration. The quality of the female is crucial, for, while a male can sire hundreds of winning stock, a female can produce only tens.

Mated judiciously to the most suitable dog available, a bitch of good quality is the key to producing a good 'family'. However, it takes a considerable amount of experience to assess the quality of a brood bitch, and successful breeders have spent many years perfecting their 'eye' and judgement.

CHOOSING A STUD DOG

When choosing an appropriate stud dog for your bitch, the help of an experienced breeder will prove invaluable.

Some facts will be obvious immediately; a small, lightly boned bitch, lacking in substance, should not be mated to a large-headed, powerfully built dog in the hope that the offspring will be of standard size. It is more likely that such a mating will produce some pups that are like the father and some that are like the mother.

Knowing your brood bitch's strengths and weaknesses is most important when choosing a mate. Although counteracting the faults of the bitch is of major importance, being positive about her good points, and mating her to a stud dog known to produce those good points, will strengthen the chances of those points being reproduced.

Taking the time to study the pedigrees of quality sires, to find the most suitable mate for your brood bitch, will prove an invaluable investment in any future breeding plans. It is only once you have fixed the strengths apparent in your bitch that you should concentrate on eliminating the unwanted points.

The stud dog should be an exceptionally good example of his breed.

If a dominant sire is present in the pedigree of your bitch, this task will be much easier, as the sire will have already sired several successful mates that can be considered for the next generation. However, if the pedigree of your bitch is somewhat mixed, aim for a mate that has been strongly linebred and dominant for the type you wish to produce.

Breeders using the 'flavour of the month' on their stock may well produce an outstanding specimen that is, nevertheless, useless in the production of a high-quality 'line'.

THE SECOND GENERATION

If the first generation from your breeding programme was sired by a dog from a particularly dominant strain, it is not wise to crossbreed with a sire from another dominant strain. Although both strains will, in their own right, produce first-class stock, bred together they may react as unrelated animals and the progeny of such matings will not bear the hallmarks of either strain.

It is only by strict, constant selection that any amelioration of the line can be achieved, so the good breeder must never lose sight of the basic, true type when trying to establish 'fancy' points.

FERTILITY

The ability of a bitch to reproduce quality stock easily and naturally is one of the considerations every breeder should take into account when planning a mating. Fertility appears to run in families; when contemplating a union, the family history of both sire and dam should be researched, allowance being made for difficult whelpings that, obviously, are not hereditary. Especial care is advised if a bitch line consistently produces only one or two pups in each litter.

BREEDING CYCLES

Generally, canines have a six-monthly breeding cycle, although this can vary a month each way. In some breeds, the first season will not happen until the bitch is more than a year old and the cycle is on an annual basis. In some of the rarer breeds, it is vital to have a successful outcome to a mating, as a whole year will pass before the next opportunity arises.

OWNING A BROOD BITCH

When the bitch comes on heat, her vulva will begin to swell. This is normally followed by some bleeding. The amount of bleeding can vary. Some bitches have a very heavy flow, while the blood loss in others is so slight it is possible to miss it until the second stage of oestrus, when the bitch is producing ova (ovulating). A white blanket placed on the dog bed at the very first signs of swelling will identify the first loss of blood. Breeders generally count this as the first day of the pro-oestrus, although the bitch will have been releasing hormones for several days previously.

As well as bleeding, the bitch may change her behaviour. She will lick herself, be more excitable than normal, and also a little confused. Possibly having some abdominal pains, she will need reassurance from her owner. She will tend to urinate more frequently, marking her territory. Male dogs will recognise the scent, known as pheromones, and be aware that she will soon be ready to mate. Tickling the bottom of the bitch's back will cause her to turn her tail and present herself to the dog, and this is a clear sign that she will be ready to mate very soon.

There is no hard and fast rule about the timing of mating a bitch. The same bitch will not necessarily ovulate at the same time every season, so the fact that her mother had successful matings on the tenth day is no indication that your bitch will be receptive on that day. The bitch will ovulate at any time from the fifth to the 21st day, although the latter is not usual. The eggs themselves are not ripe for two days after they have been shed, and they will stay alive for three days, so a bitch ovulating every day for four or five days will accept a dog during that period. The sperm ejaculated by the dog will stay alive for seven days.

PRACTICAL PRECAUTIONS

While the bitch is on heat, it is inevitable that there will be stains on the furniture and carpets unless active steps are taken to prevent this problem. A male dog will be able to pick up the scent given off by a bitch on heat, and even the best sprays and disinfectants cannot entirely mask the trace left by a bitch on heat. Therefore, it is best to buy one of the specialised products on the market that will eliminate the smell, as well as products to clean away the stains.

Where several bitches live together, it is possible that they will come into season at the same time. This is because dogs are pack animals, and, in the wild the alpha female is the only one to breed. Unless food is plentiful, pups born from other bitches are killed. However, other bitches will come into heat, producing milk and sharing the mothering duties of the alpha female.

ARTIFICIAL INSEMINATION

When a bitch is being fertilised by artificial insemination, a great deal of accuracy is needed. Once the sperm is taken from the storage flask, it will stay alive for four hours only. In many countries, special permission must be obtained from the national kennel club for artificial insemination of any bitch. In all countries, the procedure should be undertaken by a veterinarian, whose advice should be obtained well in advance.

OWNING A STUD DOG

Most novice breeders begin with a brood bitch, acquiring a good stud dog once they have more experience. However, a strongly linebred dog can prove to be a dominant force. Great stud dogs are bred for, trained and handled right from the start.

A great many male puppies enter the show ring and win enough to qualify for Crufts competition, immediately prompting their owners to dream that their 'baby' will sire a whole string of Champions. Sadly, very few fulfil this vision. However, if you have a really first-class specimen, seldom out of the cards, linebred in the purple from a really good and worthwhile sire and dam, by the time he is 10 months old, perhaps you should consider using him at stud.

More usually, breeders plan out the acquisition of a stud dog, researching the qualities of sire and dam and choosing a male dog from a litter of utmost quality. The chosen dog should have many characteristics that will strengthen those apparent in the brood bitch.

ACQUIRING THE PUPPY

When the male puppy arrives in the household, either from being part of a litter born within the pack or brought in from outside, he will be treated very sympathetically. The females will take it in turns to groom him and play with him. He will be allowed the best tidbits and enabled to take liberties with them all. However, by the time he is 10 months old and he begins to be aware he is 'male', he will learn that, while all the other bitches respect him, he must defer to the dominant bitch.

In every group, there is one bitch who hogs the best chair, sits in the sunniest part of the garden and is generally the 'boss'.

If you want peace in the household you should reinforce her dominance, making sure that she fully understands that you are the master of them all.

It takes a great deal of time and research to produce a good-quality stud.

At around 10 months of age, your stud dog's hormones are all over the place. He will be taking an interest in other dogs and bitches, and, if you have several bitches on the premises, you will need to take precautions to prevent an unwanted mating. In most cases, the male adolescent will not attempt a mating with the dominant female. The dog will retaliate against the dominant bitch being brought to him for stud, considering it the most severe provocation because of the early introduction of pack law.

THE YOUNG, UNTRIED STUD

The ideal mating for a young, untried dog is an even-tempered, mature bitch that has already had a litter. If this is successful, you should encounter few problems as your stud dog's career progresses. When the dog has successfully sired two or three litters, and, having satisfied yourself that there are no signs of congenital defects, you may feel at liberty to offer him at stud professionally. Most breed clubs issue newsletters to their members where stud advertisements can be placed. Alternatively, advertisements can be placed in show catalogues at a very reasonable rate. The Internet offers similar opportunities.

LEGAL AND FINANCIAL ARRANGEMENTS

All financial arrangements regarding the stud service should be clearly defined in writing, prior to the mating. When you put your dog to stud, you should make it clear that payment is made for the stud service and not for the results. If the bitch fails to conceive, a second mating is not 'of right' but by agreement with the stud dog owner. Likewise, should there be only one surviving pup, or if all the whelps die, a free mating can be given only if the stud dog owner agrees and has no other commitments; there is no obligation to agree to such an arrangement.

Before using your dog at stud, establish the terms of the mating with the owner of the bitch to avoid any misunderstandings.

The stud fee should be relative to the experience of the dog. Some owners choose to take the 'pick of the litter' as payment for the stud service. This does not always work out to everyone's satisfaction, and should always be agreed well in advance of the mating. You will need to consider a number of points, such as:

• What if there should be only one survivor from the litter and the bitch needed a Caesarean section to deliver the whelps?
• Who pays the veterinarian's fees?
• Suppose all the resultant puppies are of the same sex and it has been agreed that the stud dog owner takes a puppy of the opposite sex?

- It should be remembered that the selling price of a good-quality puppy is more than double that of a stud fee.
- At what stage will the stud dog owner choose the puppy? If this is left to eight weeks of age, the brood bitch owner will not be able to enter into any agreements regarding the remainder of the litter, which can make it difficult to find homes for all the offspring.

STUD DOG HEALTH

Owners of stud dogs have a duty to see that their stock is healthy, regularly wormed and treated for fleas. The stud dog should be well fed, on a reasonably high-protein, high-calcium diet. He should be exercised regularly and kept in top condition.

You should remember that a succession of bitches coming on to your premises may expose your stud dog to the odd bug. The owner of the bitch should give an undertaking to have the bitch checked by her vet prior to the mating. At the same time, she could be swabbed and treated with antibiotics if an infection is present.

Also remember that visiting dog shows will expose your stock to a number of potential infections, and you should take precautions accordingly.

Having made the decision to use your dog at stud, it is imperative that you take every step to guarantee the health of the dog. Staffords should be tested for a number of different eye conditions (e.g. PHPV and Hereditary Juvenile Cataract) as well as hip dysplasia (see Chapter Thirteen).

It behoves us all to take whatever steps we can to produce healthy puppies, and prospective breeders should never lose sight of the fact that we live in a litigious era. In future, DNA testing may indicate those factors of which responsible breeders should take note.

Enquiries from your local breed club

The stud dog should be in peak condition prior to mating.

should elicit the information you need concerning these tests.

When using your dog at stud, you must monitor his health carefully. Overuse at stud will cause him to lose condition. If he is shown regularly, you will need to maintain a balance between competition and his use at stud. The dog should be used enough to keep him on his mettle but not so much that his condition deteriorates

.

MATING

Try to arrange for two persons who are conversant with handling a stud service to conduct matters for the first two to three occasions. If you are able to obtain the services of such a capable person for all your successive matings, the small fee paid will be repaid by the confidence displayed by the dog and the ease with which your stud will accept the pattern of events. The owners of visiting bitches have travelled long distances to obtain the mating, and they will be looking for a happy and easy fulfilment of their mission. From the very first stud service it is important to set up a pattern that the young dog will learn to recognise and understand.

Decide on the place most suited for your purpose, away from any other dogs, who should be securely confined when visiting bitches are on the premises. A utility room or clean shed (remember you will be kneeling on the floor) might be suitable.

Having decided on the place you will utilise, stick to it. Your dog should then recognise that a friend visiting with a bitch in tow is not to be treated in the same way as a bitch coming for a mating, which he meets in his 'special area'. If you use the kitchen, take care that the animals are safely confined within the area and not at liberty to escape to other parts of the house.

I have known novice owners arrive with an entire family of young children, and this serves only to distract the stud dog. A stud dog owner may need tact and diplomacy to deal with the delicacy of the situation.

The most important thing to remember is that mating a dog is a perfectly natural procedure. Instinct should take over most of the time, the dog being encouraged in a quiet and reassuring way. The owner of the stud dog is in charge of the proceedings and will form a bond of understanding and trust which will be strengthened with experience.

AFTER THE MATING

Having achieved the mating, the stud dog fee should be paid and the stud dog's pedigree and the necessary paperwork provided. A record of all stud work should be kept, space being left for details of the outcome of the mating, which will be a useful reference should any queries arise. Remember that it is quite possible for a bitch mated to more than one dog to carry puppies with more than one father. DNA profiling has been accepted by kennel clubs as a sure way of identifying parentage, but this is costly and it is better to work on achieving a successful mating first time round.

A stud career can be fruitful for anything up to ten years, many a Champion coming from a mating where the sire is known as a 'veteran'

THE LITTER

Once the litter has been born, you will need to ensure that you have taken the necessary steps to avoid unwanted pregnancies. A young male becomes fertile at about seven months, and a bitch can conceive the first time she comes on heat, so it is unwise to allow litter brothers and sisters to stay together during this period. A stud dog can be fertile still at 14 years of age, so he should not be left in the company of a young bitch during this period.

10 MATING, WHELPING AND REARING

Breeding a litter of Staffords can be great fun and extremely rewarding, particularly if you have embarked on a quest to establish your own breeding programme. However, there are a number of factors to consider carefully before making the decision to breed.

POINTS TO CONSIDER

First and foremost, you must consider the overall health of the breed. Unless you know what you are doing, you may be responsible for lowering the quality of the stock, or for introducing health problems. It cannot be stressed enough that only sound, healthy stock should be bred from, and all the relevant health tests (see Chapters Twelve and Thirteen) should be carried out *before* you mate your dog or bitch.

The whole family should discuss the decision to have a litter because the entire family will be affected. A litter of puppies will disrupt the household significantly. The bitch will need a quiet area, away from the other dogs, pets, and children. She will need access to a garden, and, once the pups are slightly older, they will need a garden in which to exercise, play, and relieve themselves.

A large number of owners mate their bitch because they believe it will do her good to have one litter. Others believe that producing a litter prevents the bitch from having pyometra later in life. Many more have fallen under the spell of the breed and want to breed an identical pup just like mum, while some mistakenly believe that breeding pedigree dogs can lead to riches.

If you do not intend to breed from your bitch at regular intervals, it is probably kinder to have her spayed early on in life. The bitch will also benefit from certain health advantages – spaying completely removes the risk of pyometra, as well as reducing the risk of mammary gland tumours. Those wishing to breed a newer version of their much-loved pet would do well to remember that, just like people, no two dogs are the same – it is impossible to produce a carbon copy of any dog. There is also the risk that the bitch may have a complicated labour, and it is always a possibility that she may die.

It is very unlikely that you will make any money from breeding a litter, as the costs can be remarkably high. Veterinary fees, stud fees, food for the dam and her pups, as well as additional heating costs all serve to make breeding a litter a very costly operation.

It is also very time-consuming – remember you will have to allow approximately eight weeks before the puppies can leave their mother, and, during this time, you will have an endless round of feeding, weaning and cleaning.

The sire should have a good history of producing quality stock.

Last, but by no means least, consideration must be given to homing the pups. We are all aware of the number of unwanted dogs in rescue centres. It is a growing problem, and, unless you wish to contribute to it, you will need to ensure that you have excellent homes lined up for the pups *before* the bitch is mated.

All that said, there is, of course, a great deal of satisfaction and amusement to be gained from rearing a strong, healthy litter, and it is one of the most natural ways to teach young children responsibility.

THE BREEDING PAIR

Everyone wants to breed good stock of the highest quality, and it is important that you do some research into breeding before you begin (see Chapter Nine). However, one of the best places to start is the breeder from whom you obtained your bitch. He or she should be able to give you some sound advice, especially if you are thinking about a long-term breeding programme. They will know the dam's good qualities, and be able to recommend a list of appropriate sires for the litter. A knowledgeable breeder who is willing to assist with the mating of your bitch and the subsequent whelping will be invaluable.

If you have lost touch with your breeder, one of your local breed clubs should be able to help. Stafford people are generally very friendly and helpful, and you should have no difficulty finding a large number of people willing to help you and advise you about

breeding your first litter. During my many years as secretary of a breed club, I recall many calls for help. I remember one in particular – after a series of protracted telephone calls and a successful delivery, I was asked what my prefix was. On being told, the caller exclaimed "Wow! I've hit the jackpot!". Your national kennel club will be able to give you details of the breed clubs in your area.

FINDING A STUD DOG

Information on finding the right stud dog can be found in the previous chapter. However, remember that you should be looking for an experienced stud dog, known to sire quality stock consistently, with qualities that will complement those of your bitch. You should go along to some breed club shows to look at the winners. It will not be long before you are able to recognise family likenesses and select a sire who is dominant for those points which you wish to improve in your bitch (see Chapter Nine).

THE BITCH'S AGE

Staffordshire Bull Terriers need a sound bone structure, which takes time to mature. With this in mind, it is best not to mate your bitch before she is 15 months of age. The kennel clubs of most countries have strict rules about the minimum age at which a bitch can be bred from, as well as regulations governing the number of litters she may produce each year (normally one litter per year). Also remember that your national kennel club may refuse to register a litter from a bitch more than eight years of age at the time of whelping, or where the dam has already whelped six litters.

HEALTH CONSIDERATIONS
Under no circumstances should you breed from your bitch until she has been declared free of PHPV and Hereditary Juvenile Cataracts (see Chapter Thirteen). In addition to testing for hereditary conditions, you should ask your veterinarian to perform a general examination, checking that the bitch is healthy and in good enough condition to carry and rear a litter. Check that her inoculations are up to date and that she has been wormed prior to mating. You might consider having a vaginal swab taken to determine that there is not an excess of bacteria present. It is quite normal for bitches to carry some bacteria, but an excess can reduce the chances of a successful mating.

CHOOSING THE RIGHT TIME
Staffords generally have two seasons per annum – one every six months. This can vary slightly, with some bitches coming into season approximately every seven or eight months. Where a bitch comes into season three times in a year, it is advisable to have her tested by your veterinarian, to verify that she is not having a 'false' heat. False seasons can appear remarkably realistic. The bitch may show every indication of a normal oestrus, even standing for the dog. To ascertain if she is genuinely ovulating, your veterinarian can take swab samples and test for the oestrous hormones.

To maximise the chance of a successful mating, you will need to follow your bitch's seasons very carefully, understanding when she will be most receptive to the dog. One of the early signs that the bitch is coming on heat is a swelling around the vulva, followed by bleeding. At the first signs of swelling, it is useful to place a white towel or blanket on

her bed. This will make you aware of the first discharge, which is profuse and brightly coloured. After eight or nine days, the loss of blood will diminish and the colour be more pink, so that by day 11 to 13 of the cycle, there will be very little discharge, what there is being pale and watery.

It is at this time that the bitch will be most receptive to the dog. Prior to this stage, the bitch may show no interest in the male, and may even warn him off vehemently if he comes too close. It is generally accepted that the best time to have a successful mating is between day 10 and 14 of the season, although it is quite possible that the bitch will accept the dog as early as day 7 or as late as day 17.

An observant owner will recognise when the bitch is sexually excited and willing to mate. She will turn her tail to one side and offer herself to male and female dogs in the household. Some bitches have a very limited time when they are receptive, while others will present themselves even when they are not ovulating. In the latter case, it may be necessary for you to take veterinary advice and to test for ovulation.

The bitch should be observed closely for signs of when she is most receptive to being mated.

As the owner of the bitch, you should inform the stud dog owner on the first day that your bitch begins bleeding. This will allow the stud dog owner to leave a space on his calendar for you. Normally, the bitch travels to the dog.

If you are prepared to pay for the service, your veterinarian can test your bitch's progesterone levels, letting you known the best time for mating. If you have a long way to travel to the stud dog, you should consider this money well spent. Occasionally, your veterinarian may discover that progesterone levels remain low throughout the oestrus period, indicating that the bitch is not ovulating. In this case, it may be necessary to undertake further tests, as there may be some problems with the bitch's fertility.

MATING
If you do not have too far to travel, it is best to mate the bitch in the morning. This will ensure that both animals are fresh and alert. If the weather is very hot, try to travel during the night or very early in the morning. Avoid mating the dog to the bitch during the hottest part of the day, when both animals will be uncomfortable. Always allow the visiting dog or bitch to rest after the journey, before mating begins, and make sure that both dogs have relieved themselves before they are introduced to each other. The stud dog should not have been fed prior to the mating, as he may be sick during proceedings.

INTRODUCTIONS
Although mating is a perfectly natural phenomenon, in which instinct will take over, care needs to be taken when introducing the dog to the bitch. It is not a good idea to throw the two together, expecting them to manage affairs on their own.

To begin with, introduce the bitch to the space you have allocated for the mating and allow her to sniff around and to settle down before introducing the dog. When you are ready to introduce the dog to the bitch, there should be two handlers present, just in case problems arise. If this is your bitch's first mating, it is far easier to use an experienced stud dog. An experienced stud dog will have a regular routine, he will trust his owner, and he will know in what sequence everything will happen. An inexperienced dog, however, may not know quite what to do.

Initially, the pair should be introduced while still on a leash. In that situation the male will circle the bitch, making one or two tentative approaches and inviting the bitch to play. She will be wary of this stranger and will almost certainly warn him off. This is where the handler's experience is invaluable.

Other dogs can be a big distraction during mating, so make sure that all other dogs are safely out the way before introducing the dog to the bitch. If you are sure the bitch is at the right point in her cycle for mating, but the dogs seem a little shy of each other, it may help to take the two for a short walk, with both animals on leashes.

For territorial reasons, the bitch is invariably brought to the dog for mating.

A young female meeting a strange male dog may resent his attentions. She may be fairly aggressive, biting quite viciously to prove her point. An experienced male dog will usually remove himself from harm's reach and continue the courtship without rancour. The dog will be strutting his stuff, bright-eyed and bushy-tailed, drawing himself up to his full height and exuding masculinity. It is a pleasure to watch the courtship of a good stud dog. He will indicate his willingness to play, keeping well out of the way of her snapping jaws until she starts showing a closer interest in him. Eventually, the bitch will present herself to the dog, and at this point he should be encouraged to mount her.

MATING
Once the dog has entered the bitch, it is vital that the mating is supervised fully. The bitch should be held firmly by the collar at the side of the neck (do not choke her by holding her collar too high). The collar should be tight enough not to slide over the head, and, by being held firmly and pressing the head downwards, the bitch will not be able to bite the dog when he mounts her. At the same time, she will not be able to dislodge the dog once he has entered her.

The handler should encourage the dog to mount the bitch, and, when he penetrates the vulva, he will clasp the bitch firmly around the waist with his front legs. The glands of the dog's penis may expand, becoming so bulbous that the penis is held firmly in the bitch's vulva. This is known as a 'tie' and it can last anything from a few minutes to nearly an hour. The duration of the tie is no indication of success or failure, and, while people generally expect to achieve a tie, it must be stressed that it is not essential for the production of puppies – many maiden bitches conceive without.

During the tie, the male will release his sperm, with ejaculation occurring in three stages. The first washes the path to the oviduct. This is followed by the sperm, and, finally, an ejaculation of fluid will push the sperm further up the bitch's vagina.

It is wise to leave the dog and bitch tied for two to three minutes, after which time the dog will wish to make himself more comfortable. At this point, the dog should be turned by moving his front legs to the side of the bitch and gently lifting his hindquarters over the back of the bitch, resulting in the animals standing rear end to rear end. While this may seem strange, it is a hangover from the time before dogs were domesticated. In the wild, dog and bitch would be very vulnerable when tied. However, by standing back to back, both would be able to defend themselves, to some extent, should they be attacked.

The tie will be broken spontaneously, at which point the dog should be removed from the bitch. The handler should check that the penis has returned to the sheath, wiping it down with antiseptic if desired. The dog should be given water to drink and allowed to rest for approximately an hour. The penis should return to the sheath quite naturally after a few minutes, and a short walk will aid the process. If, after 10 to 15 minutes, the penis has not retracted, a cold compress placed against the penis will usually put the matter right. The bitch should have her hindquarters wiped down with a mild antiseptic. She should be offered water and allowed to rest. This is an ideal time to deal with the necessary paperwork relating to the mating.

MATING PROBLEMS
There are several reasons for a bitch 'missing' to a dog. In most cases (up to 80 per cent), it is due to the mating taking place at the wrong time, when the bitch is not ovulating. If the bitch seems particularly belligerent, try

introducing her to the dog the following day – sometimes, 24 hours can make all the difference.

If a number of bitches fail to conceive after mating with the same dog, it could indicate a problem with the stud dog's fertility. In such cases, it may be prudent to have the dog checked over by a veterinarian and to have a sperm count taken. There is a condition called idiopathic aspermia, meaning an absence of sperm without a reason. This can occur in dogs that have previously sired normal, healthy litters – they become sterile inexplicably. Unfortunately, the condition is irreversible. There is a suspected link between idiopathic aspermia and vaginal infection in bitches mated to the dog. This is, of course, a very good reason for leaving a suitable time frame between matings – to avoid spread of infection from one bitch to another.

AFTER MATING

The bitch should be kept away from other dogs at least until the full 21 days of her season have passed. It is quite possible that, if she was introduced to another male, she could conceive from both dogs. The only way to sort out a mixed parentage litter would be by DNA testing of the pups, which is expensive. If you have children, you will need to make sure that they know not to let out the bitch by mistake.

PREGNANCY

Approximately four weeks after mating, your veterinary surgeon will be able to feel the embryos by palpation. However, most Stafford bitches carry their young high, under the ribs, so the veterinarian will be able to do no more than establish that the bitch is pregnant. He will not be able to determine how many puppies the bitch is carrying. Ultrasound scanning is the best way to discover if the bitch is pregnant. The use of X-rays is not recommended, because they can

When walked in a public place, the bitch should be kept on a lead to ensure she does not accept another mate.

damage the embryos.

During the first four weeks of pregnancy, the bitch will be very vulnerable and sensitive to interference of any description. I am loathe to take blood samples, or to use thermometers, unless they are absolutely necessary. Remember that infection is a very real threat to the embryos at this all-important stage.

GESTATION PERIOD

The gestation period will last between 58 and 70 days, with the average being 63 days. Some bitches will reabsorb the embryos, and stress can be a big factor influencing this. Reabsorption can occur any time during the first 35 days of pregnancy.

THE PREGNANT BITCH

During the first four weeks of her pregnancy, it is unlikely that your bitch will show any

The gestation period is around nine weeks. This bitch has another two weeks to go before her big day.

outward change, although she may have a small amount of white discharge about three weeks after the mating. During this period, the bitch's routine should remain the same as normal.

Five weeks after mating, you may like your bitch to have an ultrasound examination, to provide some indication of the number of pups she is carrying. This will not affect the dam or her puppies. If it looks as though she is carrying one or two pups only, be warned. Hormonal changes and the production of prostaglandin stimulate foetal movement during parturition. If there are one or two foetuses only, the hormonal changes may produce an insufficient level of fluid, leading to inertia. In such cases, your veterinarian will usually suggest an injection of oxytocin, which should rectify the situation.

Exercise should be restricted after six weeks, and the bitch should not be allowed too much rough and tumble with other dogs; it would be sad to lose a litter through a fall. You will find that the bitch needs to relieve herself more often, and she may be unable to hold herself through the night.

FEEDING

For the first six weeks, the bitch should not be given extra food, although you must ensure that what she eats is of the highest quality. As the pregnancy progresses, you can increase her food intake to two or three meals a day. However, make sure you do not overfeed the bitch, as this will restrict muscle contraction during labour. If your bitch is fed on a complete mix or tinned (canned) food, read the manufacturer's directions for feeding the in-whelp bitch and follow them carefully. Remember to provide plenty of fresh drinking water at all times – particularly important if your bitch eats a dry, complete mix.

Ask your veterinarian for advice about feeding, to maximise the bitch's health during pregnancy. Generally, the diet will need to be well balanced, containing sufficient calcium and protein. Calcium additives, however, are not recommended at this stage, and are best left until whelping and lactation begin. Your veterinarian will advise you about this and any other steps you can take to avoid eclampsia.

Remember that, the better the condition of your bitch, the better her chance of a problem-free pregnancy and labour.

Complementary medicine has taken off in the dog world, and there are many remedies suitable for bitches in whelp. I recommend the use of raspberry leaf tablets, available from homoeopathic shops. However, never give your pregnant bitch any complementary medicine without first consulting your veterinarian.

WHELPING

Whelping or parturition may take place a week before the due time or a couple of days after. Early litters are usually large. Delayed whelping can be explained by the fact that sperm can remain in the bitch for up to 48 hours before fertilisation. However, you should consult your veterinarian if the bitch goes more than 48 hours after her due time.

WHELPING BOX

Left to her own devices, the pregnant bitch would probably choose to have her litter on your bed, or to dig a hole under the garden shed. For obvious reasons, neither of these locations is suitable.

If the bitch is a family pet, and there are no other dogs in the house, she will not want to be cut off from her family. Try to find her a spot where she will have plenty of privacy and easy access to the garden, so that she can relieve herself and come and go as she pleases. If there are other dogs in the house, care must be taken to ensure the other dogs cannot approach the whelping area.

Having found a suitable location, you will need a whelping box. There are several types on the market, available in plastic or wood. I use a wooden bed purchased some 50 years ago. Apart from the odd coat of varnish, several sets of pig rails, and the odd replacement board at the front, it has been used by many people with great satisfaction.

Pig rails are a very useful adjunct to a whelping box, especially with a first-time or clumsy dam. Instead of using wood, I use 1-inch (2.5-cm), round plastic pipe, placed about 4 inches (10 cm) from the base and sides of the box. This allows the whelps to move around freely when underneath the dam. Some dams, especially those carrying a lot of milk, will not feel the whelps underneath and can crush them. Pig rails solve this problem, and, as the pups grow, the rails can be removed easily.

As an alternative to a commercially produced whelping box, you could use a large cardboard box of the size used to contain a washing machine or fridge, etc. Although it will need regular replacing, a cardboard box has the advantage of being inexpensive and easily disposed of. Cut out

an opening to allow the bitch access. Pig rails can added, if needed, by making holes in the box and slotting broom handles through the holes.

I have seen a large tea-chest utilised for whelping, as well as an old-fashioned wardrobe with the front taken off, suitably partitioned for a whelping bed and a play area for pups. You can use almost anything to make a whelping box, the most important consideration being that it is large enough for the bitch to stretch out on her side to feed her puppies, and that it has been thoroughly disinfected before it is occupied.

The whelping box should be raised from the ground to avoid draughts, and it will need to be near an electrical point. However, make sure that the bitch – and the puppies once they are born – will not be able to make contact with any loose wires. You will need access to an electrical point for an overhead heating lamp – essential for helping to keep the newborn pups warm. Alternatively, you can purchase underbed heating pads.

The bitch should be introduced to her new quarters about 14 days before she is due to whelp. Knowing that I shall be with my bitch for two to three days, I arrange for my own comfort at the same time, and you would be well advised to do the same.

During the birth, and for the first few days afterwards, the room should be kept warm, between 25 and 30 degrees Celsius (77 and 86 degrees Fahrenheit). This is very important – the pups are unable to control their body temperature at this early stage and hypothermia is a common cause of deaths among newborns.

After the first few days, the temperature should be lowered, so the bitch does not experience any discomfort.

EQUIPMENT

As well as providing a whelping area and accustoming your bitch to it, there are a number of other, equally important preparations you will need to make. To begin with, make sure you have all the following equipment easily to hand.

- An alarm clock
- Mild antiseptic (if using a popular brand, remember that many are very strong and will need diluting)
- A pair of light, plastic gloves
- A pair of sharp scissors
- Cotton wool (cotton)
- A thermometer
- A bowl for warm water
- Towels – some to dry your hands and some old ones for clearing up mess
- A bar of soap that will produce a good lather
- An old-fashioned, stone hot-water bottle
- A cardboard box large enough to take the hot-water bottle, a warm hand towel and the pups (as they arrive)
- Some milk, glucose, and a good wedge of cheese
- Pen and paper
- Weighing scales
- Petroleum jelly
- Nutri-drops or Dopram V (both the latter can be used to stimulate or revive lifeless puppies)
- Plenty of refreshments for yourself – it is likely to be a long night!

If the ultrasound scan suggests a large litter, make sure you have a quantity of milk substitute (e.g. Welpi), in case the bitch does not produce sufficient milk. Making some enquiries locally might indicate a bitch with a very small litter. If she has a good supply of milk, and her owners are willing, she may be able to foster some of the pups if your own bitch is unable to cope.

STAGES OF LABOUR

There are three stages of labour, with the puppies being born in the final stage.

STAGE 1

In the first stage, the bitch will become very restless, panting, pacing about, and investigating her rear end. See that the whelping box is lined with clean newspaper, remove all loose bedding, and encourage the bitch to stay in the box. She may refuse her food and vomit slightly, and she may try to escape human company. If you have managed to persuade an experienced breeder to help you with the birth, now is the time to alert him or her to the situation, although help will not be needed until the second stage of her labour.

The normal temperature for a dog is 38.6 degrees Celsius (101.5 degrees Fahrenheit). As whelping becomes imminent, this will drop to approximately 36 degrees Celsius (98 degrees Fahrenheit) or below. If you take your bitch's temperature twice a day – morning and night – for a week prior to the due date, it will be possible to see a pattern.

You will notice quite quickly when that pattern changes and the bitch is beginning labour. Certainly, as soon as the bitch's temperature drops below 36 degrees Celsius (98 degrees Fahrenheit), you should not leave her alone. Puppies can be expected approximately 24 hours after this drop in temperature occurs. Temperature is usually taken via the rectum. If you are wary of using a thermometer, a good tip (given to me by my stockman) is that, as the bitch's temperature drops, her ears will grow noticeably colder.

During this first stage of labour, milk will come into the mammary glands, and, by gently squeezing the teats, a small quantity will be expelled. This is an additional indication of imminent whelping (within 24 hours).

STAGE 2

At the second stage, the bitch will begin digging frantically inside the box. She will be trying to make a bed for herself. Have a black plastic bag handy, so that you can remove the rubbish gradually. Usually, the bitch will alternate between digging and sitting, coming to you for reassurance in between. At this stage, she will be having uterine contractions. These are normally quite mild. They indicate that pressure is being exerted on the cervix, which will be gradually opening. There may be a clear discharge from the vagina. If the discharge is dark green-black in colour, you should consult your veterinarian immediately.

STAGE 3

Once the cervix is fully dilated, the bitch will have more regular contractions and begin bearing down. She may be panting, digging and be otherwise restless. She is about to start the third, final stage of labour, in which the pups will be born. Now you must note the time carefully.

After approximately an hour of this behaviour, the first pup should be engaged in the vulva. You will be able to feel the hard lump just below the tail, and you may be able to see the pup emerging. If need be, you can assist the bitch by lubricating the edge of her vagina very gently. Wash your hands in warm water and work up a good lather. Gently insert your two middle fingers into the vagina, sliding them around the pup. As the bitch pushes, ease out the pup – as gently as possible – until he comes through the birth canal. Remember to keep calm and do not rush anything.

The pup will be encased in an outer water bag, which should burst as the pup is born, to allow the fluid to escape. The pup should be presented head first; if his bottom is first, with the hind legs tucked underneath, he is termed a breech birth. The pup will arrive still enclosed in his inner membrane and attached to the placenta or afterbirth.

The bitch's first instinct will be to remove the pup from this membrane. If not, you must do so yourself, as it is essential the bag is removed, and the nose and mouth cleared, so that the pup can breathe. Break the bag in the area of the pup's head, using the nails of your index finger and thumb.

Once the pup has been removed from the bag, rub dry with a warm towel. Try to interest the bitch in the pup, encouraging her to lick him. This will remove the mucus covering the pup, allowing air into his lungs.

If the bitch has not bitten through the umbilical cord, you will need to cut it, approximately 2 inches (5 cms) from the pup's body. Push the contents of the cord towards the puppy, and tie the cord with cotton. Dab some very mild antiseptic on the cut. Alternatively, you can squeeze the cord and break it with your fingernails – this mimics the dam biting through the cord, and creates a pressure that will reduce bleeding. Providing you leave an adequate length of cord, it will not need tying.

After the birth of the first pup, the bitch will begin to have further strong contractions. Be aware of the time – the next pup should be born within an hour. Sometimes, two puppies are expelled down the birth canal together. In such cases, you must take over mothering duties for the second pup, rubbing him dry and making sure that air gets into his lungs. Encourage the bitch to take over from you as soon as possible.

The remaining pups should be born following the same pattern. Normally, a Stafford's first litter is not very large – the average containing four pups. However, it is not unknown for a bitch to have eight pups, and the largest litter of which I am aware totalled eleven (one of which became a Champion). Be aware that you may need to be with your bitch for quite some time.

If you need to assist with the delivery of a pup, remember that they are tougher than you may think. If you need to grip and pull a puppy from the bitch, as long as you work with the contractions and do not use unreasonable force, you will not harm the puppy but you will help the bitch. However, if you find yourself pulling too hard, or if the birth seems difficult, ask your veterinarian's advice.

Each puppy will be attached to its own placenta. The placenta supplies a substance called oxytocin, which stimulates the whelping of the next pup. Count the placentas to ensure that none are retained inside the bitch. If in doubt, call your veterinarian – it is better to waste his time than to lose your dam through septicaemia.

Many bitches will eat the placenta from each pup, and this is a perfectly natural behaviour. The placenta is very rich in nutrients, and will help provide the bitch with the sustenance she needs for the days ahead. However, be aware that she may have loose bowel movements for a few days after whelping.

CARING FOR THE NEWBORNS

As the pups are born, cleaned, and the umbilical cords tied, they should be placed in the cardboard box you have provided. The box should also contain the hot-water bottle (well wrapped so that it does not burn the pups), which will act as a temporary substitute for the bitch's body heat. By placing the pups in the cardboard box, the bitch will have enough room to move while the remaining pups are born.

Between whelps, take the opportunity to clear away the soiled papers and replace with clean.

It has always been my policy to handle the whelps from birth. The bitch will accept this as perfectly natural and be quite happy to let you share her family. However, never remove the newborn pups from their mother's view, as she will find this distressing.

It is rare, but some bitches object to their pups being taken away from them and placed in a box. If this happens to be your bitch, you must return her pups immediately. Your

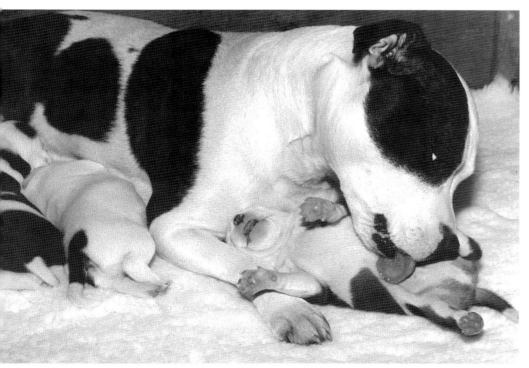

The bitch's natural impulses will take over and she will instinctively clean and feed her young. Photo: Raymond.

main priority is to keep the bitch calm during labour.

Some bitches will pick up their puppies and carry them around. There is little you can do to stop this, except try to persuade her to stay in her box. Rest assured that the imminent arrival of the next pup will soon distract her attention and she will put down the pup she is carrying.

During a lull in proceedings, offer the bitch some warm milk mixed with glucose and then make notes about the pups. You should record their markings, sex and weight, keeping a record in order to verify their growth rate. Electronic scales are the easiest to use, as well as the most accurate. After an initial loss of weight, a healthy pup will put on weight so that his birth weight is doubled within eight days.

While you are weighing the pups, you can check for deformities. Missing limbs will be obvious, but open the mouth to look for less obvious problems, such as a cleft palate (a cleft in the roof of the mouth). This is often associated with a harelip (where the two parts of the upper lips do not join). Such puppies should be set aside for your veterinarian to assess. Serious breeders will note these details for future reference.

BIRTHING COMPLICATIONS

If the bitch has been having strong contractions for an hour, and there is no sign of a pup being engaged in the vulva, call your veterinarian immediately. Do not waste time. It is quite likely that your veterinarian will ask you to bring the bitch to the surgery. You may consider this to be unnecessarily cruel and risky – exposing the bitch to infection and moving her when she is in the middle of labour. However, remember that your veterinary surgery contains all the equipment needed to solve the problem, whereas your home will not. If a Caesarean section is needed, you will be glad to be at the surgery.

CAESAREAN SECTION

Caesarean sections are not the problem they once were, and bitches soon recover from the experience, largely due to recent improvements in anaesthesia. If your bitch needs a Caesarean, decide whether or not you want to assist in resuscitating the whelps, and agree this with your veterinarian beforehand. When you take the bitch to the surgery for the procedure, remember to take along a fleece, a hot water bottle, and a box to bring home the pups.

Be aware that the bitch's behaviour may be a little erratic when she comes round after the anaesthetic. You will need to be very vigilant, as it is not unknown for the bitch to attack her whelps within the first 24 hours. Puppies born by Caesarean section should be given a small feed of glucose and bottle-fed some water, until the bitch is able to resume her duties. The pups should be kept warm using a heat pad until the bitch can gather them close.

Problems sometimes arise because pups born by Caesarean may have trouble feeding from their mother. Being blind, the pups use their sense of smell to locate the mother's teats, and the aroma of milk can be masked by the smell of antiseptic. A little condensed milk smeared on the nipples can overcome this problem. Once the pups are feeding normally, and the bitch's milk is flowing, natural instinct should almost certainly take over.

PRIMARY AND SECONDARY INERTIA

Primary inertia is when the bitch will fail to begin pushing. Normally, this occurs in bitches carrying very small litters (one to two puppies) or in older bitches whelping their first litter.

Secondary inertia is when the bitch gives up pushing, although it is obvious that she has more puppies to deliver. This tends to occur after a prolonged and difficult birth. The bitch becomes tired and the muscles simply stop contracting.

DIFFICULT BIRTHS

Difficult presentations refer to any pup born in an abnormal position, including breech births, a pup with its head bent down, and a pup with its legs bent back underneath itself. In all these circumstances, your veterinarian is your best friend. However, have the recorded time between contractions and births to hand, in order to show him that something is wrong and that you are not just panicking.

STILLBIRTHS

Delivery of a dead puppy is heartbreaking. Normally, stillbirths are preceded by a breech delivery, or a long wait between the birth of one puppy and the next, with the water bag already burst.

Although a puppy may appear inert at birth, every effort should be made to resuscitate him. Strenuous rubbing with a warm towel, pointing the puppy's head downwards, will help to kickstart the puppy's breathing by clearing the lungs. If necessary, breathe into his mouth, rocking him gently.

There is a very good video about whelping produced by the UK Guide Dogs for the Blind Association. It shows how to resuscitate a lifeless puppy by swinging it from above your head to down between your knees. The most important thing to remember is that you must support the head properly between your fingers, never allowing it to swing freely.

Additionally, there are a number of proprietary resuscitation remedies on the market, which are normally applied to the pup's tongue.

AFTERCARE

Deciding that the bitch has finished whelping may not be an easy task for the novice. However, if in doubt, contact your veterinarian, who may give an injection to clear the uterus, depending on the circumstances surrounding the whelping.

Fleecy veterinary-type bedding is warm and comfortable for dam and pups alike. Photo: Raymond.

Once the bitch has delivered all her puppies, she will be very tired. You will soon see her begin to settle. Make sure she goes outside to relieve herself. It is best if you accompany her, in case there is an unexpected late arrival. Take a torch with you if it is dark, as it is possible for a bitch to produce a final pup without the owner's awareness. Do not be surprised if your bitch seems reluctant to leave the whelping box – the bitch may need a collar and lead put on to make her go outside. Before you allow the bitch back in the whelping box, wipe over her body with antiseptic, beginning with the vulva. Also clean her feet and anus.

Clear away the soiled paper and place a piece of fleece or veterinary-type bedding in the whelping box. I tend to use an old piece of fleece for the first few days, so that I can burn it once it has been used (discharge from the bitch stains very badly). Lay the whelps on top of their mother's teats; it is astonishing how quickly they latch on to gain the nourishment they need.

199

The bitch's milk is rich in nutrients and antibodies. Photo: Raymond.

Use an overhead heating lamp if the atmosphere is very cold, as newborns are particularly susceptible to hypothermia. Alternatively, you could use an electrical heating pad, which is placed on the bedding so that the pups can lie directly on it. The pad is covered by a thin layer of sheepskin, and the wire is covered by a thick steel covering, so neither bitch nor puppies will be able to hurt themselves. Another alternative available is the type of heating pad that can be warmed in the microwave, which normally provides heat for approximately 12 hours.

For the first few days you will need to watch the dam and pups very closely. Many bitches seem unaware of the puppies feeding on them, appearing to roll over on top of the pups with scant regard for their safety. By listening to the pups, you will hear if one squeals in protest, and you can quickly check that all are present and correct.

The bitch will have a slight discharge following the birth. For the first 24 hours, this may be green in colour. This will be followed by a red-brown discharge, which will disappear slowly of its own accord. If the discharge becomes black or foul-smelling, consult your veterinarian immediately.

If the bitch begins behaving abnormally (becoming restless, lacking co-ordination, or rejecting her pups) she may be suffering from eclampsia, a condition associated with lack of calcium. Eclampsia is life-threatening and can prove fatal in a very short space of time. You should seek veterinary help immediately. While you wait for your veterinarian, try to persuade the bitch to eat some cheese, as this contains calcium that she can absorb through her stomach. On arrival, your veterinarian will inject the bitch with calcium, and the results are nothing short of miraculous.

THE LACTATING BITCH

Immediately the pups are born, the dam will produce colostrum. This first breast milk is rich in nutrients and antibodies. Following their instincts, the pups will snuggle into their mother, not only to feed, but also to keep warm. As they grow, the pups may take to lying in a heap close to the dam.

The bitch will need a high-quality diet if she is to produce sufficient milk to feed her family. She will need several small meals containing protein and calcium. Natural foods, such as fresh meat, eggs, and fish, provide these abundantly. However, you can also use a proprietary brand of food, making sure it is suitable and following the manufacturer's instructions carefully.

Milk is a popular choice to give to the lactating bitch. Some people believe goat milk to be superior to cow milk, but it is actually lower in fat and protein. If the bitch cannot tolerate milk, she will need a ready supply of water mixed with glucose (1 tablespoonful of glucose to 1 pint of water). If she is unwilling to leave the pups, feed her in the box. However, remember that separating her from the whelps temporarily – taking care to make a great fuss of her – will not only make it easier to change the bedding, but it will accustom her to accepting human handling of her pups as well.

The bitch should be encouraged to exercise for 15 minutes, twice a day. Regular exercise helps to maintain milk production. Remember to wipe the bitch's feet with an antiseptic pad before she re-enters the whelping box, and, if she is wet, see that she is towelled dry.

Be on the alert for mastitis – the bitch's mammary gland will become hard, feel hot to the touch, and she may reject her pups. Mastitis is a bacterial infection, which can be treated with a course of antibiotics supplied by your veterinarian. A little olive oil, gently rubbed over the bitch's teats, will help relieve some discomfort and prevent the teats from becoming chapped and cracked.

As the pups become more mobile, the bitch will self-regulate feeding times, and she may try to join in family activities as before. She should be given free exit from and access to the pups, as she will return at the slightest noise from the pups. During this time, you should encourage the bitch to take longer periods away from her pups, in preparation for weaning (see below).

You will notice that the pups paddle against the mammary glands to encourage the free flow of milk. To avoid the bitch being scratched, the pups should have the tips of their claws cut, very carefully, once a week. Only the very tip is removed. You should not cut the quick (the nail's blood supply and nerves) and cause bleeding. If in any doubt, consult your veterinarian.

PUPPIES

The first few days of the puppies' lives are the most important. Their bodies must adapt to very different conditions from those inside the womb. Failure to adapt may result in so-called fading puppies. It cannot be stressed enough that one of the primary needs of the pups is warmth.

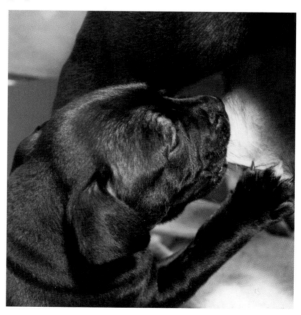

The tips of the pups' claws should be removed to avoid the bitch being scratched when suckling.

The dam will huddle the pups around her to ensure they remain warm. Photo: Raymond.

For the first 21 days, the bitch will supply her pups with all their needs. She will draw them near her for warmth and for food. She will lick them, stimulating them to urinate and to pass faeces. She will move her pups constantly, making sure they remain mobile. All pups twitch and jerk in their sleep for the first month, stretching their legs and backs and sometimes being quite vocal.

FEEDING
For the first 36 hours, the pups will gain colostrum from their mother (see above), which will give the pups some protection against disease through the natural antibodies it contains. To be sure that all the pups get the benefit of this first milk, make sure that the weakest puppies are placed on the teats nearest the bitch's hindquarters, where the supply is more plentiful.

During the first 36-hour period, you should check that the pups are gaining weight, although it is very common for puppies to lose a little weight initially. If the pups do not seem to be thriving, be prepared to take them from the bitch and hand-rear them, but as a last resort only – humans make poor substitute mothers. Powdered colostrum is available in case the bitch does not take to the pups straight away.

If the bitch has produced a large litter, you may be tempted to give the pups extra milk, using one of the proprietary milk feeds on the market. However, unless the pups are very unhappy and do not seem to be feeding well, try to avoid this. The bitch will adjust her supply to demand, and if the pups are being given a milk substitute, she will produce less milk. If the dam is well fed, she will have no difficulty supplying all her pup's milk for the first fortnight.

HAND-FEEDING
If the bitch is unwell, or milk production is insufficient, you may have to supplement with bottle-feeding. Your veterinarian will recommend the best product to you, and most pet shops will supply these products. You will need a couple of feeding bottles with an extremely small teat. Remember to be as hygienic as possible, thoroughly cleaning the bottles after use.

An old-fashioned two-edged glass bottle is easier to use than plastic ones. Position yourself comfortably, holding the puppy so that he in the same position as if he were feeding from the bitch, i.e. leaning with his head tilted upwards, with the bottle teat slanting down. You may notice the puppy paddling in mid-air, like he would do against

The pups' eyes will open at 10 days, and the ears will begin to function around 14 days. Photo: Raymond.

the bitch to stimulate the milk flow.

After the puppy has taken his fill, you will need to stimulate him to go to the toilet if the bitch is not able or willing to do this. Moisten a piece of cotton wool (cotton) with some warm water and flick it quite firmly, backwards and forwards across the anus, until you get a result. To make the puppy urinate, take a large piece of dry cotton wool and flick it carefully at the base of the stomach area – you will soon notice your cotton wool becoming wet!

PUPPY DEVELOPMENT

Stafford pups are born blind and helpless. At about 10 days of age, their eyes will open, initially as little slits, and then fully. At this age, the dam will provide all the pups's care, keeping them fed and clean; it is not advisable to clean the pups yourself without great care. A healthy puppy will smell clean, with traces of milk. He will be warm, round, and firm to the touch. Held in the palm of your hand, he will lay contentedly, usually with his tongue hanging out.

At approximately 14 days of age, the pups' ear canals will open, and the pups will be able to hear as you talk. They will begin to associate your voice with the human smell.

PARASITE CONTROL

Pups can be wormed from two-and-a-half weeks of age onwards. Buy a suitable preparation from your veterinarian and follow the instructions precisely. You should worm the mother at the same time, as well as any other dogs in the household. Treat the other dogs against fleas, but not the lactating bitch.

WEANING

If you are feeding the dam in the bed, or giving her the occasional drink of milk, the pups will soon start taking an interest. They may try to lick the dish, or, more likely, paddle into it. The bitch may encourage them. Now is the time to try a very little solid food.

Weaning should begin with some milky baby rice and a very small amount of raw, minced beef. Weaning is a messy business and should not be rushed. Let the bitch tidy up the remains so that she continues to clean her pups. However, as soon as solid food is acceptable, let the bitch leave the pups for a short while (e.g. to go out to relieve herself) and try giving the pups a meal before the bitch settles down with them.

At the start of weaning, the pups will continue to feed from their dam to supplement their diet.

By the time the pups are four weeks of age, they should be well on the way to feeding on mainly solid food, relying on their mother for the odd milk feed during the day and through the night.

While the pups are being weaned, they will become more active. You will need to restrict their ability to escape the whelping box, without interference to the dam. The pups will need a sleeping area and a playing area. By using the fleece bedding only in the sleeping area, and by laying newspaper in the play area, clean habits can be encouraged. Pups soon learn not to soil the beds. The bitch will now be regulating the number of feeds she will allow the pups and she should be provided with a sleeping bed outside the box. This way, she can hear her pups and go to them if needed, but they cannot get to her.

At four to five weeks of age, the pups should be eating four solid meals a day. When the bitch goes out to relieve herself first thing in the morning, feed a milky gruel and change the bedding. Midday meals are usually a high-quality mince or one of the proprietary foods. Choose one the pups find palatable. The third meal of the day can comprise scrambled egg, with cheese or fish mashed into it (remember to remove all the bones from the fish). The final, fourth meal should be milky – rice pudding is a good choice. As the pups grow, increase the quantity of their food and introduce a fine puppy meal, until, gradually, the bitch stops feeding her pups.

As weaning progresses, the dam will produce less milk. Once the pups have been weaned fully, the dam should cease milk production. Make sure that she is taking sufficient exercise for this to happen. You may need to decrease her liquid intake, also. If she continues to produce milk, your veterinarian can supply some medication to ease the problem.

PLAY
Once the pups are weaned, the bitch's behaviour towards them will change. She will start to play quite roughly, teaching her pups how to defend themselves. Providing a few toys for the pups will supply some stimulation, and, by having a radio or television playing in the background, the pups will be used to all the noises of an ordinary household before they go to their new owners.

FINDING NEW HOMES
Deciding on new owners for the pups is the final, most important part of rearing a litter. If you have used a well-known stud dog, whose owner is active in the breed, he or she will be able to help you.

Otherwise, you could try advertising the pups in a breed club publication (e.g. a monthly newsletter or a show catalogue), one of the weekly dog papers, or your local newspaper.

The end result: a happy mum, and a litter of healthy, happy pups. Photo: Raymond.

When people approach you, do not be afraid to quiz them. The pups depend on your ability to choose good homes. Make sure any prospective owners understand the character of the Stafford, and be sure they can manage a dog of this breed. Choosing the wrong owner means your puppy's life will be miserable, and it can also bring the breed into disrepute.

When you transfer ownership of the puppies, supply the new owners with a few days' worth of food and advice about when they require worming next, etc. Keep in touch and give advice whenever you can.

Finally, you should be prepared to take back your puppies if necessary. The fate of your puppies is your responsibility throughout their lives.

11 *SHOWING YOUR STAFFORD*

Dog showing has received something of a mixed press over the years, but there is no doubting the popularity of this activity. Crufts, which is broadcast on UK television every year, is one of the most high profile events, but dog shows and many other dog-related activities occupy enthusiasts throughout the year and all over the world. Large dog shows are held every weekend and several on weekdays. However, the world of dog shows remains a mystery to many, so what is it that attracts people to this hobby?

For many, dog showing is a way of showing off their much-loved pet in front of an audience of like-minded people. Although highly competitive, there is a great deal of camaraderie at dog shows. Most exhibitors make lifelong friends, even among rivals, and a shared interest in dogs brings people from all walks of life into contact with each other. Furthermore, dog shows are the ideal place in which to meet breed experts and dog fanciers from many other countries.

However, for the serious breeder, dog shows are on another level. While a serious breeder will enjoy a show for the same reason as a less competitive pet owner, there is the added thrill of showing a dog you have bred yourself. Breeders can spend many years in their pursuit of the perfect dog, trying to 'create' a dog that is as close as possible to the ideal laid out in the Breed Standard (a 'blueprint' of the perfect dog). Showing is a way for breeders to have the fruits of their labour assessed by their peers and other experts. Exhibiting such a dog provides a sense of excitement that today might be the winning day.

Staffords are among the most popular of breeds, and, as a result, entries at all kinds of dog show are extremely high – usually the highest among all the Terriers. Many would-be exhibitors have heard horror stories about bureaucratic breed clubs and high-powered, elitist breeders, but the Stafford fraternity is renowned for welcoming newcomers to its ranks. It is possible for an absolute beginner (provided his animal is good enough) to win all the major awards.

TYPES OF SHOW

There are many types of show, which can be very confusing for the novice exhibitor. Dog shows are run by general canine societies (clubs catering for many, if not all, breeds of dog) or by breed clubs (those specialising in one breed of dog).

GENERAL NOTES ON CLASSES

Any show affiliated to a breed club or the country's national kennel club will be subject to those clubs rules. So, for example, any dog under 6 months will be barred from entering a show affiliated to the UK Kennel Club.

These sorts of details, along with instructions for entering shows, can be found in the show schedule.

Every show has a number of different classes in which dogs compete. These vary between shows, but common classes include:
- **Breed classes:** where dogs from the same breed compete against each other
- **Group classes:** where dogs from one classified group are judged against each other (e.g. all the Terriers).
- **Any variety classes:** where dogs from any breed or group are judged against each other.
- **Age-restricted classes:** where, as the name suggests, dogs of a similar age compete against each other. For example, Minor Puppy (for puppies aged between 6 and 9 months), Puppy (from 6 to 12 months), Junior (6 to 18 months), Special Yearling (for dogs up to 24 months), and Veteran (older dogs). The age of eligibility for these classes varies between shows and will

be listed under 'Definition of Classes' in the show schedule. For example, in some countries outside the UK, special classes are scheduled for what is called Baby Puppies (i.e. 3 to 6 months of age).

UK SHOWS

All shows are divided into two main types: general canine, which are those run by a club or society catering for many breeds or Groups (e.g. Terriers, Toys, etc.); and breed clubs, which cater only for one breed (Staffordshire Bull Terriers in our case).

There are four types of show in the UK.

Exemption shows: these are the most straightforward shows available in the UK. Exemption shows are normally held in conjunction with a local fair, fete, or fundraising event. Entries are taken on the day, and, although there will be some classes for pedigree dogs, there will be other, fun classes open to mixed breeds and mongrels (e.g. the dog with the waggiest tail, or the dog the judge would most like to take home).

Limited shows: these shows are, as the name suggests, open only to members of the club running the show. There is also a limit preventing dogs with more than a certain number of wins from entering. Consequently, competition may be less fierce, and, therefore, these shows offer the best starting point for the novice. To enter a limited show, you will need to join the club hosting the show, which you can do at the same time as entering your dog.

Open shows: these shows are open to all, and you may come up against dogs that are already Champions.

The organisation of shows will vary slightly according to the country you are competing in.

Championship shows: where dogs have the opportunity to achieve Championship status.

These are the largest, most prestigious shows, and entrants will face a great deal of stiff competition.

If the show is run by a general canine society, it will schedule classes for many breeds, but, if it is run by a breed club, there will be classes for that breed and no other. As the name suggests, it is wins at this type of show that qualify a dog to become a Champion. In the Open class, Champions compete against non-Champions.

The biggest Championship show in the UK is Crufts, and, to enter, an animal must qualify. Details of the qualification requirements can be found in the show schedule.

SHOWS IN OTHER COUNTRIES

Each country will run Championship shows under the rules of that country's kennel club. In many countries, there are few dog shows other than Championship shows. Those there are tend to provide little in the way of serious competitive experience, but they are good practice for a youngster.

The kennel club and Stafford breed clubs of each country will provide details about these shows.

MAKING A CHAMPION

The rules governing the making of a show Champion vary between countries. Your national kennel club will be able to provide you with the details appropriate for your own country, and some are outlined below.

AMERICA

In the US, a Champion is made when a dog wins 15 points under three different judges. The 15 points must include two 'majors' (three-, four-, or five-point awards) given by different judges.

To win these points, a dog must be declared Winner of its respective sex. Points are decided according to the number of dogs of the same sex competing. The point count is revised annually, and the relevant rules are printed on the show catalogue.

Becoming Best of Winners, Best of Breed, or finally winning the Group, and even Best in Show, can all add to the points tally. There is a separate Champions class, so that Champions compete only for Best of Breed against non-Champions.

In the US, there are two types of show:
- **Match shows:** these are informal shows. Winners of classes at these shows take away prestige and the satisfaction of winning, but it is not possible to make a Champion out of your dog at these shows.
- **Licensed shows:** where points are on offer to make your dog into a Champion. As a result, these shows are frequently called 'point' shows.

There are two types of Licensed show – Specialty shows (which are restricted to one breed, e.g. the Staffordshire Bull Terrier) and All-breed or Group shows (which may schedule classes for Staffords).

In the US, the largest, most prestigious show is Westminster (the equivalent of Crufts in the UK).

AUSTRALIA

As in many other countries, Champions are made up on a points system. A dog must win four Challenge Certificates (CCs) under four different judges, with a total of 100 points. At least one of these CCs must be won when the dog is more than 12 months of age. A dog can become a Grand Champion by winning a total of 1,000 points.

There is a basic points score for winning the CC plus one point for every animal, of the same sex, beaten. Winning Best of Breed adds more to the total, according to the number of the opposite sex beaten. Winning the Group adds even more points to the total, with 25 points being the maximum a dog can take away from any one show.

209

Apart from Championship shows, there are parade shows, which are roughly equivalent to UK Limited shows. Champions cannot compete, and any wins here do not count towards a Championship.

Each state in Australia may hold one Royal show a year, and the most prestigious is the Sydney Royal. There are two exceptions – Tasmania holds two a year (Launceston and Hobart), as does Queensland (Toowoomba and Brisbane). Royal shows are Championship shows, and, although they may seem rather grand affairs, just as with Crufts, the prize won is the same as at any other Championship show. Unlike Crufts, however, no qualification is necessary. There is no separate class for Champions.

BRITAIN

In the UK, a dog is made a Champion when he or she wins three Challenge Certificates under three different judges, with at least one of those CCs won when the dog is more than 12 months of age.

Challenge Certificates are available at Championship shows only. Each breed has two CCs on offer, one for Best Dog and one for Best Bitch.

EIRE

As in many other countries outside the UK, a dog is made up to a Champion on a points system in Ireland. The Champion award is called a Green Star. To become a Champion, a dog must win 40 Green Star points.

In the UK, three Challenge Certificates are required to make up a Champion. Pictured: Ch. Valglo Cassanova At Crosslands.

Within those 40 points, a dog must win four 'majors', which may be calculated as follows: four 5-point Green Stars under four different judges; two 5-point awards and one Green Star under three different judges; three 5-point Green Stars and one Group win under four different judges.

Each group is allocated a Green Star index, and this figure indicates the number of dogs/bitches that must be present and exhibiting in order for the Green Star winner to receive a 5-point Green Star. This index figure is calculated and may be amended annually.

GERMANY

There are two Champion titles in Germany, one awarded by the breed clubs and one by the German Kennel Club – called the VDH. There are two official clubs for Staffords: the Gesellschaft der Bullterrierfreunde e.V and the Deutscher Club for Bullterrier e.V.

To become a Champion under the rules of the German Kennel Club the dog must win a total of four CACs under at least three different judges and between the first and the last there must be a period of one year and one day.

To win the CAC, a dog must win the Open Class or the Championship Class with an 'Excellent' qualification. Where there are entrants in both the Open and Champion Classes, two CACs are awarded.

It should be noted that because the minimum age of entry into an Open Class is 15 months, and a dog cannot become a Champion in Germany untill the age of 27 months and one day.

As in other European countries there is an award of Youth (or Junior) Champion. The dog must win the Youth Class – restricted to dogs of 9 to 18 months of age and be graded excellent.

The dog is then given a Youth CAC and the number required to make the dog a Youth Champion varies from club to club.

Reserve CACs are awarded, but, as in the UK, these do not count towards a Championship, no matter how many are won. The nearest award in the UK to the Youth Championship is the Junior Warrant. This is given on a points system which must be won at a combination of Open and Championship Shows while the dog is between 6-18 months of age.

The points are awarded according to the number of animals competing. The award allows the dog to have JW after its name and an entry into the Kennel Club Stud Book, although there is no official title of 'Junior Champion'.

NEW ZEALAND

To become a Champion, a dog must win eight Challenge Certificates under at least five different judges, with at least one CC achieved after the dog has passed 12 months of age. Each CC is worth one point. There is no separate class for Champions.

SOUTH AFRICA

In South Africa, there are many Open shows, offering good practice for novice exhibitors and judges. These shows often schedule Baby Puppy classes, for dogs between four and six months of age.

To become a Champion, a dog must win five CC points. If a dog wins his CC from an entry of less than 10 exhibits of the same sex, he will win a 1-point CC. If the entry is from more than 10 dogs of the same sex, the CC will be worth 2 points.

Once a dog has achieved Champion status, he cannot compete for further CCs. Instead, there is a separate Champion class. However, Champions will compete against CC winners for the titles of Best of Breed and Reserve Best of Breed.

The most well known of the South African Championship shows is Goldfields, held in its own show ground close to Johannesburg. However, Staffords are so popular in South Africa that the country boasts seven breed clubs, and all of these hold Championship shows as well.

CHAMPIONS IN EUROPE
European countries run dog shows under their own rules, but some shows are held under the rules of the FCI (Fédération Cynologique Internationale or World Canine Organisation), notably International Championship Shows.

At most European shows, each dog is graded according to its quality as gauged against the Breed Standard. This occurs during each class and is accompanied by a written critique. When every dog in the class has been examined, graded, and a critique has been written, the entire class returns and the steward tells the exhibitors which dogs received the highest grade. Only these dogs are asked to remain in the ring, to be compared with each other – as in the UK – and placed in order of merit.

Challenge Certificates are awarded at the end of judging but before the Best of Breed award is made. At national shows, these certificates are called CACs. In some countries, Champions will compete against non-Champions, while, in others, Champions will compete only against non-Champions for the Best of Breed award.

A third possibility is where Champions and non-Champions compete together in the Open class. In this case, however, once the judge has placed the dogs in order of merit, if the dog standing first is already a Champion, the CC will awarded to the highest placed non-Champion in the line-up. All European countries vary slightly in their rules for gaining Championship status.

At international shows, CACIBs are given. These are awarded after the main breed judging is completed. To be eligible for

competition, an animal must be more than 15 months of age and have won either the CC or the Champion quality award in the breed judging. Winning a CACIB is a step towards becoming an International Champion. Veteran dogs and dogs who are already International Champions are not eligible.

The biggest shows run by the FCI are the World shows. These rotate annually, with a committee visiting countries that wish to host the event.

Of course, it is not always possible for dogs from every country to attend, because of quarantine restrictions, etc., so, in many ways, the term 'World show' is something of a misnomer.

INTERNATIONAL CHAMPIONS
International Champions are dogs who have become Champions in more than one country. There is, for example, a Stafford – Ch. Rolona's Domino von Fraud – who is a Champion in the US, Mexico, Venezuela, Cuba, Guatemala, Salvador, Honduras, Nicaragua, and a few more countries. Most Staffords are campaigned only in one or two countries, however, and so this multi-Champion title is not sought-after by many owners.

GETTING STARTED
Having done the research, and made the decision to show your dog, the process of getting started may seem more than a little daunting. However, you can help matters by starting your exhibition career slowly, taking a step at a time.

FINDING SHOWS
By joining a breed club, you will be notified of all the latest developments affecting your breed, as well as given details about forthcoming shows. In some countries, there may be no clubs specifically for Staffords, and

a general terrier club will look after the breed's interests instead. However, in most countries where a significant number of Staffords have been registered, there will be at least one club catering especially for the breed. Addresses of club secretaries will be available from the national kennel club.

In addition, you can contact your national kennel club for a show list, or you could buy one of the weekly or monthly dog papers, which carry advertisements for shows. Remember that, as entries for some shows close well in advance of the show date, you will need to be organised if you wish to enter. Write or telephone the show secretary to ask for a schedule, which will arrive with an entry form. The form should be completed with care, and, if you are uncertain about anything, contact the show secretary or someone with experience of showing dogs. It is better to complete the entry form correctly first time, as it may not be possible to alter something on the day.

CHOOSING YOUR FIRST SHOW

If you have never competed in a dog show, you should try a few lesser shows (e.g. Limited or Open shows). Your dog might win many prizes at the lower level, but never win at Championship shows. Some regard this as failure, while other (more sensible) fanciers have enormous fun, winning numerous prize cards and rosettes without the pressure that accompanies large events.

When you enter your first 'serious' show, try not to enter too many classes – you and your dog will be exhausted. In some countries, there is a restriction on the number of classes each exhibit can enter.

ENTRY FEES

Entry fees for Championship shows are normally higher than those of any other type of show, reflecting the costs involved in staging the event.

Observe experienced handlers in the show ring to see how they present their dogs.

RING TRAINING

Showing Staffords is highly competitive. Therefore, it is very important that you give your dog the best possible chance by presenting him in as good a light as possible. This will not make a truly inferior dog into an outstanding one, but a mediocre dog, looking at his very best, might beat an otherwise superior dog that is out of condition or being poorly handled.

It is a very good idea to visit some shows as a spectator before entering as an exhibitor. By watching more experienced handlers show their Staffords, you will be able to see how correct handling can show off a dog to his best advantage.

Ideally, training should start when your puppy is very small. The earlier he is taught to perform in a show ring, the greater his chances of success.

If he has come from a good breeder, he may have some preliminary experience. Unlike most breeds, the Stafford is shown presenting his face to the judge; almost all

213

Start them young: place your pup's legs four-square and get him used to this position with short, frequent show-training sessions.

other breeds are shown presented sideways.

Once your pup has received all his injections and he can mix with other dogs, you should enrol him at ring-training classes. Your breed club will probably hold regular classes, and there may be handling classes for all breeds in your locality.

These all-breed classes can be very good, especially for the youngster, as they help with socialisation enormously. However, if any of the other dogs are aggressive, stop going – you do not want your pup to have a bad experience at this young age.

Your instructor will teach you and your puppy everything you need to know to perform in the show ring, but, by practising at home, you can help things along. However, make sure you do not train bad habits to your dog – if in doubt, show your instructor what you are doing so that he can correct you if necessary.

STANDING AND STACKING
Stacking is when the dog is placed into position manually, with the handler placing each foot in the correct position individually.

In the past, Staffords were shown free on a lead, and very few were stacked. Many people would prefer the old practice, but the large entries in each class leaves little room for manoeuvre in the ring, so it is necessary for you to stack your dog.

There are two ways you can stand your dog – by stacking (where you place him in the correct position), or by teaching him to stand correctly by himself (freestanding).

Many handlers use a method halfway between stacking and freestanding, stacking the dog initially and then standing back, leaving the dog free on the lead in the stacked position.

Alternatively, the handler might crouch beside the dog, stack him, and then, holding the lead above the dog's head in one hand, use the other hand (containing a tidbit) to attract the dog's attention, so that his ears are shown to best advantage.

Using a tidbit to keep your dog's attention will help enormously. However, avoid holding the tidbit above your dog's head as this will cause him to look up too far, creating a dip in his back.

Begin your puppy's training by standing him on all four legs and asking him to stand still for a few seconds. Practise this repeatedly, extending the time he must remain still. It is a good idea for your pup to practise standing on a table, which should have a non-slip surface. Your pup will concentrate more when he is away from distractions on the floor. It is also easier for you to handle him at this level. Teaching your pup to stand on a table and be handled also has advantages beyond the show ring, as he will be more likely to stand still at the veterinary surgery and during grooming. After he has learned to stand still on the table, and once he is a little bigger, you can transfer the standing lesson to the floor.

You will be taught how to stack (stand) your dog correctly at ring-training classes, but you can encourage him into the correct position at a very early age.

- Place one hand between your pup's front legs and the other between his rear legs.
- Lift him an inch (2.5 cms) from the ground, and then place him down again gently.
- Your pup should now be standing in the correct position – with his four legs parallel, creating a rectangular shape. Each leg should appear to drop straight from the shoulder or hip, and not at an angle. Do not let your pup's front legs stand back from his shoulders – this will push his sternum forward, creating an ugly shape.
- Do not stretch the pup's body. Try to keep his legs positioned in a square shape, so that his topline (back) is level, not dipped or arched.
- Your pup's head should be held low, parallel to the floor, with his eyes facing directly forward. The Stafford has a rather short neck, so you should never stretch your pup's neck with your lead. Instead, allow his head and neck to be held in an alert, but relaxed manner.

- Do not practise for too long and always finish on a positive note, i.e. when the dog has performed his task correctly.

As a novice exhibitor, you may be uncertain about the view presented to the judge when your dog is stacked. Ask a knowledgeable friend to give his opinion or use the old trick of a mirror. Stand your dog in front of a mirror and see what differences are made to his overall appearance if, for example, you move his back foot slightly, or you widen his front legs a little, etc.

EXAMINING
When your dog is in the ring, the judge will want to examine him. It is vital that your pup is properly socialised so that he will accept the judge's handling.
- While you teach your puppy to stand, get him into the habit of being examined.
- Talking to him gently, to reassure him, run your hands gently over his body.
- Get a friend to go over him in the same fashion, so that your pup becomes used to strangers touching him all over.
- Make sure your pup is handled on his head, down his neck, across his shoulders and down his legs.
- Squeeze his hind legs, pick up a foot and gently squeeze it, and run your hands along both sides of the pup's ribs to his waist.
- Do not forget to measure your puppy's tail, which should come down to his hock.

Two important – and sometimes difficult – areas to examine, are the 'top and tail'. All dogs will have their mouths examined by the judge, and all male dogs must be examined to ensure they have two, fully descended testicles. Unless a dog is accustomed to being handled around the mouth and genitalia, he will undoubtedly wriggle away.

Initially, stack your pup on a table, where you can place him in the required position and encourage him to stay.

Once he stacks well on a table, you can move him to the ground.

With practice, your dog will no longer need to be held, and the correct position will come naturally to him.

Ask a friend to observe how you stack your Stafford, or practise in front of a mirror to see if the dog's position can be improved.

SHOW EXAMINATION

It is important to accustom your dog to being examined all over to prepare him for being assessed by a judge (or vet) when he is older.

Accustom your puppy to having his mouth and teeth checked from an early age.

Dogs can be sensitive about having their ears touched, but early training can prevent this.

Dogs can have tickly toes too! Touching the feet should always be followed with a tasty treat.

To look at a dog's mouth, the judge will lift the top and bottom lips, looking first at the front and then at both sides. You should aim to teach your puppy to accept this as early as possible (it also has advantages for teeth care). However, your pup's mouth may be very sore around the time he loses his milk teeth, and, if this seems to be the case, leave his mouth alone until it is no longer sore.

Never get involved in a struggle to look in a young animal's mouth, and, when things go smoothly, remember to praise your pup effusively. Some people like to use a word (e.g. "Teeth") before the mouth is examined, so that the dog knows what is expected of him and behaves accordingly. When you are training your puppy, make sure that anyone examining the pup's mouth will be gentle. If you hear a judge has a reputation for being heavy-handed, do not take your youngster under him or her. Do not practise for too long and always finish on a positive note, i.e. when the dog has performed his task correctly.

MOVING
You should have taught your young puppy to walk on a lead correctly (see Chapter Five). However, in the show ring he will need to walk slightly differently – at your side, but slightly apart. The idea is to present your dog without attracting too much attention to yourself. As a tip, where there is a rubber mat on the floor (there will be at most indoor shows), make sure your dog is walking on the mat and you are just off it. It is best to hold your dog's lead in your left hand.

It is important you discover the correct pace for your dog. Staffords have a variety of

A lively pace is required to show off your dog's powerful drive.

walks. If you walk very slowly, you may find your dog 'poddling', rolling along like a lazy sailor. As you quicken your pace, his movement should become snappier, with more drive from behind. At optimum pace, a Stafford should walk beautifully, driving from behind. There will be very little lift of his front feet and his rear legs will be parallel with the front, so that anyone looking from behind will see a clear tunnel between the dog's legs. If you go faster than this, the rear legs will close inwards and the dog will prepare to run. It is worth getting a friend to stand behind you when you start walking. Start slowly and build up your pace. Your friend can shout when you and the dog hit the correct speed. After practice, you will be able to feel when you and your dog are moving in harmony at the right speed.

Some Staffords take off far too quickly, before their owners get a chance to achieve the correct speed. You can help to overcome this by continuing training while your dog is out on a walk. During the walk, keep a sedate pace and change direction frequently. Initially, your dog may try to pull you after him, or he will struggle to catch up with you. Eventually, however, he will learn to watch you, trying to keep to your side so he does not have too much ground to make up if you change direction again.

If your Stafford is 'crabbing' (walking with his hind legs to one side of the front), try walking him on your opposite side for a while. If he is usually on your right, put him on your left. Again, the element of surprise can achieve remarkable results.

Normally, Staffords are asked to walk straight up the ring and back again, possibly repeating this for a second time so that the judge may go to the side of the ring to see the dog from the side. Make sure your dog is on the side nearest the judge – it is your dog's legs the judge wants to see, not yours! Be aware that any imperfections in your dog's build or gait will be very obvious when the judge sees a side view of your dog on the move.

Sometimes, a judge may ask the dogs to walk in a triangle (to save time if he or she has a large entry). To walk in a triangle correctly, you should walk at an angle away from the judge, go across the ring to the next corner, and return at an angle to where you started. Again, you must be careful that your dog is on the side nearest the judge at all times.

GROOMING AND APPEARANCE
One of the big advantages to owning a Stafford as a pet is that the breed requires little in the way of coat care. Equally, this is a big advantage in showing the breed. Most Stafford owners do not know how lucky they are compared with those who show long-coated breeds.

However, appearance is everything in the show ring, and it is not limited to coat care. Physical fitness and a good outline are of great importance for the Stafford. Your Stafford will do well in the show ring if he has a tucked-in waist, firm muscles (especially in the hindquarters), and a gleaming coat. To achieve these qualities, your Stafford will require a great deal of dedication from you – looking fit, with a gleaming coat, begins weeks (if not months) before you get to the show ring. You will need to keep him free from parasites (see Chapter Twelve), feed him high-quality food (see Chapter Six), and give him plenty of exercise throughout his life.

FEEDING AND EXERCISE
Introducing some cod-liver-oil pills, or the odd tin of oily fish, will help to add gloss to your Stafford's coat, although a lovely sheen should be already present if your dog is well cared for and healthy. Balancing the amount of food against the level of exercise is the secret to producing a good body outline.

A good-quality feeding and exercise regime are essential for a healthy coat and physique.

Overfeeding combined with lack of exercise will produce a fat dog with no waist and soft, floppy muscle tone. Too little food will produce a slim dog without vitality. Achieving the right balance will produce a trim dog glowing with health.

Exercise should be tailored to each individual dog, as some require more than others. You should remember that too much exercise will cause as much damage as too little, especially when your Stafford is young. For the first six months, your puppy should go for short, regular walks. The emphasis should be on giving him as many new experiences as possible, rather than distance. From six months of age onwards, the distance may be increased.

Once your Stafford nears adulthood, he should receive lots of strenuous exercise, taking care you feed him to match (see Chapter Six). Your Stafford will enjoy a five-mile walk enormously, but he will gain just as much benefit from 20 minutes of exercise running after a ball.

I knew a Stafford who went by car the 10 minutes to the local park, where his master sat on a bench, smoked a cigarette, and threw a ball for 20 minutes or so – in fact, until his arm ached. Then, dog and master got back in the car and drove home. This dog was as hard as nails!

GROOMING

As mentioned above, Staffordshire Bull Terriers do not require a great deal of coat care – a healthy lifestyle being the main factor contributing to a beautiful sheen. However, there are a number of grooming practices you should carry out in the weeks leading up to a show.

COAT CARE

You should ensure that your Stafford's coat is clean and dust-free for the judge to touch. If your Stafford has some white in his coat, it is almost certain that he will need bathing before a show.

Bathing your dog on a regular basis is not recommended, but shampoos designed for frequent bathing, which will not damage the natural oils in your dog's coat, are now available.

Many owners prefer to bathe their dogs a few days before a show, giving the coat time to 'settle down'. This is particularly advisable if your dog has a black coat. After a bath, dogs produce dandruff, which is very unsightly on a dark coat.

During the summer, bathing your Stafford in a tin bath (tub) in the garden is fine. During the winter, however, it is best to bathe your dog indoors.

Filling and emptying a tin bath is time-consuming, hard work. Lifting the dog into your own bath is far better. Special dog baths are available, but these are very expensive. I find using my shower is the simplest and most efficient way to bathe my own Staffords.

Whatever method you adopt, make sure you have all your supplies (e.g. shampoo, towels, etc.) in place before you start.

- Test the water temperature carefully before immersing your dog.
- Place a rubber mat or towel on any surface that is slippery or that you do not want to get scratched, particularly acrylic surfaces.
- Once you have made all your preparations, wet your dog all over and apply a dog shampoo.
- Be careful to avoid getting shampoo in the eyes and try to keep water out of the ears.
- Staffords do not develop ear trouble very often, but this is the ideal opportunity to check for excess wax or mites. The best test is with your nose – dirty ears smell very mousy and stale.
- If you think the ears need cleaning, do not be tempted to use cotton buds; seek veterinary assistance.
- Having lathered your dog all over, be sure to rinse away all the foam.
- Thorough rinsing is essential.
- When you have finished, your dog's first instinct will be to shake himself vigorously. A towel held roof-like above him will keep most of the droplets contained.
- Towel-dry him thoroughly, and brush his coat with a stiff brush or rubber glove to remove any loose hair.
- A hand massage will help to bring out the oils in the coat and a stiff brush will remove most dead hair.
- Chalking, dyeing, or using any substance that alters the appearance of a dog's coat is forbidden in most countries, and could result in disqualification.

TRIMMING

Many owners trim the hair on the underneath and sides of the tail, making sure the tail tapers to a fine point at the end. This produces the whippy tail described in the Standard, giving the dog a clean, workmanlike appearance.

To trim the tail you should use scissors or a razor. This procedure is best done a few days before a show. Some Staffords become very proud of their tails after trimming, holding them too high, or, to use a dog fraternity term, 'gay'.

In the past, fanciers have trimmed whiskers from the Stafford's foreface, believing it made for a cleaner outline. This is rarely, if ever, done today.

NAILS

Staffords do not have their dewclaws removed, but you should check that they are short and neat, along with the toenails.

Adequate exercise on hard surfaces will ensure that your Stafford's nails remain short without human interference. However, if the nails need clipping, you can use a pair of clippers designed for the task. Make sure you avoid cutting the quick (the nail's blood supply and nerves); this is painful for the dog and cuts in this area bleed profusely. Alternatively, the nails can be filed.

TEETH

When the judge examines your dog's mouth, you do not want to be let down by poor dental hygiene. You should ensure that your dog's teeth are cleaned regularly (see Chapter Four).

ACCESSORIES

Most Staffords wear a leather collar and lead when they are exhibited, with many owners choosing a traditional-style collar with some additional furnishings (e.g. the Staffordshire knot in brass or silver).

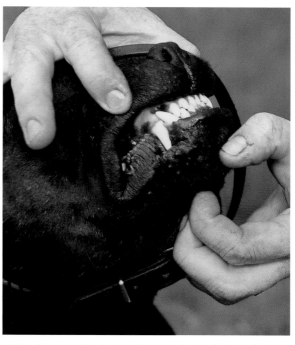

Check your dog's teeth are gleaming before the show.

At one time, these collars were broad and very ornate, but today's fashion is for narrower, less ornate collars.

However, yesterday's exhibitors were thinking about far more than the collar's style. For example, a broad collar can disguise an overly long neck, while a narrow collar will elongate a neck that appears stuffy and short.

The collar and lead may be of any colour, with brown and black predominating at present (most people use black for a dark-brindled dog, for example).

Make sure your leather lead is soft and can be screwed up in your hand with ease. You do not want yards of lead dangling untidily when you are showing your dog.

Never try to use a chain or half-chain lead, as these are cumbersome and will hurt your hands. Kennel Club rules demand the dog is kept on a lead throughout the show, except in Obedience competition.

SHOW PREPARATIONS

CLOTHES

What you wear is an important consideration. You must be dressed comfortably, sensibly, and smartly. You will be stretching up and down, so men should avoid trousers (pants) with a tendency to slip down, and women should avoid short skirts. If the show will be held outdoors, make sure you are covered for every eventuality of the weather, which includes sun protection as well as a raincoat and waterproof boots. The chief concern at open-air shows is footwear – even if the weather is glorious, the ground can be treacherous underfoot if there has been rain on the days before the show.

Another consideration is the colour of your clothes. Wearing black trousers when showing a black dog will result in the dog's outline sinking into the background. However, red, green or fawn trousers will throw his silhouette into relief.

If you use tidbits to keep your dog's attention, try to wear something with pockets. Alternatively, you could buy a small purse that clips around your waist.

EQUIPMENT

One essential piece of equipment is the show clip – the means by which you fix your ring number on to yourself – and show rules stipulate that every exhibitor must display his ring number. You will find your dog's ring number by reference to your exhibitor's passes in a large show, or by looking in the catalogue at smaller or breed club shows. It will be helpful to have the schedule with you, to remind you of the exact location and name of the venue. At larger shows you will receive an exhibitor's pass and a removal order. It should be necessary for you to show the removal order to security when you leave the show.

For the dog, you will need to take a show cage. These are collapsible and fit into the wooden benches supplied at larger shows. In the UK, the size of the bench for Staffords accommodates a cage measuring 24 inches wide. Most breed club and non-Championship shows provide no benching, and you will need a cage in which to leave the dog during the day. These cages are made of metal and are collapsible for easy carriage. If in doubt, check the show schedule, as this will tell you (usually on the front cover) whether or not the show is benched. It is a good idea to take a sheet to cover the cage, or to buy a special cage cover. This will be useful if there is a cold wind blowing or if there are distractions that could deny your dog proper rest.

As well as a cage, you will need to take some tidbits, if you use them, and a water bowl. Access to water should be provided, but there is no reason why you cannot take your own, if you prefer. Take a towel in case of rain, as well as a wet flannel, which will be useful if the ground is dusty or muddy. A Stafford's nails should be black, and a layer of dry mud could make them look teak-coloured and badly pigmented. Most important of all, take some bags to clear up your dog's mess. Nothing upsets the general public more than having their favourite pathways fouled by dogs, and dog fouling has caused more than one venue to refuse future dog shows.

THE DAY OF THE SHOW

It is a good idea to arrive early. This will give you a chance to look around and to recover from the journey. First of all, you should go to your bench and make your dog comfortable. If you find two numbers on your bench, one will be your ring number, intended for you to wear in the ring; the other being the number that signifies your bench. If there is only one number on the bench, you will be given your ring number when you go to your class. Check your dog's

Watch some classes to glean some tips on how the judge is organising the ring.

details have been entered in the show catalogue correctly, and that you have been entered into the right class. If you have any queries, see the show manager immediately.

Having settled your dog and made sure everything is in order, it is a very good idea to watch some of the other classes being judged (provided, of course, that yours is not the first class). This will give you some idea about how the judge is organising the ring. However, make sure you do not get too caught up in events – it is your responsibility to get your dog to his class in time, and if you miss the class, there is no redress.

There are a multitude of rules and regulations governing dog shows, and, as a newcomer, you cannot possibly know them all. Most are the responsibility of the show manager, but a few will be yours. If in doubt, ask the steward or the show manager. As well

as taking responsibility to get your dog to his class on time, you are also responsible for clearing up your dog's mess, and there are a number of things you must not do. These include impeding other exhibitors and double handling (i.e. you must not let your family stand outside the ring to attract the dog's attention). You must do as the steward asks you, as he in turn will be taking his instructions from the judge.

IN THE RING

When you enter the ring, everyone will stand in a circle. The steward will confirm your number or give you your number to put on. Once the judge is ready to begin the class, everyone will stack their dog and wait for the judge's instructions. The judge will take some time going round the ring and looking at all the dogs. He will repeat this by going behind all the dogs to get a clear view of their rear ends. At this stage, most handlers go to the front of their dogs, so they do not impede the judge's view. This initial examination is extremely important, and most judges will have an idea of the dogs in which they are most interested after this first look.

Following the initial assessment, the judge will examine each dog individually. When you first begin showing it is best to give others the chance to go first. This gives you an opportunity to see what will be expected from you. While you wait, do not be tempted to keep your dog stock-still – he will become bored and more difficult to manage. Let him relax and look at his surroundings. However, make sure he does not present himself badly when doing so (see below).

Just before your turn, you will, in most cases, be asked to stack your dog ready for the judge. There may be a special piece of mat set aside for this purpose; if not, the steward will indicate where you should stand. If the judge is walking a dog twice, wait for the second walk before stacking your dog.

After the initial assessment, the judge will examine all the dogs individually.

Do not rush – the longer you keep your dog waiting, the greater his chance of moving out of position. If your dog moves when the judge turns to look at him, do not panic. Keeping calm, start again and stack your dog.

The judge will examine your dog from the front to the back. He will want to look at the dog's teeth – at the front and at the side. After the head, he will examine the front legs and feet, before going over the dog's shoulders, rib, and waist. He will feel the muscles and check the alignment of the dog's hindquarters, checking the tail, and, in male dogs, the testicles. He will probably ask the dog's age (certainly in the age classes).

When the judge has finished his examination, he will ask you to move around the ring. Listen carefully, as the judge will make it quite clear whether you should move in a straight line or in a triangle. Take your time to collect your dog's lead, and, remembering to use the ideal pace for your dog, take him on his walk. When this finishes, some judges will ask you to restack your dog, and may even perform a second examination. Other judges prefer to see the dog freestanding, and will try to attract a dog's attention to check his ear carriage.

Once the judge has seen your dog, you should return to your place and wait for him to examine the others. A good steward will warn everyone when the last dog is being examined and this will give you time to prepare yourself for the judge's decision. A

The judge assesses the dog's bite.

The ground is very rough at outdoor shows, so look for the most level ground on which to stack your Stafford.

judge may, where the class is very large, select some dogs for a second consideration. Those the judge is interested in will be brought into the centre of the ring. Those not selected will be asked to leave the ring. The dogs remaining in the centre of the ring will be asked by the steward to move to the side, where they should be presented again for the judge to make his final selection.

When the judge is ready to announce his decision, he will place the chosen dogs in the centre of the ring. In the UK, dogs are placed left to right in descending order, but this can vary in other countries. The steward will hand out any prize cards and rosettes while the judge fills in his judging book. The first two animals will be asked to stay behind for a few minutes while the judge writes a critique on them. These critiques will be published in the dog papers. If the show is hosted by a breed club, the club may ask for a copy to be published in their newsletter.

SHOWING IN OTHER COUNTRIES

In some countries – notably in Europe – a different procedure is adopted. Once the judge has taken a look at the whole class, he will examine each dog individually, as at UK shows. However, each dog will be graded at this point and each dog will have a critique written about him. At the completion of this process, dogs with low grades are dismissed and those with high grades are placed in order of merit.

This style of judging is very lengthy, but it can be of enormous value, especially if the critiques are helpful and meaningful. It should be remembered that, while Britons have the opportunity to see 200 to 300 Staffords at one show, in other countries this is not the case. It can be difficult to assess the results of your breeding programme when there is little with which to compare. It is helpful for fanciers from countries where Staffords are not popular to be assured they are on the right lines.

COMMON MISTAKES AND PROBLEMS

Think about what you are doing. A common mistake among newcomers is to place themselves between the dog and the judge – particularly on the walk. When stacking your dog, be careful not to crowd him, and never impede the judge when he is trying to examine your dog.

At outdoor shows the ground is often rough, so look for the most level piece of ground near to you. Standing on level ground will show off your dog to advantage, whereas uneven ground could make him look as though his back end is higher than his front.

Even when taking the opportunity to relax your dog in the ring, never let him show off his bad points. Experienced judges cast their eyes around the ring at all times, and will definitely spot a 'drop' ear, a roached topline, and weak pasterns – to name but a few

Mirror the judge to avoid impeding his view of your Stafford. If he moves to the dog's rear, move to the dog's front.

common faults while the handler is off-guard.

The Stafford is not the easiest dog to handle. He is primarily a pet and his natural instincts are to be with his family, having a game or lying in front of the fire. If yours becomes bored, he may present a lethargic appearance. If you cannot hold your dog's attention in the ring, think about giving him a rest from showing. There are shows every week, and it is far too easy for the dog to lose interest if he attends too many. By giving him a break from showing, his interest should be renewed when you begin again at a later date.

A dog that is shy of the ring will try to draw back, shrinking into himself. This is the hardest problem to overcome, requiring a great deal of patience. It may help if you withdraw from serious competitions, attending smaller, fun shows instead. At these events there will be no pressure. The dog can stand as he likes and look around to see what is happening. Hopefully, this will encourage him to feel more relaxed about the whole thing. A good handling class with plenty of people to encourage him will also help.

An overactive dog is hard work, but if you

get him under control you could have an excellent animal to show – one that stands up on his toes, alive and happy. However, never use force to dampen his exuberance – this will put off a Stafford from showing indefinitely. Staffords are tough physically, but they are easily hurt by aggressive, uncaring behaviour from their owners.

WINNING AND LOSING

Whatever the type of show, and wherever in the world it is held, the process of finding the ultimate winner is always the same. When all the classes have been judged, every first-prize winner will be asked to return to the ring. These are called 'unbeaten dogs' and from these the judge will select the Best Dog and the Best Bitch. It could be that the judge will ask the second-prize winner in the class from which he has chosen the winner to come back and stand with all the remaining unbeaten animals. From these, he will choose the Reserve best of sex.

Following this, the Best Dog and Best Bitchy come forward to compete against each other for Best in Show or Best of Breed. At a breed show, the second to these will compete for Reserve Best in Show. There may be further awards, especially at a breed club show – Best Puppy certainly, but there may also be a Best Junior, Best Veteran, etc. You should look at the schedule to see what prizes are on offer.

At a general canine society show, the Best of Breeds will go forward to compete for Best in Show, usually via the Group. The Stafford's Group is, of course, the Terrier Group. All the Group winners will then compete against each other so that a final Best in Show can be selected.

Winning at shows is not the lucrative business many imagine. Most wins result in nothing more than a prize card and rosette, possibly accompanied by a trophy that will have to be returned in 12 months. The real

Win or lose, you know you are taking the best dog home with you.

prize is the kudos of winning. For an aspiring breeder, a Championship win adds prestige, and the stud fee for a Champion could be higher than a non-Champion.

Learning to be a good loser is a prime requirement of dog showing. Even if you disagree with the judge's decision you must accept it unconditionally. Swallow your pride and remember to congratulate the winners. Above all, remember all the other reasons why you entered – to have a fun day out, to meet friends, to exchange gossip and ideas, and, hopefully, to see some animals you admire.

12 *HEALTH CARE*

The Staffordshire Bull Terrier is a very robust breed, which can make detecting ill health a problem. Staffords have a high pain threshold, and, indeed, it is common for a Stafford with a broken leg to show little or no sign of pain.

It is, therefore, very important that owners are able to detect early signs of ill health in their dogs, such as a change in behaviour, increased or decreased thirst and appetite, or changes in toilet habits. The early detection of illness greatly increases the chances of successful treatment.

REGULAR CHECKS

As part of his routine care, your Stafford should be examined regularly for any abnormalities. This will increase the likelihood of your picking up early warning signs of illness.

The ideal time to perform these checks is when you groom your dog. Once you are familiar with what is normal for your dog, detecting early signs of illness becomes much easier.

When you suspect a problem in your Staffordshire Bull Terrier, consult your veterinarian – it is better to be safe than sorry. In some cases, it may not be necessary to travel to the veterinary surgery, as your veterinarian may be able to offer advice over the telephone.

SKIN

Hair loss, signs of dandruff, areas of redness or inflammation, and unexplained lumps are all causes for concern, and should be investigated further by a veterinarian. In addition, the coat should be regularly checked for fleas and ticks.

EYES

The eyes should appear clear and bright with no discharge in the corner of the eye. There should be no overflow of tears on to the hair below the eye. The white of the eye should be checked for any redness or change in colour.

Grooming presents a perfect opportunity to check your dog for any abnormalities.

EARS

Ear infections can be very painful, and your Stafford may try to avoid having his ear touched. Signs of an ear infection include inflammation of the pinna (earflap) and the ear canal. There may be an increased production of earwax, and, occasionally, a green, purulent discharge. There may also be a pungent smell caused by a yeast infection. If the ear is infected, veterinary attention will be necessary, so you should make an appointment to see your veterinarian as soon as possible.

Build-up of wax, leading to blockage, is a common cause of ear infection. This can be avoided by using an ear cleaner prepared for dogs. The cleaner acts as a solvent, making removal of the wax far easier. Ask your veterinarian to recommend a suitable product and make sure you follow the manufacturer's instructions carefully.

MOUTH

In a healthy dog, the gums will be a healthy pink colour. You should check your dog's gums regularly, so you notice any changes immediately they become apparent. If the gums appear paler than normal, it may indicate anaemia (a reduction in the number of red blood cells) or circulatory problems.

Like humans, dogs have an initial set of milk teeth that are later replaced by permanent teeth. In dogs, this happens between four and six months of age. Dental disease is the most common complaint affecting dogs more than two years of age, and approximately 80 per cent of dogs over this age show some signs of dental disease.

Problems begin when plaque and tartar build up on the teeth. Unchecked, this leads to gingivitis (a painful condition of inflamed gums), and, eventually, abscesses may form under teeth.

The best way to prevent dental disease is to brush the dog's teeth regularly. If your Stafford has been well socialised, he should be accustomed to this (see page 79). Never use toothpaste designed for human use, as dogs can develop health problems after swallowing the toothpaste.

GENITALIA

Check your dog's anus regularly, as this is one of the first places in which ill health can become apparent.

Look for the presence of any discharge from the anal glands, which will have a pungent smell. Tapeworm segments, which look similar to grains of rice, may also be seen near the anus.

A bitch's vulva should be free of discharge, except when in season, and a male dog should not have any discharge from his penis.

FEET

Every time you take your dog for a walk, you should check his paws on your return. This is particularly important during the summer, when grass seeds are a problem. Check for cuts or any areas of inflammation. You should ensure that your dog's nails are kept short and neat, which may mean clipping occasionally (see page 79).

CHOOSING A VETERINARIAN

Selecting the right veterinarian is very important. Many people choose their nearest veterinary practice due to convenience. However, it is advisable to enquire about the facilities available at the practice before making a decision.

The cost of treatment varies between practices depending on the facilities available. A veterinary hospital, providing 24-hour nursing and a range of diagnostic equipment, will charge more than a smaller surgery performing routine procedures only (e.g. vaccination and neutering), and referring cases to other practices for the more complicated procedures.

When it comes to choosing the best veterinarian for your needs, there is no better recommendation than word of mouth. Other owners of Staffords will be more than happy to advise you, and your local breed club may have a list of appropriate veterinarians too. Staffords are popular dogs, and you may be pleasantly surprised to discover that a local veterinarian has a particular interest in the breed.

INSURANCE

In recent years, the cost of veterinary treatment has risen faster than the rate of inflation. In part, this is due to advances in veterinary science. Surgeons are able to treat more complaints than ever, with a greater degree of success, but these advances have a cost.

Insuring your Stafford means that, should he need treatment, you will be able to afford the best available, rather than a less effective compromise that suits your budget. The peace of mind afforded by taking out an insurance policy is worth an awful lot.

The number of companies offering pet insurance has grown significantly, and policies are competitively priced as a result.

However, do not choose the least expensive policy without checking that it covers all your needs. Some policies provide cover for life, which means they will pay for the treatment of a particular condition throughout the dog's life. However, other policies may pay a specified amount for different conditions.

Be aware of the restrictions in the policy. Some will refuse to cover any condition known about before the policy was sold, while other companies refuse to insure pets over a certain age. Make sure you buy the best policy for your particular pet.

VACCINATIONS

Canine vaccines have been responsible for a dramatic reduction in the incidence of many canine diseases. There are two main groups of vaccinations – those that should be administered as standard, and those administered for specific purposes.

Until your pup is vaccinated at eight to ten weeks of age, he should be kept away from any possible sources of infection.

STANDARD VACCINATIONS

Puppies receive some immunity from their mother, but this normally disappears by 16 weeks of age. It is essential to get your puppy vaccinated. Regimes vary slightly between practices, but, in most cases, the first vaccine will be administered at 8 to 10 weeks of age and the second at 12 weeks. Dogs are vaccinated against distemper, canine parvovirus, canine viral hepatitis, leptospirosis and canine parainfluenza, with vaccinations against adenovirus, rabies and canine coronavirus being administered additionally in the US. Dogs may also be vaccinated against Lyme's Disease if they live in an at-risk area.

Your puppy will take vaccinations in his stride. Some people believe that these initial vaccinations protect their dog for life, but the immunity provided by a vaccine decreases over time – eventually, the dog will become susceptible.

The only effective way to protect your dog throughout his life is through regular booster vaccinations (your veterinarian will advise).

DISTEMPER

Distemper is a highly contagious virus. It causes coughing, diarrhoea, vomiting, a purulent discharge from the nose and eyes, pneumonia, central nervous problems (especially fits), and, ultimately, death. The virus can cause a dog's paw pads to change, hence its old name of 'hardpad'. Distemper can affect dogs of all ages, but is most common among puppies.

CANINE PARVOVIRUS

This virus has a very sudden onset, producing haemorrhagic (bloody) diarrhoea and vomiting, which quickly lead to dehydration and death. The virus also attacks the dog's immune system, killing the white blood cells that normally fight infection.

Parvo is extremely contagious, and, when outbreaks occur, it is very difficult to eradicate. The virus can be carried on the soles of a person's shoes, picked up when that person walks over an area where an infected dog has defecated previously, and the virus can remain active for several months.

Many canine diseases are transmitted easily from dog to dog, so vaccination and regular boosters are vital.

Parvovirus is easily prevented by vaccination, and, because it is so easily transmitted, it is essential that all dogs are vaccinated against it.

CANINE VIRAL HEPATITIS

Like many viruses, this is highly contagious and can be fatal. Clinical signs include a high fever, vomiting, and stomach pains. Fortunately, the disease has become quite rare due to vaccination.

LEPTOSPIROSIS

Leptospirosis is caused by two types of bacteria, transmitted by contact with urine from an infected animal. A particular source of infection is rat urine. Leptospirosis causes liver and kidney failure and can be fatal. The same bacteria can cause Weils disease in humans.

CANINE PARAINFLUENZA

This is one of the viruses that causes infectious bronchitis, commonly known as kennel cough. Infected dogs develop a persistent, harsh cough, which can last for several days. In most cases the disease is not serious, but some dogs will develop pneumonia.

Kennel cough is so called because dogs commonly contract it while in boarding kennels. This is because dogs in kennels are under stress, which lowers their immunity to infections, and they are in close contact with other dogs. It is advisable to accustom your dog to going into kennels while he is still young. Many boarding kennels have introduced a policy where dogs are refused unless their owners can prove that vaccinations are up to date.

When you leave your dog at a boarding kennel, do not forget to leave important information with the manager. This includes a contact number for you, a list of any medication your dog receives (as well as full instructions about dosages), a description of your dog's normal diet (following this will prevent an occurrence of vomiting and diarrhoea), and the name and telephone number of your veterinarian. If the dog has a favourite toy or blanket, leaving these will make your dog feel more at home, making him less stressed, and, hopefully, less prone to infection.

OTHER VACCINATIONS

As well as the above, you may wish to have your puppy vaccinated against some other strains of kennel cough, and rabies.

KENNEL COUGH VACCINATION

Bordetella bronchiseptica is a bacterium that causes infectious bronchitis or kennel cough. It is possible to vaccinate against by means of a nasal vaccine. The vaccine encourages antibodies to develop on the lining of the nasal cavity, and these fight off infection. This vaccine should be given at least two weeks before entering boarding kennels, and immunity will last for six months.

A kennel cough vaccination is especially important if you exhibit your dog, as the condition is easily spread at shows.

THE PET TRAVEL SCHEME

The Pet Travel Scheme, which allows dogs to enter Britain without a period of quarantine, was introduced to the UK in February 2000. Dogs can enter the UK from Europe, the US and Canada, as well as other rabies-free, small, free islands around the world. Details of which countries are part of the scheme can be obtained from The Department of the Environment, Food and Rural Affairs.

There are certain conditions dogs must satisfy before being granted entry into Britain. Every dog must:

- Be microchipped (see below)
- Be vaccinated against rabies
- Be treated for ticks and tapeworm within 24 hours of entering the country.

The most important part of the scheme for dog owners is the rabies vaccination, as it takes several months to prove the vaccine is effective and dogs must remain in quarantine until immunity can be demonstrated satisfactorily. A blood sample is taken 30 days after the vaccination, and the vaccine is considered successful only if the rabies antibodies have reached a specified level.

Dogs may enter the UK using approved routes only, and they must be accompanied by the appropriate certificates. A small number of dogs that have visited Europe have returned with some diseases contracted abroad, such as babesiosis, a blood-borne parasite contracted via a bite from an infected tick. Contact your veterinarian before travelling to Europe, to gain advice on preventing this and other conditions.

SOCIALISATION CLASSES

Many veterinary practices run socialisation classes for puppies that have not yet completed their vaccinations. These classes allow the puppy to socialise with other dogs and people in a controlled environment, without exposing your pet to potentially fatal diseases before he has developed immunity.

You may feel happier leaving socialisation classes until your dog has finished his vaccination course, but this is not to be recommended. The way a dog reacts to other dogs and people is based on his experiences between 6 and 14 weeks of age – the sensitive developmental period.

Unfortunately, vaccination regimes stop puppies attending standard socialisation classes until the sensitive development period is nearly over, which can cause problems later.

Behavioural problems are a common reason for euthanasia in young, adult dogs. Therefore, it is strongly recommended that you take your puppy to socialisation classes provided by your veterinarian.

IDENTIFICATION

There are two main methods available to identify dogs, and they can provide enormous peace of mind for the owner. Identification

Identification, such as a microchip, is essential if you are to be reunited with a lost pet.

234

means a dog can be reunited with his owner if he has been lost or has strayed accidentally.

Identification can also be used to prove ownership, in cases where a pedigree dog has been stolen and recovered, for example.

A popular form of identification is the creation of a tattoo on the skin inside the dog's ear flap. The tattoo consists of a series of letters and numbers, and it is easily read. However, tattoos can be defaced by dog thieves or by accidents that damage the ear flap. Many owners choose to have their dogs microchipped as well as being tattooed.

A microchip is a small implant approximately the size of a grain of rice. It is implanted under the skin between the shoulder blades. Each chip carries a unique number, which is read by a special scanning device. Once implanted, the chip cannot be altered. The scanners are used routinely by rescue kennels, dog wardens and larger animal charities, so microchipping greatly increases the chance of your being reunited with your dog. Ideally, dogs should be tattooed and microchipped.

NUTRITION

There is a huge choice of dog food available, with something to suit every dog and budget. Full details about nutrition can be found in Chapter Six, but these points merit attention:

- Unless you know what you are doing, do not feed your Stafford a home-made diet. A dog's nutritional needs are complex, and are best provided by a commercially prepared dog food.
- If you feed your dog on tinned food, always remember to add a mixer.
- Any food created specifically for puppies should contain extra calcium and phosphorus as standard, to help with bone formation. Do not add extra. More problems are caused by oversupplementing than by deficiency.

A tinned food should always be fed with mixer to create a balanced diet.

- It is as important for an older dog to have a diet tailored to his needs as it is for a puppy. Commercially prepared foods for older dogs contain reduced amounts of phosphorus and salt.

Excess phosphorus exacerbates kidney damage in older dogs, while too much salt can contribute to high blood pressure, which will make heart or kidney problems worse.

PARASITE CONTROL

There is a large number of parasites that can affect dogs, falling into two groups – endoparasites (internal) and ectoparasites (external). Fortunately, there are many effective products to control parasites, although you should never forget that prevention is far better than cure. Your veterinarian will happily advise you about various products.

INTERNAL PARASITES

This group includes roundworm, tapeworm, *Giardia* species and lungworm.

ROUNDWORM

Roundworm or *Toxocara canis* is one of the most common endoparasites. The worms look like strands of spaghetti, and can measure up to 7 inches (18 cms) in length. A dog becomes infected when he ingests eggs during licking and cleaning. The eggs hatch into larvae in the dog's intestines, travelling through the liver to the bloodstream. Once in the bloodstream, the larvae enter the lungs, from where they are coughed up and swallowed. Once back in the intestines, the larvae develop into adults, producing more eggs that are passed out in faeces, so becoming a source of infection to other dogs.

Some larvae will form cysts in the dog's muscles, becoming active only during times of stress, such as pregnancy. Roundworm infestation is common among newborn puppies. They are infected by the bitch in the womb, and will contract more larvae from the bitches' milk. Roundworm infestation can be prevented in a litter of puppies by worming the bitch with a specific anthelmintic (wormer) during pregnancy. This is available from your veterinarian.

Puppies remain at risk even when weaned. Signs of an infestation include vomiting, diarrhoea, a swollen abdomen, and a loss of weight and condition. Puppies should be wormed regularly from 2 to 12 weeks of age, with the frequency dependent on the product used. From 12 weeks of age onwards, the young dog should be wormed every three months for the rest of his life.

Adult dogs with roundworms may not show any signs of illness unless there is a heavy infestation. Vomiting, diarrhoea and weight loss are indicative of an infection.

There is a wide range of worming products on the market, available from pet stores and your veterinarian. In general, a preparation provided by your veterinarian will prove more effective. Before any worming preparation is given, it is essential to weigh your Stafford, particularly as a puppy. Dosages are based on the dog's weight, and it is important to get it right – do not guess.

Staffords are great scavengers, so a regular worming routine is important.

Roundworms can affect humans, and there has been much written about this by the media. Worm eggs can lead to toxocariasis in children, with extreme cases causing severe illness and blindness. These cases are extremely rare, but sensible precautions are advised.

Dogs should be prevented from licking children's faces, and it is also advisable to wash your hands after handling your dog. Dogs should be discouraged from fouling in public places and children's play areas, but, as a responsible dog owner, you should be enforcing this habit already.

TAPEWORMS

Tapeworms look like long strings of flattened rice grains. They can grow more than 1.5 feet (500 cms) in length. Tapeworms are more common among adult dogs than puppies. The tapeworm attaches itself to the wall of the intestine, and the segments, which contain the eggs, are passed out through the rectum, often in the faeces. The segments look like grains of rice and are one of the main signs of an infestation. Once the segments have reached the outer environment, they will split, releasing the eggs contained inside them, which are not visible.

Tapeworms require an intermediate host to complete the life cycle. In the case of the most common canine tapeworm *(Dipylidium caninum)*, the intermediate host is the flea, and tapeworm eggs are eaten by flea larvae. Once ingested, the tapeworm egg develops into an adult. When a dog eats an infected flea (during licking and cleaning), he becomes infected with tapeworm, so completing the cycle.

Heavy infestations of tapeworms cause diarrhoea, leading to weight loss and a loss of condition. However, tapeworms are easy to eradicate, and suitable drugs are available from your veterinarian. Dogs should be wormed routinely every three months, using a wormer effective against roundworms and tapeworms.

GIARDIA

This is a one-cell parasite that can cause diarrhoea in dogs and in humans. The usual sources of infection are stagnant water and unhygienic kennel conditions. Its presence can be detected by examining a faecal sample under the microscope. Once diagnosed, it is easily eradicated.

LUNGWORM

The lungworm has a complicated life cycle. Adult worms are found in the dog's lungs, where they produce eggs. Once the eggs hatch, the larvae are coughed up and swallowed, to be excreted in the faeces. The larvae are eaten by slugs and snails, which are then eaten by dogs. Once inside the dog, the larvae migrate from the intestines to the lungs, where they develop into adults.

Lungworm can cause severe lung damage. The symptoms include a cough and difficulty breathing. The disease is treated using a drug called Fenbendazole.

HEARTWORM

This type of roundworm is called *Dirofilaria immitis*, which is 12 inches (30 cm) long and lives in the main artery supplying the lungs from the heart (the pulmonary artery). The diesease in common in Southern Europe and in some American states. It appears in the UK only in imported dogs.

A dog affected by heartworm will have difficulty breathing, a cough, and reduced exercise tolerance. He will also suffer weight loss and premature death. Unfortunately, treatment success is very variable, as it can complicate things further (e.g. the development of a thromboembolism).

Prevention is better than cure, and there are a number of preventative treatments

Some flea preparations can be used safely on puppies.

available, including oral agents (e.g. ivomec) and topical applications (e.g. selamectin). There is also an injection available (moxidectin), which last for six months.

EXTERNAL PARASITES
Ectoparasites live on a dog's skin. They are a common cause of skin diseases and problems.

FLEAS
The most common flea found in the UK is the cat flea, which lives on dogs as well as cats. The adult fleas lay their eggs on the dog. The eggs fall off in the surrounding environment (carpets and bedding, etc.), where they can lie dormant for several months. The eggs hatch and develop only when conditions are suitable – warm, moist, and with a suitable host.

Fleas are very small and can be difficult to spot. It is much easier to look for flea droppings. Using a very fine comb and piece of wet, white paper, comb the coat so that any debris lands on the paper. If there are fleas present, small red dots will appear on the paper, dissolving within a few seconds. The red dots consist of digested blood.

Fleas cause irritation and itchiness, which can lead to bacterial dermatitis (severe inflammation of the skin). Some dogs seem able to tolerate a large flea burden while others become itchy with only one flea present. It is clear that some dogs have an allergy to the saliva the flea injects into the skin to help extract blood.

Infestations of fleas can be extremely difficult to eradicate; unless the entire environment is treated, the problem will recur. Therefore, treatment is two-fold. Firstly, all cats and dogs will need to be treated with a suitable product prescribed by your veterinarian. Secondly, you will need to destroy any fleas in the dog's environment. It has been estimated that 95 per cent of the flea population in an infested house is in the form of eggs, larvae and pupae. The most effective method of killing all these life stages of the flea is by using an aerosol spray.

It is far better to prevent flea infestations from ever arising. Your veterinarian will advise you about this. Remember that flea shampoos work for a limited time only, and products that interfere with the flea's life cycle are more effective. These products include a once-monthly tablet given to dogs that will prevent fleas from breeding. The tablet contains an insect growth hormone called luferon, which prevents flea eggs from hatching. This product contains no insecticide. Also available are spray or spot-on insecticides.

TICKS
Ticks look like pieces of sweetcorn and are found attached to the dog's skin. They remain attached for a few days, while they feed, and then drop off. The most common ticks are sheep ticks and hedgehog ticks, with dogs living in sheep-farming areas most at risk.

Ticks and mites can be picked up when out on a walk, so post-walk checks are recommended.

Ticks attach firmly to the dog's skin, and can cause a severe reaction if removed incorrectly. Ticks can be removed using a special tool available from your vet, who will show you how to use it properly. Applying an insecticide called fipronil every four weeks will help to prevent ticks attaching to your dog. In the US, ticks can be responsible for transmitting Lyme's Diseases, but there is a vaccination available.

LICE
Lice are visible to the naked eye, and will be easily spotted when you groom your Stafford. They look like tiny grains of rice attached to the side of the dog's hairs. They are most common among puppies, and live their whole lives on the dog. A severe infestation can cause itchiness and anaemia, but they are easily controlled by applying an appropriate insecticide.

MITES
There are two forms of mites that affect dogs – *Demodex* and *Sarcoptes*. Examining skin samples under the microscope will determine if these mites are present. There is a blood test available to diagnose *Sarcoptes*.

Demodex is the most common mite to affect Staffords. All dogs have *Demodex* mites on their skin but demodectic mange affects certain individuals only. It causes patches of hair loss and occasional itchiness. It is more common among younger dogs, and treatment with baths is usually successful. Occasionally, it is seen in adult dogs, when it can become a severe problem. Frequently, there is an underlying medical problem that reduces the dog's resistance to the mites.

Sarcoptes cause scabies, a very contagious skin disease. Affected dogs have very itchy skin, with the edges of the ear flap the area affected in most cases. People in contact with an infected dog may develop small red spots on their skin, especially on the forearm. However, canine scabies cannot lead to human scabies. Canine scabies is easily treated with insecticides, and there is a product available in the form of a spot-on treatment.

CHEYLETIELLA
This mite causes skin irritation and appears as severe dandruff, especially on the dog's back. It can cause red spots on human skin, especially on the forearms. It is easily treated using an appropriate insecticide.

MALASEZZIA
This is a yeast infection. In the majority of dogs it does not cause a problem, but it can become significant if there is an underlying

skin allergy. It can be found by examining a skin sample under a microscope. Inflamed skin in the groin and between the toes, possibly with a concurrent ear infection, are the main clinical signs. Malasezzia can be treated with shampoos, and ear drops if there is an ear infection.

RINGWORM

This fungal infection is contracted by coming into contact with fungal spores. Ringworm normally presents as circular areas of hair loss – hence the name. Diagnosis can be made by culturing the fungus, which takes up to 14 days. An ultraviolet light can be used to detect ringworm, but is only accurate in 50 per cent of cases. Ringworm is treated with antifungal creams or the antifungal drug griseofulvin, which is available in tablet form. It is possible for people to catch ringworm, so good hygiene is essential when handling a dog with ringworm.

NEUTERING

Neutering is a controversial subject, with many arguments to support both sides of the debate. The main risk comes from anaesthesia, as both male and female dogs require a general anaesthetic in order to have surgery performed. All general anaesthetics involve some risk (your veterinarian will discuss this with you) but the anaesthetics used today are much safer than those used previously, and highly sophisticated monitoring equipment is now available.

A frequent point raised by owners is that some dogs, and bitches in particular, are prone to weight gain after neutering. This occurs due to the loss of sex hormones, which burn off extra calories. However, weight gain is avoidable by reducing food intake slightly. It has been claimed that neutering can alter a dog's personality, although the evidence for this remains anecdotal.

Neutering pet females reduces the chances of them developing a life-threatening womb infection in later life.

CASTRATION

Castration involves removal of the testicles. A vasectomy is not performed, as it can be difficult to guarantee that it has been successful and it does not reduce the male hormones produced by the testicles. It is the reduction of these hormones that reduces the incidence of the male behavioural problems that some owners wish to curb by having their dog neutered.

Overdominance, aggression, and hypersexuality are common behavioural problems that can be reduced by castration. Without his male hormones, a male dog should be less likely to run away after a bitch in season. If a male dog is being neutered for behavioural reasons, the operation should be carried out as early as possible, between 6 and 12 months of age. The optimum age for castration is nine months, when the dog's long bones have finished growing, but behavioural patterns have not become imprinted on his brain. Later than 12 months, castration will have less effect, as behavioural patterns are imprinted on the dog's brain over time.

Castration has significant health implications, greatly reducing the incidence of prostatic disease in older dogs. The prostate is a small gland situated near the urethra (the outflow tube from the bladder). It increases in size as the male dog ages, as a result of stimulation from the male hormones. Without such stimulation, there is no increase in the size of the prostate and the risk of cancer is greatly reduced.

Older dogs can suffer from small tumours around the anus, known as anal adenomas. These tumours are rarely malignant, but they can cause severe problems due to ulceration. They are caused by the stimulation of tiny glands around the anus by male hormones, and will not develop in a neutered dog.

SPAYING

An ovariohysterectomy, or spaying, involves removal of the ovaries and uterus (womb). Bitches usually recover within a few days.

A spayed bitch should not show any signs of being in season, and this is one of the main reasons for spaying. An unplanned pregnancy is also avoided by spaying. Spaying will also prevent false pregnancies (see below).

Spaying reduces the incidence of mammary tumours (breast cancer) in later life. If a bitch is spayed before her first season, the risk is reduced by 50 per cent. If the bitch is spayed between the first and second seasons, the reduction is 25 per cent.

Furthermore, a spayed bitch will not develop pyometra (a life-threatening infection in which the womb fills with pus, particularly common in older bitches). The symptoms are an increased thirst, vomiting, lethargy and a purulent vulval discharge.

Treatment is spaying. However, if the bitch is spayed when she is unwell, there are increased risks involved with the surgery.

Spayed bitches are less likely to develop diabetes mellitus (sugar diabetes). This is because the female hormones interact with insulin, which controls glucose metabolism. Bitches can be spayed at any age from six months onwards. It is best to spay a bitch when she is not in season. This is because the blood supply to the ovaries and uterus is greater during a season.

FALSE PREGNANCY

False pregnancy or pseudopregnancy is a condition that can affect a bitch after she has been in season. The symptoms vary. Some bitches become irritable, nervous and aggressive, while others may be depressed, introverted and refuse to eat.

In the latter stages, the bitch may prepare a nest, adopting household objects (e.g. soft toys) as her 'puppies'. Some bitches may produce milk.

False pregnancies occur because hormonal changes after a season are similar in pregnant and non-pregnant bitches. If the bitch begins to lactate, veterinary advice should be sought. Lactation can lead to mastitis, an infection in the mammary glands. Drugs are available to stop false pregnancy, but spaying will solve the problem permanently.

COMMON AILMENTS

The following are some of the more commonly encountered illnesses. It should be emphasised that it is important to seek advice from your veterinarian regarding any health problems. A delay in treatment can often increase the length of treatment required, and, in some cases, reduce the chances of recovery.

Eating unsuitable food is a common cause of diarrhoea.

VOMITING AND DIARRHOEA

Gastrointestinal upsets are very common, especially in younger dogs. This is because young dogs tend to explore their environment more closely, eating any discarded food they discover. If a dog vomits once, it is not usually a cause for concern.

However, if vomiting persists, there is a danger of the dog becoming dehydrated. No food should be given, but small amounts of water should be offered.

A salt and glucose powder can be added to the water. Milk should be avoided, as any bacteria present in the intestine will feed on the milk. If vomiting does not cease within a few hours, contact your veterinarian. The presence of any blood in the vomit should be noted.

Diarrhoea is common in dogs, caused by infections, a change of diet, exposure to toxins, or an underlying metabolic problem. Common infections include *Salmonella*, *Campylobacter* and the O157 strain of *E. coli*. The practice of feeding raw eggs to dogs should be avoided due to the risk of *Salmonella*.

Dehydration is the major complicating factor of diarrhoea. Water should always be available to a dog with diarrhoea. Giving food to a dog with diarrhoea is controversial. Traditional practice has been to starve the dog for 24 hours, but recent research suggests that feeding a highly digestible diet may help repair any damaged gut lining. Your veterinarian will recommend a prescription diet that contains easily digestible food.

CONSTIPATION

It is important to check if an apparently constipated dog is passing very hard faeces or small amounts of diarrhoea. This is because dogs suffering from inflammation of the colon (colitis) will often present as a constipated dog. A dog suffering from colitis should receive veterinary treatment immediately.

If a dog is truly constipated, he will pass very hard faeces. Giving liquid paraffin, which acts as a lubricant to help the faeces pass through the intestine, can treat this. Feeding cooked bones to a dog is a common cause of constipation. Only raw bones should be given to dogs, and, if necessary, they can be sterilised in boiling water for 30 seconds.

HEAT STROKE

This is a relatively common condition among Staffords. Heat stroke occurs when dogs are left in cars on hot days, or after too much exercise on a hot day. Dogs are ill equipped to deal with high temperatures, as they lose excess heat only through their paws and by panting. As the dog's temperature increases,

Although Staffords enjoy sunbathing, care should be taken that they do not overheat.

these heat loss areas are insufficient, and the dog's temperature regulation mechanisms fail.

A dog suffering from heat stroke will pant rapidly, and his tongue may appear blue. The normal temperature for a dog is 38.5 degrees Celsius (101.5 degrees Fahrenheit), but with heat stroke it can reach 42.5 degrees Celsius (108 degrees Fahrenheit). This can prove fatal in less than one hour.

Dogs suffering from heat stroke should be cooled down immediately, with baths of cold water and plenty of cold water to drink. Staffords should never be left unattended in a car in warm weather, and avoid overexertion during warm weather.

WASP STINGS

These tend to be more common in late summer. The most common areas to be stung are the face and paws. Some dogs will suffer only a few minutes' discomfort, while others will develop large swellings. In some cases, there may be a severe allergic reaction, in which case veterinary attention should be sought immediately. Normally, stings are treated with antihistamines, with steroids used to treat severe reactions.

ROAD TRAFFIC ACCIDENTS

Any dog involved in an accident should be approached with care – dogs are more likely to bite when frightened and in pain. It is advisable to take the dog to a veterinarian, even if the dog appears to have sustained no injuries, as internal bleeding can take some time to manifest.

Injuries to the chest can be life-threatening, and fractures of the limb bones and pelvis are also common. If a spinal injury is suspected, the dog should be lifted carefully and placed on a flat, rigid surface. If there is bleeding from a wound, pressure should be applied to stop the bleeding until the veterinarian can provide expert assistance.

13 BREED-RELATED CONDITIONS

The Stafford is a healthy, robust dog, but, like all breeds, there are some conditions to which he is more prone.

SKIN DISEASES

ATOPIC DERMATITIS

An atopic dog is one that has inherited a susceptibility to allergic reactions. A dog suffering from atopic dermatitis is genetically predisposed to develop the condition after exposure to allergens that would create no reaction in other dogs. Common allergens in dogs include grass, tree and weed pollens, house dust mites, and flea saliva. When these allergens come into contact with an atopic dog they induce an allergic skin reaction. A helpful analogy is hay fever in people.

Atopy is on the increase, and it has serious consequences for dogs, owners, and breeders. The condition is unpleasant for the dog, costly for the owner to keep under control, and can ruin a breeding programme. If one parent has the disease, up to 40 per cent of the pups may develop it. If both parents have the disease, up to 90 per cent of their pups could be affected. Therefore, affected dogs should not be bred from.

Staffords normally develop the disease between six months and three years of age. Pruritis (severe itching of the skin) is the main sign. It usually affects the face and paws, but any region, including the ears and eyes, may be affected. Mildly affected dogs will lick their paws occasionally, while severely affected dogs will have hair loss with thickened, smelly skin. Persistent scratching results in secondary infection, causing the dog to scratch further.

Atopy is diagnosed by intradermal skin testing and by blood tests. Intradermal skin testing involves injecting various allergens into the skin to see if there is a reaction. It is a means of determining which allergens a dog produces a response to. Blood tests measure the amount of antibody produced by various allergens; the greater the number of antibodies, the more severe the allergic reaction. Veterinarians need to know which allergens are responsible, and the degree of reaction they produce, before appropriate treatment can be administered.

There are various treatments available to atopic dogs, with immunotherapy being one of the most popular. Immunotherapy injections work by increasing the dog's resistance to allergens, following a similar principle to vaccination. The substance to which the dog is allergic is injected into the dog so that the dog develops a greater immunity to it. Immunotherapy is effective in 70 to 80 per cent of cases, but the dog will need injections once a month throughout his life.

Grass pollen is a common cause of skin allergies.

In some cases, it is possible to remove the dog from the source of the allergy. For example, a dog allergic to house dust mites will benefit from being kept in an outdoor kennel. However, this is not always practical. Staffords allergic to flea saliva should be treated, once a month, with spot-on flea treatments provided by your veterinarian. The dog's environment must be treated also.

Any Stafford suffering from secondary infections will require antibiotics on a daily basis for up to three months. Secondary infection with the yeast malasezzia can be controlled with a shampoo, eardrops, or tablets. With effective immunotherapy, this will solve many cases. However, some dogs require treatment for life – receiving antibiotics for two days in each week.

One of the difficulties with treating atopic dermatitis is breaking the itch-scratch cycle. Glucocorticoids (steroids) can be used to break the scratch reflex. Dogs respond very well to steroids and usually stop scratching within a few days. Possible side effects of steroids include diabetes mellitus, renal and liver problems, Cushing's disease, eating, drinking and urinating more, and skin problems. For these reasons, veterinarians prescribe oral medication rather than injections – if there are side effects, oral medication can be withdrawn immediately, but injections can last for up to a month. Steroids also prevent further allergy testing.

Antihistamines are not licensed for use in dogs, but are used regularly with few side effects. They can be very effective at reducing itchiness. Diet can also help matters. Essential fatty acids (EFAs) are essential for normal skin metabolism, and, when combined with other treatments, help to reduce itching. Special shampoos from your veterinarian will help to remove skin debris and restore the normal microenvironment of the skin.

DEMODICOSIS

This is a skin disorder caused by *Demodex canis,* a host-specific mite and a normal inhabitant of canine hair follicles. The mites cause skin disease in some dogs but not in others. Problems arise when the mite population grows unchecked. It is a fairly common disease in Staffords. The mite is transferred from a lactating bitch to her newborn pups.

Demodicosis normally develops between six and nine months of age, when puppies begin to reach sexual maturity. It is common for a bitch to develop the condition after her first season. For this reason, it is thought that changing hormonal levels may be responsible. However, the factors that trigger unchecked growth of the mites are not entirely understood. Another possible cause is a suppressed immune system, often as the result of steroids or as an inherited factor.

Staffords tend to present with localised, non-itchy hair loss around the face and forelimbs. In many cases – up to 90 per cent – the dog will recover by himself, but in the remaining 10 per cent of cases the condition may spread over most of the body. These cases develop secondary bacterial infections, which cause the dog to scratch. An affected dog will appear depressed and off his food.

Demodicosis can be treated by killing the mites responsible. The dog will be washed in a chemical solution that opens the hair follicles in which the mite lives. This is followed by an application of insecticide every seven days for several months.

Demodicosis is fairly common in the Stafford.

Unfortunately, the mite seems to be developing some resistant to the solution. Recently, veterinarians have discovered a cattle wormer that works very well, and this may be used more frequently in the future. Antibiotics will be required to cure any secondary bacterial infection.

Demodicosis normally responds well to treatment, but, in rare cases, there is no cure and euthanasia is required. Dogs with the disease should not be bred from, as a hereditary factor is probable.

Some skin problems are triggered by hormonal changes as the puppy matures.

ORTHOPAEDIC DISEASES

LUXATING PATELLA

The patella (kneecap) is covered by cartilage, sitting in a large tendon that crosses the front of the stifle (knee). The tendon allows the knee to flex and extend, while the patella prevents the tendon from disintegrating when the knee moves. There is a special groove in the femur where the patella sits. If the patella luxates (i.e. pops out of the groove), it results in an inability to flex the knee, leaving the affected dog with a leg locked straight. There are two types of luxation – medial (inside) and lateral (outside). Staffords normally present with a medial luxation, and both hind limbs are usually affected. The condition is growth related, so most cases occur at a young age.

There are varying degrees of severity. In some Staffords, the patella will luxate but return to its groove almost immediately. Characteristically, the dog will be lame for a few strides, until the patella pops back in place and the dog walks normally. Mild cases do not require treatment.

More serious luxating patella can be caused by a number of factors and will require treatment. Trauma is a common factor, but hereditary causes, and abnormal development are also responsible. Where hereditary factors are believed responsible, affected dogs should not be bred from. Frequently, medial luxation occurs as a result of too shallow a groove in the femur and the tendon inserting into the tibia at the wrong angle.

In cases where treatment is required, surgery is the only answer. The results are normally very good. The groove in the femur will be deepened and the part of the tibia into which the tendon is inserted will be cut off and moved laterally. This stabilises the joint, preventing it from luxating.

A major problem is that the condition causes secondary oesteoarthritis in the knee, which can lead to lameness when the dog is older. To avoid this, any dog that has suffered from a luxating patella should be subject to careful weight management. It is essential to feed a high-quality diet that will not result in weight gain. If osteoarthritis develops, artificial cartilage supplements can help to slow down its progression (see below).

CRUCIATE DISEASE

There are two ligaments in the stifle (knee) joint that help to stabilise the joint. They are called the cranial and caudal cruciate ligaments. Among Staffords, disease normally presents in the cranial cruciate ligament.

In young dogs, the ligament degenerates over many months, eventually leading to tearing or rupture. This causes severe lameness and both stifles are normally affected. Cruciate disease is accompanied by osteoarthritis, but it is not clear whether osteoarthritis causes the ligament to degenerate, or if ligament degeneration causes osteoarthritis.

In some cases, the ligament ruptures following trauma. For example, a dog running at speed could trap his leg in a hole, severely wrenching the ligament. However, most cases are caused by degeneration of the ligament over time, leading to rupture. Hereditary factors have not been demonstrated.

Cruciate disease must be treated by surgery. There are several different methods, but, in most cases, the diseased ligament is replaced with an artificial one. In addition, the joint will be checked for any other damage and flushed with sterile fluid to remove inflammatory mediators. Although both stifles are normally affected, surgery will not be performed at the same time on each stifle. Surgery produces good results, but owners need to be aware of the importance of managing any subsequent osteoarthritis.

Osteoarthritis is, in essence, a degeneration of articular cartilage in a joint. Articular

Staffords enjoy free-running, but gentle, controlled, on-lead walks are recommended for those with hip dysplasia.

cartilage is responsible for preventing the bones in a joint from rubbing against each other, which is very painful. Long-term management of osteoarthritis involves controlled exercise, pain relief when required, maintenance of the correct weight, and the use of artificial cartilage supplements. These supplements are effective at slowing degeneration, but they are very expensive and need to be taken for the whole of the dog's life. Steroids should not be used as they exacerbate cartilage degeneration.

HIP DYSPLASIA

The hip joint is a ball-and-socket joint. The ball is the round, femoral head (the top of the thigh) and the socket is the pelvis (acetabulum). The socket should cover the ball, allowing normal, pain-free movement of the hip joint. Hip dysplasia is a developmental joint disease where the socket does not cover the ball sufficiently. This results in laxity in the hip joint, causing pain and restricting movement.

Staffords are not the most susceptible

breed to hip dysplasia, but incidences are fairly common. Fortunately, most dogs will grow out of the disease when they reach 14 months of age. In a minority of cases, surgery will be required. Only qualified veterinary orthopaedic surgeons should perform these complicated procedures. In all cases of hip dysplasia, secondary osteoarthritis must be controlled (see above).

PANOESTEITIS

This is a developmental bone disease that occurs in Staffordshire Bull Terriers. The cause is unknown.

The disease has a characteristic pattern of lameness in the forelimbs, shifting from one leg to the other over time. This is because the disease affects the same bone in both forelimbs, but at different times – one month the dog will be lame on the left forelimb, while the right forelimb will be affected in the following month.

Panoesteitis normally clears by itself when the Stafford reaches 14 months of age. Most cases are not serious, an analogy being 'growing pains' in human children.

The condition can be confirmed by radiography, but treatment involves little more than rest and pain relief in most cases.

OSTEOCHONDROSIS

This developmental joint disease is occasionally seen in Staffords. Osteochondrosis is when the articular cartilage covering bone in a joint is not formed properly. This leads to flattening of the cartilage, and, eventually, a flap of cartilage will form.

This flap may be released into the joint (referred to as a joint mouse), causing lameness and a great deal of pain. Osteochondrosis normally develops in the shoulder, elbow and knee joints. Normally, both joints are affected.

Treatment for osteochondrosis depends on its severity. Rest and pain relief will suffice in mild cases. In more severe cases, where a cartilage flap has formed, the flap will be removed by surgery and the joint will be flushed with sterile fluid.

Osteochondrosis predisposes the dog to secondary osteoarthritis, and this will need to be managed for the remainder of the dog's life (see above).

EYE DISEASES

HEREDITARY DISEASES

Two hereditary eye diseases affect Staffords, these being hereditary cataracts and PHPV (see below). Hereditary diseases may be congenital (present at birth) or they may take months, or even years, to appear. To understand how these diseases are inherited, it is important to understand some basic genetics.

The dog has 78 chromosomes, 39 inherited from his dam and 39 inherited from his sire, linking together to form 39 pairs. Chromosomes are contained in the nucleus of every cell in the body. Chromosomes contain genes, which are made up of DNA (deoxyribonucleic acid), so each nucleus contains two copies of a particular gene, one inherited from the sire, and one from the dam.

Although there are two copies of each particular gene, some will be dominant and some will be recessive (see page 174 for an example). If both genes are identical (i.e. both are dominant or both are recessive), the particular characteristic for which they are responsible will be manifested. If they are different (i.e. one is dominant, and the other is recessive), the dominant gene will override the recessive one.

Some inherited diseases are carried in the dominant strain of a gene, while others are carried in the recessive. Unfortunately, where an inherited disease is due to a dominant gene, only one such gene needs to be present for the disease to manifest itself. Where an inherited disease is due to a recessive gene, two identical genes must be present for the disease to manifest itself.

Diseases carried in recessive genes may be carried without manifesting themselves. Carriers have one recessive gene and one normal gene, but because two recessive genes are required for a recessive condition to manifest itself, carriers appear normal. However, if they mate with another carrier, the condition may manifest itself in the resulting offspring.

TESTING

The British Veterinary Association and the Kennel Club run an eye-testing scheme. It is hoped that testing will alert breeders to affected dogs, so that they can be removed from any breeding programme. Over time, this should result in a significant decrease in the number of dogs suffering from hereditary eye conditions.

Under the scheme, pedigree dogs are examined by a panel of experienced

Screening should help to eliminate eye problems in the breed.

ophthalmologists. Staffords are tested for hereditary cataracts and PHPV (see below). Dogs are issued a certificate giving their status – affected or clear.

Hereditary cataracts do not develop until the puppy is several months old, so breeders cannot test their litters before sending them to new homes. However, no Stafford should be bred from until this condition has been tested for.

HEREDITARY CATARACTS

A cataract is opacity of the lens or its capsule. Cataracts can develop without any underlying genetic involvement, but Staffords suffer from this inherited form as well. The cataracts affect both eyes, and the disease is progressive, leading to complete blindness by the time the dog is two to four years of age.

As the condition is recessive, both parents must be carriers. The following examples show how genes from each parent combine in their offspring. 'A' represents a healthy

gene free of the hereditary condition, while 'a' represents a faulty, recessive gene.

	A	A
A	AA (healthy)	AA (healthy)
a	Aa (unaffected but a carrier)	Aa (unaffected but a carrier)

In the above example, all the dogs will appear normal, never developing the disease, but 50 per cent of the litter are carriers. If the two Aa carriers produce offspring, one could expect the following results.

	A	a
A	AA (healthy)	Aa (unaffected but a carrier)
a	Aa (unaffected but a carrier)	aa (affected)

However, genes combine randomly during conception, so an actual litter will not have the same percentages as the example given above. It may be that the entire litter possess AA or Aa combinations, with no puppies affected. However, over time, an aa dog will arise, affected by hereditary cataracts. The chances of this happening are increased by inbreeding, which increases levels of recessive genes within a population of related dogs.

Hereditary cataracts can be removed by surgery. The cost is high, but results are very effective when an experienced ophthalmic surgeon has performed the operation.

PERSISTENT HYPERPLASTIC PRIMARY VITREOUS (PHPV)

This is an inherited, congenital defect, manifesting itself in Staffords as young as six weeks old. PHPV causes visual impairment and can lead to total blindness.

While the puppy is in his mother's womb, the developing eye is supplied by a network of blood vessels. The major part of these

The eye disorder PHPV can manifest itself in pups as young as six weeks.

blood vessels are located behind the lens of the eye, known as the primary vitreous. These blood vessels regress near the end of gestation, with regression complete before birth. In a dog affected by PHPV, regression does not complete. At birth, some of the blood vessels may remain and plaque formation may build up on the back of the lens.

PHPV can be extremely mild, having no effect on vision, or it can be severe, causing haemorrhage (bleeding) within the lens. Severe PHPV may cause the lens to be abnormally shaped and cataracts may also be present at birth. Usually, both eyes are affected. Surgery can restore the sight in affected dogs, but it is not always successful.

The mode of inheritance governing PHPV is extremely complex. Although PHPV is carried in a dominant gene, the gene will activate the disease only under particular circumstances. Some dogs with the PHPV gene are affected while others are not, and the reasons behind this are not yet understood.

NON-HEREDITARY DISEASES

ENTROPION
This disease of the eyelids is not common among Staffords, but will present at veterinary surgeries from time to time. Entropion is the name given to an inversion or inward rolling of the eyelid. As a result, hair-bearing skin can rub against the cornea (the surface of the eyeball), leading to pain, blinking, fear of light, excess tear production, mucous discharge from the eye, and corneal ulceration. The condition can affect both eyelids.

Surgery achieves good results, and, provided that the condition is assessed and treated immediately it becomes noticeable, affected dogs should live normal, healthy lives with unaffected vision. Some breeds develop a form of entropion that is thought to be inherited, but this has not been proven in Staffords.

ECTROPION
Ectropion – outward turning of the eyelid margin, usually affecting the lower eyelid – is rare among Staffords. It is often the result of overcorrective surgery for entropion. Ectropion can lead to reddening of the eye, chronic conjunctivitis, and discharge from the eye, but surgery, if required, achieves good results.

DISTICHIASIS
This is a condition in which eyelash hairs are able to touch the cornea, which may lead to inflammation and corneal ulceration. It is rarely seen in Staffords, although it is inherited in some breeds. It may occur following inflammation of the eyelids, but many cases are idiopathic (i.e. the cause is unknown).

It can be difficult to see the offending eyelashes with the naked eye, so owners may be unaware of the problem. However, under magnification, the eyelashes touching the cornea will be more obvious. Treatment involves surgical removal of the hair root, and repeat procedures may be necessary for a complete cure.

TRICHIASIS

Trichiasis, which is rare among Staffords, is a condition in which normal facial hair (usually from the eyelids) is abnormally angled so that it contacts the cornea. It can lead to inflammation, soreness, excess tear production, and corneal ulceration. Surgical correction achieves good results.

REPRODUCTIVE PROBLEMS

FEMALE

To understand reproductive diseases it is necessary to have some knowledge of the oestrous cycle. A bitch will undergo the following changes in the course of her life.

- **Puberty:** a bitch will have her first season between the ages of 6 and 20 months. Smaller breeds generally come into season

A bitch undergoes many hormonal changes throughout her life.

earlier than larger breeds, with Stafford bitches having their first season between 6 and 12 months of age.

- **Pro-oestrus:** the beginning of a season. It lasts, on average, for nine days, but this is very variable. The bitch's vulva will become swollen and reddened, and there will be a brightly coloured bloody discharge. The quantity of the discharge varies greatly and is of no clinical significance. The bitch will pass small quantities of urine to disseminate pheromones (hormones that attract and sexually excite dogs). Pheromones may bring other bitches in the kennels into season as well. Ovulation (release of the eggs) may occur towards the end of pro-oestrus but normally occurs during oestrus.
- **Oestrus:** this stage begins when the bitch will stand to be mated and ends when she refuses. It lasts for approximately nine days, but again, this is very variable. The bloody discharge tends to become less copious and less bloody, but this is not a constant feature. Ovulation normally occurs during the beginning of oestrus, but it can happen during pro-oestrus.
- **Metoestrus:** this stage begins when the bitch first refuses to be mated and lasts for approximately 60 days. Vulval swelling and discharge decrease. Pregnancy, false pregnancies, and pyometra may occur during this stage.
- **Anoestrus:** when there is no activity in the ovaries or uterus, lasting between the end of metoestrus or pregnancy and the beginning of the next pro-oestrus. It usually lasts for four months, but this can vary from one month to one year.

PYOMETRA (CYSTIC ENDOMETRIAL HYPERPLASIA)

Pyometra is a pus-filled, infected womb. The condition is common among Stafford bitches, but is not thought to be inherited.

There are two types of pyometra – open and closed. In an open pyometra, the cervix is open, so pus and blood can pass out through the vagina. In a closed pyometra, the cervix is closed and there is no vaginal discharge.

During oestrus, the cervix is open to allow sperm into the uterus. Unfortunately, bacteria can enter the uterus through the same path. High blood progesterone levels released at this time reduce the effectiveness of the normal defence mechanisms, and the bacteria will multiply over the course of a few weeks, producing pus and toxins. The most common bacterium is *Escherichia coli*. There is no relationship between pyometra and irregular oestrus cycles or false pregnancies. Indeed, using progestogens and oestrogens to regulate the cycle may predispose a bitch to pyometra.

Pyometra manifests itself during metoestrus. The affected bitch will drink and urinate more, vomit, refuse food, and become depressed. If she has an open pyometra, she will have a vaginal discharge. As well as the clinical signs, a veterinarian will take blood samples, and use radiography, ultrasonography, and abdominal palpation to diagnose pyometra.

Ovariohysterectomy (spaying) is the treatment of choice, accompanied by intravenous fluid therapy (drip-feeding), antibiotics and pain relief. It is also possible to treat pyometra medically. In some countries, prostaglandins are used, but they can have side effects. In other countries, progesterone receptor antagonists are used with good results, and progesterone and prostaglandins may also be used in conjunction with one another.

VAGINAL HYPERPLASIA (PROTRUSION)

Occasionally seen in the Stafford, this condition occurs in the first stage of the oestrous cycle. Oestrogens released during pro-oestrus cause the vaginal wall to thicken, possibly resulting in protrusion from the vagina. As a consequence of vaginal hyperplasia, a bitch may develop urinary incontinence.

The condition tends to settle down after oestrus, only to recur during successive heats. However, it should be treated before the bitch is next mated because mating may cause the bitch to bleed. The dog will find it difficult to introduce his penis into the vaginal cavity, and the bitch will experience some pain. The protrusion can be surgically removed during oestrus, or the bitch may be spayed afterwards.

PREGNANCY TESTING

A bitch mated between days 11 and 13 of the oestrous cycle should have an 80 per cent chance of becoming pregnant. Eggs are fertile for up to three days, while sperm is viable for up to seven days in the bitch's reproductive tract, so the chances of egg and sperm meeting are high (see chapter Thirteen for more details).

The most common reason behind failure to conceive is that the bitch was mated at the wrong time. To overcome this, breeders can ask their veterinarian to perform a number of tests. These include vaginal cytology and blood tests. Vaginal cytology involves taking cell samples from the bitch's vagina, staining them, and examining them under a microscope. When 80 per cent of these cells are cornified (i.e. contain no nucleus), it is the ideal time to mate the bitch. Blood tests will measure the level of progesterone in the blood, which rises during the bitch's season. Together, these tests give a very good indication of ovulation, having a success rate of more than 95 per cent (provided the stud dog is fertile).

Vaginal cytology and progesterone testing should be performed as standard if a bitch is to receive artificial insemination. In some

The main reason for a dog's failure to conceive is a wrongly-timed mating.

countries, permission must be obtained from the national kennel club before performing artificial insemination.

MALE

CRYPTORCHIDISM

In the uterus, a male puppy's testicles are located next to the kidneys. After birth, the testicles migrate through the abdomen, to become located in the scrotum by 5 to 10 weeks of age. This does not happen in some dogs, and one or both testicles may be retained in the body. As the dog ages, the chances of a retained testicle descending normally greatly decrease. It is very rare after one year of age.

If one testicle is retained, the dog has unilateral cryptorchidism. If both testicles are retained, the dog has bilateral cryptorchidism. Cryptorchidism is not the same as anorchism (the congenital absence of both testicles) or monorchidism (the presence of one testicle only), as the testicles are retained in cryptorchidism, whereas they are absent completely in anorchism and monorchidism.

Most dogs with retained testicles are infertile, as the high temperature inside the abdomen inhibits sperm production. However, this does not apply to all cryptorchid dogs, and, in cases of unilateral cryptorchidism, the normally descended testicle may produce sperm. As the condition is hereditary, cryptorchid dogs should be prevented from breeding, which may necessitate castration of retained and normal testicles. This is necessary not only to prevent the condition from being passed on, but also because there is a high risk of testicular cancer in testes remaining in the abdomen.

MISCELLANEOUS COMPLAINTS

FOOD ALLERGIES

The main signs include chronic itching and intestinal problems, such as diarrhoea. Many people make the mistake of assuming their dog is allergic to a particular brand of food. However, the allergic response is produced by a particular food (e.g. milk or beef), not the way it is prepared.

There are two ways of diagnosing food allergies – blood tests and food trials. Blood tests are extremely accurate, but expensive. Consequently, many owners choose to carry out a food trial, which can last for up to 12 weeks. The dog is placed on a special diet until the allergic reaction disappears. Once this happens, the dog's normal diet is introduced slowly, with one food added at a time. If skin and intestinal problems return after the reintroduction of a certain food, the allergy has been discovered.

Food allergies can be managed effectively by careful control over the dog's diet.

OVERLONG SOFT PALATE.
The hard palate forms the roof of the mouth and is composed of bone covered in mucosa. The soft palate is the end of the hard palate, located at the back of the mouth. It is composed of soft tissue.

The soft palate is regarded as overlong if it hangs behind the epiglottis in the opening to the trachea (windpipe).

An overlong soft palate causes injury to itself and to the back of the mouth, leading to inflammatory oedema (swelling). In addition, it prevents sufficient air from travelling into the trachea and therefore the lungs. Consequently, affected dogs will show signs of gagging and coughing, frequently accompanied by rattling or snoring during breathing. In very rare cases, the dog can collapse (usually after exercise in hot weather). Normally, surgical resection is the treatment of choice for an overlong soft palate.

Some people believe this is common among Staffords, especially those from particular lines. However, from my own experience, and from speaking to a leading soft tissue veterinary surgeon, incidence is low in the breed. No studies have shown the condition to be hereditary, although the pronounced vertical stop of the head may be responsible in part. This has not been proven, however.

Although the Stafford suffers from some breed-prone problems, it is generally a healthy, hardy breed.